AMERICAN
A·L·I·Y·A

AMERICAN A·L·I·Y·A

Portrait of an Innovative Migration Movement

CHAIM I. WAXMAN

WAYNE STATE UNIVERSITY PRESS   DETROIT   1989

Library of Congress Cataloging-in-Publication Data

Waxman, Chaim Isaac.
   American aliya : portrait of an innovative migration
movement / Chaim I. Waxman.
     p. cm.
   Includes index.
   ISBN 978-0-8143-4342-5 (paperback);
   ISBN 978-0-8143-4341-8 (ebook)
   1. Jews, American–Israel. 2. Zionism–United States.
3. Immigrants–Israel. 4. United States–Emigration and
immigration. 5. Israel–Emmigration and immigration.
6. Israel–Ethnic relations. I. Title.
DS113.8.A4W38 1989
956.94'004924073–dcl9   88-38114
                                           CIP

National Endowment for the Humanities

THE ANDREW W. MELLON FOUNDATION

The publication of this volume in a freely accessible
digital format has been made possible by a major grant
from the National Endowment for the Humanities and the
Mellon Foundation through their Humanities Open Book
Program.

http://wsupress.wayne.edu/

In Honor of
Ari & Sandy, Shani & Noam, and Dani

Contents

Tables   8

Preface   11

Introduction   15

PART I

1   Zion in Jewish Culture   27

2   Messianism and the Forerunners of Zionism
in the Nineteenth Century   39

3   American Jewry and the Land of Israel in
Eighteenth and Nineteenth Centuries   50

PART II

4   Early Twentieth Century American Zionism   65

5   American Aliya Before the Six-Day War   77

6   American Aliya, 1967–1987   88

PART III

7   The Centrality of Israel in American Jewish Life   105

8   Orthodox Judaism in Modern American Society   119

PART IV

9   The Acculturation of American Israelis   139

10   American Israelis in "the Territories"   150

11   The Return Migration of American Olim   169

12   Families Apart: Parents of American Olim   186

13   Aliya and the Priorities of the American Jewish Community   195

Notes   203

Index   204

Tables

Table 1. Distribution of Most Important Reasons Given for
American Aliya, Pre–1948   82

Table 2. American Immigrants to Israel, 1950–1987   82

Table 3. Regional Distribution of American Olim and Jewish
Population in the U.S.   90

Table 4. Occupational Distribution, 1970   95

Table 5. Olim Aged 15 and Over by Continent of Residence and
Occupation Abroad, 1986   95

Table 6. Occupational Distribution of American Olim and Israeli
Jewish Labor Force   96

Table 7. Denominational Distribution   99

Table 8. Number of Hebrew Day Schools, Types, and
Enrollments   122

Table 9. Fulfillment of Expectations of American Olim, 1972 and
1975 (%)   148

Table 10. Distribution of American Israelis in the Territories by
Age and Sex   151

Table 11. Number of Children in Families of American Israelis in
the Territories   151

Table 12. Distribution of American Israelis in the Territories by
Education and Sex   151

Table 13. Distribution of American Israelis in the Territories by
Parents' Affiliation   152

Table 14. Distribution of American Israelis in the Territories by
Jewish Education   153

Table 15. Jewish Youth Group Affiliations of American Israelis in
the Territories   154

Table 16. Distribution of American Israelis in the Territories by
Period of Aliya   154

Table 17. Feelings about the U.S. among American Israelis in the
          Territories   155
Table 18. Primary Motivations of American Israelis for Moving to
          Territories   155
Table 19. Support of American Israelis in the Territories for
          Democracy as a Value   156
Table 20. Ideas on Dealing with Arabs in Territories among
          American Israelis There   157
Table 21. Attitudes toward Kach among American Israelis in the
          Territories   157
Table 22. Attitudes toward Gush Emunim among American
          Israelis in the Territories   158
Table 23. Belief among American Israelis in the Territories in Equal
          Rights for Arabs   158
Table 24. Belief among American Israelis in Territories that Now Is
          Period of Messiah   159
Table 25. Occupational Status Before, During, and After Stay in
          Israel   173
Table 26. Intentions upon Arrival (%)   174
Table 27. Visa Status upon Arrival (%)   174
Table 28. Reasons for Aliya Rated as "Very or Somewhat
          Important" (%)   175
Table 29. Reported Reasons for Return (%)   177
Table 30. Reasons for Returning to the U.S. Rated as "Very or
          Somewhat Important" (%)   178
Table 31. Distribution of Push and Pull Factors in Decision to
          Return   180
Table 32. Arrangements Before Israel and Return (%)   180
Table 33. Synagogue Affiliation Before and After Israel (%)   181
Table 34. Frequency of Synagogue Attendance Before and After
          Israel (%)   181
Table 35. Planned or Current Jewish Education of Children of
          Returnees (%)   181
Table 36. Jewish/Israel Activities and Feelings Before and After
          Israel   183
Table 37. Zionist Self-identification Before and After Israel (%)
          184
Table 38. Probability of Reattempting Aliya   184
Table 39. Agreement or Disagreement with Aliya-related
          Statements (%)   185

Preface

The research and writing of this book were inspired by one event and two individuals. The event was what began as a one-year sabbatical from Rutgers University and ended up as a two-year stay in Israel for me, my wife, and our children. From 1982 to 1984 we lived in Rechovot, a city south of Tel Aviv with a significant population of Americans, in which we were made to feel very welcome and in which we made many dear friends. That stay in Israel sparked my interest in several of the topics and issues covered in this book.

Just before I left for Israel, in the spring of 1982, Yehuda Rosenman, late director of the Jewish Communal Affairs Department of the American Jewish Committee and a dear friend, asked my advice about a research project on the subject of American aliya, immigration to Israel, and the return to the United States of many of those immigrants. Yehuda had a burning love for both the land and people of Israel, Eretz Israel and Am Israel, and he was one of the first American Jewish communal leaders to argue that the American Jewish community should support American aliya, that it need not fear that such aliya would deplete its future leadership; on the contrary, he argued, support for American aliya would strengthen American Jewry. At the time and in subsequent letters I told Yehuda what I felt would be necessary for such a project. He encouraged me to keep abreast of the issue of American aliya and also that of the return migration of American olim. Ultimately, Yehuda and Bert Gold, executive vice-president of the American Jewish Committee and director of its Institute on American Jewish-Israeli Relations, engaged me in a study of the return migration of American olim, upon which Chapter 11 of this book is based. I am deeply grateful to both of them for their personal and institutional support of the subject of American aliya and for their friendship. I will sorely miss Yehuda Rosenman's wisdom, wit, and warmth; his passing was a great loss for his family, his many friends, and the entire American Jewish community.

Another dear friend who, at a later stage, was a source of encouragement and assistance in completing this book is Moshe Davis, founding director of the Hebrew University's Institute of Contemporary Jewry and director of the America–Holy Land Studies Project. His friendship and support are appreciated.

Many people assisted me in my research for this book and I wish to thank all of them. The staff at the research libraries of Rutgers University, Yeshiva University, Hebrew Union College, Jewish Theological Seminary, and the New York Public Library were very helpful. Three librarians in particular deserve special mention for assistance beyond the call of duty: Edith Lubetski, head of the Hedi Steinberg Library of Yeshiva University's Stern College for Women; Cyma Horowitz, director of the American Jewish Committee's Blaustein Library; and Shoshana Kaufmann, Associate Director of the Paul Klapper Library of Queens College–CUNY. Also, Shoshana Kaufmann's compilation *American Immigrants in Israel: A Selected Annotated Bibliography, 1948–85*, published by the American Jewish Committee's Institute on American Jewish-Israeli Relations, was very helpful in tracking down various books and articles on different topics.

Several other individuals gave me important technical assistance and deserve special mention. Irving (Isser) Green, president of Skan Teknologies, Inc., is much more than a friend. All else aside, the technical assistance he and his staff so graciously provided is deeply appreciated. Benjamin Sporn, attorney, and Anne D. Wade, market analyst, both of AT&T, graciously provided me with relevant telephone data. Rabbis Herschel Billet and Jay Goldberg, rabbis of the Young Israel of Woodmere and Young Israel of Wavecrest and Bayswater respectively, helped me track down several items from responsa literature. Bernice M. Salzman, editor of *The Bridge*, the newsletter of Parents of North American Israelis (PNAI), graciously loaned me all of the back issues of that publication. Ephraim Tabory, senior lecturer in Sociology at Bar Ilan University, kindly allowed me to refer to his as yet unpublished research on PNAI. My good friend and Bitnet correspondent in Rechovot, Ellen Wachtel, was always there to help track down information not readily available outside of Israel. Throughout the writing of this book Gershon, Suri, and Yaacov Blank, who are also much more than friends, provided me with a variety of technical assistance, all of which is deeply appreciated. And to Natalie, Naomi, Shirley, Myrna, Rita, and George, many thanks for everything. Also, the willing participation of all of the interviewees is duly noted.

Even before the book was written I had consulted with Robert A. Mandel, director of Wayne State University Press, whom I knew from his previous position. He was very supportive of the project, and he encouraged me to devote myself to it and write the book that I had initially thought would be too taxing to write on my own. For his personal concern I am very grateful. Likewise, the editorial skills and invaluable suggestions of Lois Krieger and Kathryn Wildfong are very much appreciated.

A grant from the Lucius N. Littauer Foundation enabled me to complete the manuscript on time, and I am grateful for that support. I also thank the Foundation for Middle East Peace, the Jewish Agency for Israel, the Jerusalem Center for Public Affairs, and the Sociology Department of Tel Aviv University for grants which enabled me to conduct the original research upon which Chapter 10 is based.

As in many of my previous writings, I have benefited greatly from the thoughtful comments of Egon Mayer. A long-time friend and colleague, he read the entire manuscript and made many valuable suggestions.

Portions of this book are revisions of writings of mine that have appeared elsewhere, and I am grateful to the publications in which they originally appeared for permission to use the material here. Earlier versions of Chapter 2 appeared in *Modern Judaism* and *Morasha;* Chapters 7 and 8 appeared in earlier versions in *Judaism* and *Yearbook of Religious Zionism, 1985–86;* earlier versions of Chapter 10 appeared in the *Middle East Review* and *Midstream;* and an earlier version of Chapter 11 was written with Michael Appel and published by the American Jewish Committee's Institute on American Jewish-Israeli Relations.

Finally, words alone could never express my deepest love and appreciation to my wife, Chaya, and our children, Ari & Sandy, Shani & Noam, and Dani. More than anyone can ever know, they have a major share in both the research and the writing of this book.

Introduction

Since human beings appear to be creatures of habit, we would expect them to remain in the place where they were born unless there was a strong incentive to move elsewhere. The fact that people have always migrated from one city, state, and even country to another merely indicates that there have always been, and continue to be, strong incentives for people to move. Although there are many reasons people migrate from one place to another, migration is not a random phenomenon. Different types of migration seem to be characteristic of different types of societies.

Within the sociological literature on international migration there is a central conceptual distinction between "push" and "pull" factors. That is, immigration is sometimes motivated by dissatisfaction with one's native country as the result of hardships there, while at other times immigration may be motivated by an attraction to another country because of special opportunities and conditions there. Because of the variations in patterns of migration, contemporary sociologists are skeptical of explanations that postulate such "psychological universals" as "wanderlust."[1] On the other hand, the economic motive, as either push or pull or both, has usually been taken to be the major incentive for migration. In the earlier part of this century this was probably due to the fact that most Europeans who migrated to the United States during the period of peak immigration, at the end of the nineteenth and beginning of the twentieth century, did so for economic reasons.[2] Subsequent studies point to the continued importance of the economic factor as the motivation of voluntary migration. As Beijer says, following his extensive survey of the subject, "The economic factor is clearly one of the most important factors in voluntary international migration."[3]

Obviously, not all international migration is voluntary. To this day there continue to be waves of involuntary migration to and from various countries. They, too, must be accounted for. In an effort to explain different types of migration by more adequately considering the factors involved in each, William Petersen has developed a "general typology of migration,"[4] which consists of five different classes of migration. Those classes are: "primitive," "forced," "implied," "free," and "mass." Each of them can be subdivided into two types: "innovating," in which people "migrate as a means of achieving something new," and "conservative," in which, in response to changed conditions in their homelands, people migrate "in order to retain what they have had; they move geographically in order to remain where they are in all other respects."[5]

Interestingly, the most recent example of free migration Petersen cites is that of the migration of Swedes to the United States during the nineteenth century.[6] He offers no twentieth-century examples, nor any involving migration from the United States. Such examples do exist, however, as Ada Finifter clearly demonstrates.[7] In fact, she documents a dramatic rise of emigration from the United States during the 1960s (after Petersen's typology was published), which has been largely motivated by dissatisfaction with American society, especially political dissatisfaction.

At first glance it seems obvious that American Jews who have migrated to Israel, have "made aliya"–at least those who have done so since the late 1960s–have done so as the result of pull factors, because of the special attraction Israel had for them, and not because of any push from American society. After all, contemporary American society offers its Jews a measure of economic, political, and religious freedom unprecedented in Jewish history. America's Jews enjoy very high socioeconomic status. Anti-Semitism, although clearly present, shows signs of continual decline and overt anti-Semitism has not been personally experienced by most contemporary young American Jews. There has been a marked decline in the stigma of ethnicity, and America is today much more receptive to ethnic and religious pluralism than ever before.[8] Obviously, then, those American Jews who have gone on aliya, some sixty-thousand since the Six-

Day War of June 1967, were not pushed from American society. They were pulled by an attraction to Israel.

The issue, however, is considerably more complex than it appears. Push and pull factors are most frequently not contrasts. Rather, there are elements of both for almost all immigrants. As S. N. Eisenstadt suggests, "Every migratory movement is motivated by the migrant's feeling of some kind of insecurity and inadequacy in his original social setting."[9] If one is attracted to migrate to another society, for whatever the reason, that implicitly indicates that there was a perceived inadequacy in the "original social setting" from which the migrant emigrated.

Nevertheless, we can still differentiate between push and pull factors if we understand them as the primary motivations as perceived by the migrant. Thus, it would be valid to speak of American olim, immigrants to Israel, as being motivated by pull factors if they perceived their experience in American society as essentially positive and their aliya not as a manifestation of any push from American society, but as the fulfillment of some challenge, dream, or ideology they saw as being fulfilled in Israel. That the vast majority of American olim, especially since 1967, are in fact primarily drawn to Israel by those kinds of special attractions is evident from several recent studies, as will be seen in Chapter 6.

How one views American aliya will of course vary, depending on whether it is approached from an ideological or a sociological perspective. To those who are ideologically committed to Zionism and believe that all Jews have an obligation to migrate to Israel, the phenomenon of American aliya is significant in a negative way. That is, what is viewed as the paucity of American aliya–less than two thousand per year or less than one-twentieth of 1 percent of America's Jews per year migrate to Israel–is seen as significant only because it is so meager. For most Zionist ideologues, the low rate of American aliya only highlights the qualitative weakness of the American Jewish community and reinforces the perception of the impending total assimilation and disappearance of America's Jews within the larger American population. Do traditional Jews, the ideologues argue, not pray three times each day, facing Jerusalem, for the rebuilding of Jerusalem and the return to Zion? Do traditional Jews not cry out, "Next year in Jerusalem!" at the conclusion of the ritual order at the seder feast each Passover? Do traditional Jews not show their yearning for Zion by fasting several times each year to commemorate losses in Jerusalem? And from a political Zionist perspective, is Israel not desperate for increased Jewish immigration, surrounded and vastly outnumbered as it is by states that are, at best, unenthusiastic about its existence? Even within Israel itself, is Israel's Jewish character not threatened by the significant non-Jewish minority that lives there? Do America's Jews not realize, he or she continues, that they are in the best position to "go on aliya," to migrate to Israel, since they are the most populous Jewish community in the diaspora and they are so affluent? From such a perspective, American aliya is indeed pathetically small, and it is tragic.

A social scientific perspective, on the other hand, would more likely view the phenomenon of American aliya in comparative perspective. It would begin not with normative imperatives but with empirical observations. It would ask not why don't many more American Jews go on aliya but, rather, who are those who do go on aliya? Why do they go? Their migration is of particular interest because it is so rare to see a wave of immigration consisting of a group of people who are free and affluent immigrating to a country in which the economic and many of the political conditions are manifestly poorer than in their original country.

For the sociology of migration, thus, the phenomenon of American aliya appears to be a deviant case; that is, it does not fit into any of the modal types of immigration. American immigration to Israel is obviously not of the primitive, forced, or impelled type. Nor is it a mass movement. It is closest to the class of free migration. But even as such, American aliya, especially in recent years, does not appear to be primarily motivated by any explicit dissatisfaction with the American political system. Nor does it appear to be primarily motivated by any changed conditions in American society. It is, rather, motivated much more by the religious, ethnic, and/or nationalistic pull to Israel. It may, in fact, be viewed as one of the very few, if not only, contemporary examples of what Petersen calls free, innovating migration.

This, of course, does not mean that other factors, such as the economic and/or occupational situation in the United States or economic conditions in Israel, play no role. They clearly do. Many of the American olim had decided to immigrate only after they experienced problems in their jobs, such as teachers in the New York City public school system following the implementation of community control and the subsequent teachers' strike in 1968,[10] or engineers who lost their jobs during the massive layoffs of engineers in the early 1970s. Also, it has been convincingly demonstrated that aliya figures from the West certainly do fluctuate in accordance with economic conditions in Israel.[11] But neither economic conditions nor occupational situation constitutes sufficient cause for aliya. Both can influence the rate of aliya, but neither provides sufficient motivation for aliya itself.

American aliya, thus, is a more explicit example of free migration of the innovating type and suggests that the push-pull dichotomy is even more inadequate than heretofore assumed. If "push" has any meaning, especially as it relates to its counterpart, "pull," it refers to a push from the society of emigration. If, however, migrants state that they felt comfortable in the society of emigration, even while being not wholly satisfied within their subcultural ethnic or religious group, and that they migrated in order to more fully realize their subcultural values, then that migration cannot be defined as a consequence of push factors. Free migrants of the innovating type can, thus, be considered motivated by pull factors in that their migration is not precipitated by any alienation from the structures of the society from which they emigrated.

The purpose of this volume is twofold. The first is to examine and explain the phenomenon of American aliya for its own sake. The second is to show the extent to which the existing knowledge base in the study of international migration remains limited as long as there is no comprehensive theory that also accounts for the complexities of American aliya. Accordingly, Part I provides the historical and cultural background for the ideology of aliya. Chapter 1 analyzes the extent to which Zion and aliya have traditionally been central to both Judaism and the Jewish experience. Chapter 2 discusses the extent to which the messianic yearnings of the nineteenth century contributed to the ideology and reality of Jewish settlement in the Holy Land, Eretz Israel. Chapter 3 examines the writings and orations of a number of prominent leaders of the Jewish community in the United States during the nineteenth century. The analysis demonstrates that not only did they subscribe to the traditional Jewish yearnings for Zion, but several of them became active in efforts to resettle the Holy Land and regain Jewish sovereignty over it. These preinstitutionalized Zionist notions and activities helped pave the way for the organization of the Zionist movement at the end of the nineteenth century, and it is largely within the context of them that American immigration into Israel takes place.

Part II begins by showing how the organized American Zionist movement, from its very inception, took an independent stance on the ideologies of Diaspora and aliya. In contrast to the mainstream

Zionist Organization, which was headquartered in Europe and defined both individual and collective aliya from all Diaspora lands as a central imperative of Zionism, American Zionism in both its political and cultural versions staunchly avoided any expression of Zionism that might detract from the legitimacy of communal Jewish life in America. Chapters 5 and 6 provide an extensive analysis of twentieth-century American aliya, from the beginning of the century through 1987. They present social and demographic analyses of American olim during different periods, which indicate the significant shifts in the type of American Jew most likely to go on aliya and the changing cultural and religious motives for aliya. Chapter 6, which provides an analysis of contemporary American olim, also indicates the complexity of American aliya; it is affected by a variety of factors, including religion, economics, politics, education, occupation, age, marital and family status, and more. Wherever feasible, the chapter also shows the extent to which the factors affecting American aliya are similar to those generally affecting international migration.

The data do indicate that religiosity, although not prominent until relatively recently, is becoming an increasingly differentiating variable. Not only are the Orthodox disproportionately represented among American olim, but there is some evidence that the majority of recent American olim are Orthodox. Part III analyzes this phenomenon and offers a number of hypotheses as to why an increasing proportion of American olim are Orthodox–given that Orthodoxy Jewry is actually not as homogeneous as it is thought to be–and, indeed, what type of Orthodox are likely to be drawn to aliya.

Chapters 9 and 10 focus on American Jews in Israel. Chapter 9 analyzes the acculturation process of American olim and, once again, shows how different American immigrants to Israel are from the typical international migrants. Whereas, as Jackson reminds us, "migrants, especially international migrants, characteristically find themselves in minority groups within the receiving society,"[12] this is clearly not the case with American immigrants in Israel. Although they may not immediately be accepted into native Israeli friendship groups and are most definitely a numerical minority in Israel, and a small one at that, they are also unquestionably part of the dominant segments of Israeli society. If anything, American olim are an elite group there. They are, thus, once again "off the graph" with respect to typical patterns of international migration. Chapter 10 deals with a specific group of American olim, one that, in certain respects, is even more of an elite group than American Israelis as a whole, namely,

those who have settled "beyond the Green Line," in the Administered Territories of Judea, Samaria, and the Gaza Strip. The data in
this chapter show how different these settlers are from the stereotyp-
ical image of them prevalent both in the American Jewish community
and in Israeli society at large.

One other aspect of American aliya that is important within the
larger context of international migration is that of return migration.
As Bovenkerk says, the phenomenon of return migration was already
observed in the nineteenth century, and the noted Anglo-German
geographer and statistician Ernst G. Ravenstein included it in his
essays "The Laws of Migration" in 1885 and 1889.[13] Since then many
studies have included discussions of return migration. Most of the
literature, however, and especially the theories and laws of return
migration, relate only to internal migration–that is, migration within
the same society–rather than international migration. The reason,
according to Bovenkerk, is that "there are so many indeterminate factors in international migration that they pose analytically serious
obstacles."[14] Only three generalizations from patterns of internal
return migration appear to also hold for international return migration: "the shorter the distance of emigration, the higher the incidence
of return migration"; "the longer the emigrants stay away the less
chance they will return"; and "changes in the economic balance
between the place of origin and the place of destination directly affect
the volume of return migration."[15]

Given the state of affairs of the whole study of the phenomenon
of international return migration, Chapter 11 contributes to that body
of knowledge by exploring the return migration of American Jews
from Israel. This chapter looks at the rate of return, who returns,
reasons for return, and the impact of these returnees on the American
Jewish community after their return. As was the case with their initial
migration, these migrants are a rare contemporary example of free
migration of the innovating type. Within the context of international
return migration, those cases of return migration of the innovating
type in which the United States is involved invariably occur when the
United States is the country from which the returnees migrate. As
Bovenkerk surveys them, there are studies of Greek, Italian, and Third
World returnees who had initially migrated from their native countries to the United States and then returned to their native countries.
In some cases, the studies do focus upon the extent to which the
returnees are able to use that which they learned or achieved in the
United States to have an impact on their native countries.[16] American

aliya is, again, unique in that it provides an opportunity to examine the impact of the stay in the nonnative country, Israel, on Americans who return to the United States.

The sociological novelty of the phenomenon of American aliya is suggested by the fact that there is almost nothing in P. Neal Ritchey's extensive survey of explanations of migration that relates conceptually or theoretically to the migration of American Jews to Israel.[17] This book, therefore, underscores the need for greater conceptual clarity and more careful empirical research in the field of international migration. By demonstrating and explaining both the unique and typical aspects of the migration of American Jews to Israel, it implicitly seconds Ritchey's charge to scholars in the area:

> Research must deal more rigorously with the three basic classes of factors which general models of behavior suggest constrain behavior: aspects of the social structure, the status or position of individuals in the social structure, and values or attitudes of individuals. In migration research these variables are referred to as the conditions of areas, structural attributes, and social psychological attributes, respectively. The primary requirements are more precise operational definitions of these factor types and simultaneous empirical consideration of their effects on migration.[18]

Chapter 12 adds another dimension to the study of international migration. Although some attention has been paid to the impact of migration on the country and community from which the migrants leave, there are virtually no empirical studies of the impact of that migration on the families and family ties of those involved. This chapter, therefore, focuses on the reactions of the parents in America to the aliya of their children. Are they supportive, accepting, or resentful of their children's migration? Has their children's aliya changed their lives in any significant ways? What practical changes have taken place in terms of their relationship with their children? What has happened to the quality of the relationship between themselves and their children, and what measures have they undertaken to retain the quality of their relationship with their children? This chapter, then, may also be seen as part of a study of families across national boundaries that, in the final analysis, is one consequence of international migration.

The last chapter begins with a move from the core of the study of the sociology of international migration to that of social policy, not in the sense of public, governmental policy but the social policy of an organized voluntary group, the Jewish community. The chapter then examines some of the structural, organizational weaknesses of current aliya efforts and explores the prospects and possibilities of developing and implementing alternatives that might result in increases in the numbers of American Jews who migrate to Israel, who go on aliya. Assuming that it is unreasonable to assume that there will be any major increases in the rate of American aliya at the present time, one issue within the traditional subject matter of the sociology of migration—namely, the possible negative impact of migration on the country and community of emigration—is moot. At this point, the potential impact of increased American aliya on American society would be virtually inconsequential. As for the American Jewish community, increased American aliya would be highly functional in terms of its stated goals: survival and the strengthening of Jewish identity and identification.

PART I

1

Zion in Jewish Culture

Although the destruction of the Temple and the loss of Jerusalem to Rome in 70 c.e. resulted in the end of Jewish sovereignty in the Holy Land and the onset of the dispersion of Jews and Jewish communities to distant countries throughout the world, the Holy Land, Eretz Israel, was never far from the consciousness of Jews during the almost two-thousand-year absence of Jewish sovereignty in the land. Throughout almost that entire period Eretz Israel played a central role in traditional Jewish culture. Small Jewish communities in such cities as Jerusalem and Safed persevered, aided by contributions from Diaspora Jewish communities. Some Diaspora Jews managed to visit Eretz Israel, and others actually managed to move there on a more permanent basis. And for Jews around the world the Hold Land and the dream of return were embedded in daily religious rituals and prayers as well as in law and lore. Three days each year of the Jewish ritual calendar were set aside as fast days commemorating a significant part of the destruction of the Temple and the loss of the Holy Land. Likewise, the loss of Jerusalem is symbolized in the rituals of the Jewish marriage ceremony. The daily prayers are recited facing east, toward Jerusalem. The service at the Passover seder concludes with the prayer "Next year in Jerusalem!" These served as constant reminders and sustained the persistent yearning for both being in Eretz Israel and the ultimate messianic redemption.

Talmudic lore is replete with statements affirming the superior status of the Holy Land, the obligation to live there, and the absolute faith in the ultimate collective return of the Jewish people to their rightful land. Thus, the Talmud states, "One should always live in Eretz Israel, even in a city in which the majority of the population is gentile, and one should not live outside of the Land, even in a city in which the majority is Jewish . . . to teach you that whoever lives outside of the Land is as if he were commiting idolatry."[1]

Likewise, the *Yalkut Shimoni*[2] relates: "It happened that Rabbi Yehuda ben Beteira, Rabbi Matia ben Cheresh, Rabbi Chanina ben Achi, Rabbi Yehoshua and Rabbi Yonatan were walking in the Diaspora and reached Flatus and remembered Eretz Israel. They lifted their eyes, shed their tears, rended their clothes, and read this verse: 'And you shall possess it and you shall dwell therein. And you shall observe to do all the statutes . . .' (Deut. 11:31–32) They said, 'Dwelling in Eretz Israel is equal to all of the commandments in the Torah.'"

Each day, in the morning, afternoon, and evening prayers, as well as in the blessings recited after each meal, Jews prayed for the return to Zion and the rebuilding of Jerusalem. And they remained confident of the ultimate return, which was guaranteed in a variety of authoritative passages. As Heschel eloquently put it:

> Throughout the ages we said No to all the conquerers of Palestine. We said No before God and man emphatically, daily. We objected to the occupations, we rejected their claims, we deepened our attachment, knowing that the occupation by the conquerors was a passing adventure, while our attachment to the land was an eternal link.
>
> The Jewish people has never ceased to assert its right, its title, to the land of Israel. This continuous, uninterrupted insistence, an intimate ingredient of Jewish consciousness, is at the core of Jewish history, a vital element of Jewish faith.
>
> How did the Jews contest and call into question the occupation of the land by the might empires of the East and West? How did they assert their own title to the land?
>
> Our protest was not heard in the public squares of the large cities. It was uttered in our homes, in our sanctuaries, in our books, in our prayers. Indeed, our very existence as a people was a proclamation of our link to the land, or our certainty of return.[3]

Part of this attachment to Eretz Israel was the strong religious rejection of the Diaspora–*galut*–which was a major theme of most Jewish philosophers.[4] Although there were differences among scholar-rabbis in terms of the degree to which they explicitly emphasized the negative nature of Diaspora existence and, concomitantly, the degree to which they emphasized the drive to return to Eretz Israel, there was virtually no Jewish religious authority until the modern era who even remotely suggested *galut* existence as an ideal. Without exception, *galut* was defined as an ultimately negative existence; Zion was the unequivocal ideal.

There is, however, an important qualification that must be added. Historically, there have been variations in the degree to which that link was overtly expressed, and it does appear that an important variable in determining the emphasis placed on Eretz Israel was and is the degree of security experienced by the Jews in the Diaspora. As will be discussed, during periods in which the physical conditions of Jewish life in the Diaspora deteriorated there was usually an increase in emphasis on and yearning for the Holy Land and, as discussed in Chapter 2, messianism.

Nevertheless, although there have been periodic fluctuations in the extent of emphasis on the theme of Eretz Israel, virtually all streams of traditional Judaism throughout the history of the dispersion, despite their many variations, resolutely expressed the supreme holiness of and love for Eretz Israel. To illustrate the depths of these expressions, four representative thinkers, representing four different streams within Judaism, have been selected for analysis. In each case their writings about Eretz Israel and their personal involvement with it will be highlighted. The first two, Rabbi Yehuda Halevi and Rabbi Moses ben Maimon (Maimonides), were both Sephardim; Halevi was more of a mystic and poet, and Maimonides was a rational legalist. The other two, Rabbi Judah Loew (the Maharal) of Prague and Rabbi Nachman of Bratslav (Breslov), were both Ashkenazim; the Maharal was a prolific writer with strong mystical overtones and Nachman was an early Chasidic leader.[5]

In terms of literary craftsmanship there is probably no one who equaled the beauty and eloquence of the mystical and poetic philosophy of Rabbi Yehuda Halevi (1086–1141). Yehuda Halevi's most famous work, *The Kuzari,* was written in the form of a dialogue with the king of Khazars,[6] Al Khazari, and was an extensive apologetic analysis of the logic and rationale of Judaism. In the second chapter, after having elaborated on the unity of God, the author engages in a lengthy analysis that attempts to systematically prove the preeminent character of Eretz Israel.[7] He presents what he deems to be scientific proof of that preeminence and then continues with a "discourse on the advantages of the Land of Israel." Following that lengthy discourse, Al Khazari offers a strong rebuke to Yehuda Halevi:

> If this be so, thou fallest short of the duty laid down in thy law, by not endeavouring to reach that place, and making it thy abode in life and death, although thou sayest: "Have mercy on Zion, for it is the house of our life," and believest that the shekhinah will return thither. And had it no other preference than that the Shekhinah dwelt there five hundred years, this is sufficient reason for men's souls to retire thither and find purification there, as happens near the abodes of the pious and prophets. Is it not "the gate of heaven"? All nations agree on this point. . . . Everybody turns to it in prayer and visits it in pilgrimage. Thy bowing and kneeling in the direction of it is either mere appearance or thoughtless worship. Yet your first forefathers chose it as an abode in preference to their birthplaces, and lived there as strangers, rather than as citizens of their own country. This they did even at a time when the Shekhinah was yet visible, but the country was full of unchastity, impurity, and idolatry. Your fathers, however, had no other desire than to remain in it. Neither did they leave it in times of dearth and famine except by God's permission. Finally, they directed their bones to be buried there.[8]

With the validity of this strong rebuke Yehuda Halevi had no argument. On the contrary, he reinforced the king's reproach by elaborating on what the Jewish people had lost by not heeding God's call for return because they do not even realize what they are saying in their own prayers. And at the conclusion of the book, he announced to the king that he was leaving for the Holy Land. The king, however, did not want him to leave and challenged him with a number of practical questions: "What can be sought in Palestine nowadays, since the divine reflex is absent from it, whilst, with a pure mind and desire, one can approach God in any place? Why wilt thou run into danger on land and water and among various peoples?"[9]

The rabbi then responded:

> Palestine is especially distinguished by the Lord of Israel, and no function can be perfect except there. . . . Thus the longing for it is awakened with disinterested motives, especially for him who wishes to live there, and to atone for past transgressions. . . . He who incurs even greater danger on account of his ardent desire to obtain forgiveness is free from reproach. . . . He braves danger, and if he escapes he praises God gratefully. . . . This sacred place serves to remind men and to stimulate them to love God, being a reward and a promise. . . . This means that Jerusalem can only be rebuilt when Israel yearns for it to such an extent that they embrace her stones and dust.[10]

The book closes with the king's reaction to the rabbi's response: "If this be so, it would be a sin to hinder thee. It is, on the contrary, a merit to assist thee. May God grant thee His help, and be thy protector and friend. May He favour thee in His mercy."[11]

Whereas *The Kuzari* was Yehuda Halevi's philosophical explication of Judaism, including its strong ties to the Holy Land, the author communicated his deep longings for Eretz Israel even more vividly in his more poetic works. Of the many of them, two poems in particular have become so much a part of Jewish tradition and ritual that it is often forgotten that Yehuda Halevi authored them. The first line of one, "My heart is in the east, and I am in the uttermost west," has been repeated often throughout the centuries by thousands of other Jews who used this line to express their longings for the Holy Land. The poem continues:

> How can I find savour in food? How shall it be sweet to me?
> How shall I render my vows and my bonds, while yet
> Zion lieth beneath the fetter of Edom, and I am in Arab chains?
> A light thing would it seem to me to leave all the good things of Spain—
> Seeing how precious in mine eyes to behold the dust of the desolate sanctuary.[12]

Another, "Ode to Zion," was incorporated into the traditional liturgy for Tishah B'av, the ninth day of the Hebrew month of Av, the day of mourning that commemorates the destruction of the Temple of Jerusalem. Its first lines read:

> Zion! wilt thou not ask if peace be with thy captives
> That seek they peace—that are the remnants of thy flocks?
> From east and west, from north and south—the greeting
> "Peace" from far and near, take thou from every side;
> And greeting from the captive of desire, giving his tears like dew
> Of Hermon, and longing to let them fall upon thine hills.[13]

Ultimately, Yehuda Halevi did immigrate to Eretz Israel. For centuries the story has been told that he was killed at the gates of Jerusalem just as he was about to realize his lifelong dream. The veracity of this tale is highly questionable. It is known that he left his native Spain for the Holy Land just before the Almohades, an Arab sect, invaded Spain and destroyed the Jewish communities of Andalusia.[14]

Rabbi Moses ben Maimon, Rambam, or Maimonides (1135–1204), was born just a few years before Yehuda Halevi's death and grew up to become the most prominent intellectual figure that Jewry produced during the medieval period. Master of both Jewish religious law, halakhah, and philosophy, he was widely revered as *the* leader of Jewry. His followers sang about him: "From Moses (who led the Jews out of Egypt and received the Torah at Sinai) until Moses (ben Maimon) there was none like Moses." In contrast to Yehuda Halevi, for whom the yearning for Eretz Israel was personal and rooted in mysticism, philosophy, and emotion, for Maimonides its unique character and status was defined within the framework of religious law.[15] Indeed, Maimonides hardly refers to Eretz Israel in his philosophical work.

When we turn to the religio-legalistic or halakhic work of Maimonides, specifically, *The Book of the Commandments* and *Yad Hachazakah: Mishneh Torah* (the law as codified by him), we find emphasis on the sanctity and sacred status of the land and the ultimate return to it. For example, in his enumeration of the positive commandments, he lists the "Commandment of the Sanctification of the New Moon,"[16] and emphasizes the unique status of Eretz Israel in the observance of that commandment: "That duty is never to be performed by anyone except the Great Court, and must be performed in the Land of Israel and nowhere else. . . . To-day we make calculations only in order to know what day the inhabitants of the Land of Israel fixed. . . . It is on their decisions that we rely, not on our calculations."[17]

He then elaborates: "Suppose we were to assume, for example, that the inhabitants of the Land of Israel disappeared–which God forbid, *since He has promised that He will not altogether wipe out and uproot the remnant of the nation*–and that there was no Court there, and that outside the Land there was no Court which had received ordination in the Land of Israel: in that case our calculations would be of no use to us whatsoever, because we are not to make calculations outside the Land" (emphasis added).[18]

Maimonides is known to have been very careful with his choice of terminology. From his comment on the hypothetical situation he raised, of the disappearance of the Jewish inhabitants from the Land, it is apparent he believed that the destiny of the entire Jewish people was dependent on there being at least some Jewish settlement in the Land of Israel. Indeed, at least one prominent rabbinic commentator specifically asserts that Maimonides maintained that the absence of a

Jewish population from the Land, even though there were Jews living in the Diaspora communities, would mean the destruction of the Jewish people.[19]

As a rule, Maimonides dealt with the status of Eretz Israel within a religio-legalistic or halakhic context, rather than within a philosophic one. Even in the case just cited, although the comment is not, strictly speaking, religio-legalistic, it was made within the larger religio-legalistic context. When we turn to the other places in which Maimonides dealt with the unique status of the Land, we find that they are almost exclusively within that context, in his codification of the Law, the *Mishneh Torah*. There the status of Eretz Israel is presented within the discussion of such laws as a slave who wishes to go to the Land; purchasing land in Eretz Israel from a heathen on Sabbath; a wife who wants to go there while her husband does not, and vice versa; and more.[20] From all of these it is obvious that for Maimonides Eretz Israel is sacred; it retains its sacred status even when the Jewish people do not have sovereignty in the Land; and even though he did not specify it as such in his enumeration of the commandments, there is a special obligation to settle in the Land.[21]

As for himself, Maimonides did dwell in the Holy Land for a while. He was born in Cordoba, Spain, from which his father escaped with his family in 1148, when Maimonides was thirteen years old, then lived in various other places in Spain for the next twelve years and another five or six years in Fez, Morocco, each time escaping just before the Almohades conquered. His father and family arrived in Eretz Israel in 1165. They lived in Acre for about five months, during which time they visited most of the holy places in the Land. The physical and spiritual conditions of the country, however, were apparently too difficult for them–there was harsh persecution, poverty was rampant, the soil was barren, there was a very meager Jewish community because few Jews lived there–and the family then moved to Egypt. The Land, however, remained dear to Maimonides, and after his death, in 1204, he was buried in the Galileean city of Tiberias.

One of the most outstanding rabbinic figures of the sixteenth century was Rabbi Judah Loew ben Bezalel, the Maharal, of Prague (ca. 1525–1609). The Maharal is known to the masses as the most famous golem creator,[22] but empirically he is much more deserving of renown as the most wide-ranging and prolific Jewish scholar and philosopher of the sixteenth century.[23] Although the Maharal's writings are not explicitly kabbalistic, they do contain strong mystical overtones.[24] For our purposes, two of his books, *Netzach Israel* (The Eternity of Israel) and *Ner Mitzvah* (The Mitzvah Candle), are particularly relevant.

In his book *Ner Mitzvah*, the Maharal formulates a Jewish theory of the sociopolitical history of civilizations,[25] which, in terms of the theme of this chapter, serves as the background for his perspectives on Eretz Israel. While emphasizing the Greek empire and the significance of the holiday of Chanukah, he also attempts to explain the history and development of the Babylonian, Persian, Roman, and Arabian empires by pointing to the unique characteristics of each of these cultures and the interrelationships between them.[26] Through the use of key mystical concepts, the Maharal then distinguished between these empires and the empire of Israel. Israel's reestablishment is rooted in its unique and holy character, and although the human intellect cannot reckon the time of the redemption, its inevitability is assured in Scripture.[27]

Netzach Israel, as noted on its title page, discusses in detail the beliefs that God will not forsake His people, that He will send the Messiah, and that the Temple in Jerusalem will be rebuilt. The Maharal begins the book by asserting:

> One cannot explain the final redemption without first explaining the subject of the dispersion, the *Galut* and the destruction . . . because the exile, *Galut*, itself is clear proof of the Redemption since there is no doubt that the *Galut* is the exception and deviation from the order that God set, each nation in its appropriate place, and He set Israel in the place which is most appropriate for them, Eretz Israel. Exile from their natural place is a complete deviation, and everything which departs from its natural place . . . has not standing in the unnatural place because if it remained in the unnatural place, the unnatural would become natural, and that is an impossibility.[28]

After discussing various reasons for the exile and dispersion,[29] the Maharal devotes a good part of a chapter in praise of Eretz Israel. He cites one of the biblical verses that refers to the Holy Land as "the land of the hart," and the Midrash, which elaborates, "Just as a hart has a rapid pace, so the Land hastens to ripen its fruit." He interprets the analogy to the hart in yet another way, in a perspective reminiscent of that of Rabbi Yehuda Halevi:

> Just as the hart, when its hide is on its body it expands . . . when it is on the living hart it stretches and when it is removed from its body the hide contracts because it is no longer alive, so the Holy Land,

when its rightful dwellers are on the Land it has an exceptional quality in that it has the a capacity to accommodate all of them. . . . But only when its rightful dwellers are on it, because when they are on it, that is its life. . . . When Israel, which is a holy nation, is upon it and it thus has an additional quality.[30]

The Maharal is the only one of the four scholars discussed in this chapter who did not even manage to visit Eretz Israel, but his thought is very much Zion-oriented in that he saw the Holy Land as the natural territorial center of the Jewish people and he repeatedly assured the Jewish masses of the ultimate redemption and return.

Rabbi Nachman of Bratslav (1772–1810) was the great-grandson of Rabbi Israel ben Eliezer, the Baal Shem Tov or Besht, the founder of the Chasidic movement, who himself became the leader of a major Chasidic sect. On the subject of Eretz Israel he also spoke from experience. In 1798 he traveled to the Holy Land, and the trip became for him one of the most important events of his life. Indeed, he dismissed as virtually worthless all of his teachings prior to that journey.[31]

As a number of Rabbi Nachman's modern biographers have noted, his whole life was characterized by religious struggle, not so much with others as with himself and between his conception of self and God.[32] Both chronologically and philosophically, he stood on the threshold of the transition from the medieval to the modern period, and this may be one of the sources of that conflict. His sayings about Eretz Israel manifest attachments to a land that has both spiritual and physical qualities, and his approach to it appears as a synthesis of the medieval mystical and the modern physical. Thus, in line with his predecessors, he said: "Eretz Israel is the most inclusive and perfect holiness of all holinesses."[33] Or: "There is no wisdom like the wisdom of Eretz Israel, and every Jew has a portion in Eretz Israel, and each according to his portion in Eretz Israel, so he receives and suckles from the brains of Eretz Israel."[34]

At other times, however, Rabbi Nachman spoke of Eretz Israel as of a very real land and his sayings have a much more modern tone to them. For example: "If one wishes to be a true Jew, that is to go from level to level, it is impossible without Eretz Israel. This Eretz Israel, plainly and simply, with these houses and yards."[35]

In even more explicitly modern terms he said: "Even though the gentiles stole our land and our inheritance from us and we do not have the power to take it away from them, because of a blemish in our actions, we pray and scream that Eretz Israel is ours, it is our inheritance. We thereby reply to "the other side" that the claim of the gentiles is no claim at all. Eretz Israel is ours and ultimately we will take it away from their hands, with God's help."[36]

And as if to dispel any idealistic fantasies about the Land, he said: "Physically, by using human eyesight, no difference between Eretz Israel and other countries can be seen. Only the one who is worthy to believe in its holiness can make somewhat of a distinction."[37]

To those of his colleagues and students who tried to discourage him from making his journey to Eretz Israel he responded: "I want to travel to Eretz Israel, and I know the enormity of the many barriers which I will have to making this journey. But as long as my soul is in me and the spirit of life is in my nostrils, I will sacrifice myself and I will harness all of my strength to go there. As long as there is life within me I will go there, and the Good God will do as He sees fit."[38]

Although Rabbi Nachman and, centuries earlier, Maimonides did not, each for his own reasons, remain in Eretz Israel, the traditional Jewish dream of aliya was not merely hypothetical; it was often translated into empirical reality. In fact, even after the destruction of the Temple in 70 C.E. and well into the talmudic era, there was a steady flow of rabbinic scholars who left the Babylonian Jewish community and settled in the Holy Land. It was only with the persecutions of the Jews in Palestine by Constantine the Great, during the fourth century, that there was a sharp decline in aliya. For the next several centuries there was only individual aliya. There was no wave of aliya, no mass aliya, nor even any group aliya to speak of. At most, a very small number of people came as individuals.

When there was group aliya, it was invariably related to persecution or other treacherous conditions in the country of emigration. Thus, when the Almohades persecuted Jews in North Africa during the twelfth century, some of them went to Eretz Israel. Even then, not all that many went, as witness the fact that the Jewish population in the Holy Land in the middle of the twelfth century consisted of approximately one thousand families.[39]

From the very end of the twelfth century, when the Arabs forced the Crusaders from the Holy Land, the Jewish population increased. According to a well-known Jewish traveler of that time, Yehuda Alcharizi, in 1190 (or 1187) Saladin sent in his armies and after the Arab conquest he issued an invitation to the Jews to settle there.[40] Tradition has it, for example, that in 1211, a group of more than three hundred Tosafists, rabbis in France and England, went to Eretz Israel. Although that figure is, apparently, somewhat inflated, there seems to be no question that a group of rabbis did go at that time, due in part, no doubt, to the more hospitable conditions under the Arabs, which began with Saladin's capture of Jerusalem and his subsequent invitation to Jews to settle there.[41]

In 1267 Rabbi Moses ben Nachman, Nachmanides, left his native Spain under an order of exile because of his disputations with the church and arrived in the Holy Land, which had several years earlier been ransacked and left to waste by Mongolian invaders. Although he died a short time later, in 1270, the three years he lived in Eretz Israel were very productive ones for him–he completed his commentary on the Torah there–and very important ones for the small remnant of a Jewish community that remained there. He was the recognized religious leader of the Land, and his presence and activity served to revitalize Jewish life there, so much so that it is said that since his time there has been a continuous Jewish presence in the Holy Land. He, therefore, earned the title "patriarch of the community of settlement."

Jewish immigration to the Holy Land increased steadily during the following centuries, with Jews coming from many different lands. During the early fifteenth century there was a marked increase in aliya of Jews from Spain due to a sharp rise in messianism.[42] Later in that century the Inquisition contributed to another rise in immigration from Spain.[43]

One of the most noted olim of the late fifteenth century was Rabbi Ovadia of Bartenura, the Italian scholar whose commentary on the Mishnah is *the* standard work and who arrived in Eretz Israel in 1488. He became very active in the communal life of Jerusalem Jewry and was a source of inspiration for the aliya of other Italian Jews.

Jerusalem, however, was not the major Jewish center in Eretz Israel at the turn of the sixteenth century. In 1500 there was an estimated ten thousand Jews living in the Safed region of the country.[44] As a result of the expulsion from Spain, Jewish mysticism, Kabbalah, spread widely. As Gershom Scholem puts it: "The expulsion from Spain in 1492 produced a crucial change in the history of the Kabbalah. The profound upheaval in the Jewish consciousness caused by this catastrophe also made the Kabbalah public property."[45] Safed, which was the center of Kabbalah teaching, now attracted growing numbers of Jews from many countries, from both the Spanish (Sephardi) and German (Ashkenazi) centers in Europe as well as from North Africa. During the second half of the sixteenth century, the attraction of Safed as the center of Kabbalah grew even stronger under the influence of Rabbi Isaac Luria, the "Holy Ari" (1534–72), "the most important kabbalistic mystic after the explusion."[46] Although Luria only lived in Safed for the last two of three years of his life, his charismatic personality enabled him to have a profound influence on his colleagues and students, and his teachings long outlived his own short life.

In 1700 Rabbi Judah the Saint (1658–1718), a scholar who was highly regarded by both Sephardim and his fellow Ashkenazim, led a group of some 1500 Jews to Eretz Israel. Their aliya was primarily the result of the severe strife and difficulties caused by the growth of the Sabbatian movement.[47]

The next major, and not totally unrelated, group aliya was that of the early Chasidim in 1764, among whom were such notables as Rabbi Nachman of Horodenka and Rabbi Menachem Mendel of Peremishlyany.[48] Earlier some colleagues of the founder of modern Chasidism, Rabbi Israel Baal Shem Tov, the Besht (1700–1760), had gone on aliya; for example, Rabbi Abraham Gershon of Kitov, who was a brother-in-law of the Besht, and Rabbi Yaacov Yukel of Mezhibuz.[49] In 1777 an even larger Chasidic aliya was led by Rabbi Menachem Mendel of Vitebsk and Rabbi Abraham of Kalisk, who settled in Safed and Tiberias and became the recognized leaders of the Chasidim in Eretz Israel; they were shortly followed by many other major Chasidic figures who went on aliya.[50] The Chasidic settlement was limited to the Galilee region until a group of Chabad (Lubavitch) Chasidim came and settled in Hebron in 1823,[51] and that community remained in Hebron until the riots of 1929.

At the turn of the century the Chasidic aliya began to trickle off considerably, apparently due to both ideological and situational reasons. Conditions in the Holy Land were very difficult, and the new generation of Chasidic leaders in Eastern Europe was much less Zion-oriented than were its predecessors. Perhaps not completely coincidentally, the aliya of the "Prushim," the non-Chasidic Ashkenazi Jews, many of whom were students of Rabbi Elijah, the Gaon, of Vilna, which began in the beginning of the eighteenth century (see Chapter 2), started just as the Chasidic aliya declined.[52]

2

Messianism and the Forerunners of Zionism in the Nineteenth Century

Although there may be no explicit reference to messianism in *Tanakh*, the Bible, belief in the Messiah and the ultimate redemption of the children of Israel is an integral part of Jewish belief, at least since the talmudic period. In the Talmud itself there are numerous references to *Mashiach* and *Yemot Hamashiach*, the period of the Messiah, as well as attempts to calculate precisely when the Messiah will arrive.[1] Despite the strong condemnations of attempts to calculate the precise date of the arrival of the Messiah, by Rabbi Shmuel Bar Nachmani and Rabbi Yonatan,[2] and centuries later by Maimonides[3] and others, messianic speculation continued full force through the seventeenth century, until the disasters of Shabbtai Zvi and the Frankists.[4] Those debacles strengthened the position of those who opposed such speculation. This did not mean, however, that Jews ceased to believe in the ultimate coming of the Messiah. That belief, set down by Maimonides as one of the thirteen cardinal Jewish beliefs recited daily by observant Jews–*Ani maamin beemunah shlemah beviat hamashiach* (I firmly believe in the coming of the Messiah)–remained as strong as ever. It was the engaging in calculations that was scorned by most scholars, not the belief itself.[5]

Despite the official scorning of messianic calculation, there was widespread anticipation in virtually every Jewish community throughout the world that the year 5600, or 1840, would mark the onset of the arrival of the Messiah. For example, as Jacob Katz points out, "In all of the Balkan countries, as well as in all of those of Eastern

Europe, there was widespread opinion that the forthcoming year, 5600, will be the year of redemption."[6] This belief, apparently based on statements in both the Talmud[7] and the *Zohar*,[8] spanned world Jewish communities from Africa to Asia and from eastern to western Europe.[9] It was precisely within this atmosphere of messianic anticipation that the students of Rabbi Elijah, the Gaon, of Vilna, left Lithuania and immigrated to Safed and Jerusalem in Eretz Israel. The available evidence strongly suggests that the Gaon not only condoned their aliya but actually decreed it, because he was convinced that the year 1840 was to be the year of *atchalta degeulah*, "the beginning of the redemption," and he wanted his students to begin preparing the setting for the arrival of the Messiah.[10] Tradition has it that the Gaon himself seriously intended to go on aliya and in fact began to, but for unknown reasons turned back midcourse. This lends further credence to the claim that his students were acting with his blessings and according to his wishes.

It was within this air of messianic anticipation, too, that the founding fathers of religious Zionism-Rabbi Zvi Hirsch Kalischer, the Ashkenazi, and Rabbi Yehuda Chai Alkalai, the Sephardi–emerged as authoritative critics of the popular notion that the Messiah would arrive suddenly through a momentous act of divine intervention. Kalischer (1795–1874) was born and raised in western Poland, moved to Germany, studied with the most prominent scholars of halakhah of the late nineteenth century, and developed into one of the most learned Orthodox rabbis of his generation. He was, however, atypical in that he did not adopt the characteristic Eastern European Orthodox approach of rejecting modernity out of hand. As will be discussed below, he was able to speak the language of modernists and to develop and retain close relationships even with those who rejected Orthodoxy.[11] In this respect, his approach to the world at large was much more characteristic of German than of Eastern European Orthodoxy.

Four years before the widely anticipated date of the redemption, Kalischer wrote a letter to Asher Anshel (Anselm Mayer) Rothschild, the head of the Frankfurt branch of the Rothschild family banks, in which, based on his position on the Messiah and redemption, he turned to Rothschild for assistance. Perhaps the most novel aspect of Kalischer's approach was in his conviction that the Messiah would arrive through natural processes and by human efforts:

No one should think that the redemption of Israel and our Messiah, whom we await each day, will arrive through God's sudden descension upon Earth saying to His people, "Go out," or that He will suddenly send His Messiah from Heaven to blow on a big *shofar* over the dispersed of Israel. . . .

The beginning of the redemption will be through natural causes and by the will of the governments to gather some of the dispersed of Israel to the Holy Land. . . .

Then, when many of the dispersed of Israel will be in the Holy Land and Jerusalem, the Merciful One will comfort us to bring about for us complete redemption and everlasting happiness. At that time, there will be wars over the Land of Israel, and then will arrive [the Redeemer].[12]

After his lengthy discussion of the Messiah and redemption, Kalischer turns to Rothschild and suggests to him that he buy a different piece of land for Muhammad Ali, the Egyptian ruler who then controlled Eretz Israel, so that Ali would give Eretz Israel to the Jews, where, through the help of many wealthy Jews, they would be able to establish a government of Israel and build up the country for the many dispersed Jews who would flock to it.[13]

Although Rothschild's response, if any, is unknown, it is known that Kalischer subsequently wrote to Sir Moses Montefiore, apparently in 1839,[14] and also to Abraham (Albert) Cohen, the *gabbai zedakah,* manager of philanthropic funds, of the Rothschild family in Paris, in 1860.[15] In 1860 Kalischer joined an organization founded by Dr. Chaim Lurie, the Society for the Colonization of Palestine in Franfurt on the Oder.[16] Finally, in 1862, Kalischer's major and highly influential work, *Drishat Zion,* was published and it came to be a seminal work in the literature of religious Zionism.

The uniqueness of Kalischer's messianism lies in his espousal of the natural process of the redemption, and the fact that he combined his vision with pragmatism, that is, he suggested specific ways to settle the land and undertook efforts to realize those suggestions. He not only wrote to wealthy Jews in an effort to enlist their financial assistance in building up the land; he also detailed the directions that building should take. It is significant that two of his suggestions–the establishment of an agricultural cooperative as the economic foundation of settlement and the establishment of an agricultural school in Eretz Israel–were both seconded by Moses Hess[17] and became realities in later years. The second goal was realized when the Alliance Israelite Universelle founded the well-known agricultural school

Mikveh Israel in 1870; and the first when the Palestine Office of the World Zionist Organization adopted an emphasis on agricultural development in the early 1900s.

Kalischer's slightly younger contemporary, Rabbi Yehuda Alkalai (1798–1878), was born in Sarajevo, Serbia, which is now in Yugoslavia but was then under Turkish rule, and where his father, Shlomo Chai, was a teacher. In contrast to the halakhic scholarship of Kalischer, Alkalai was a student of Midrash (homiletics) and Kabbalah, which he apparently learned from his teachers Rabbis Yaacov Finzi and Eliezer Pappo, as well as from his travels throughout the large Sephardic communities in the Balkans.[18]

Alkalai began his adult life in the footsteps of his father, by becoming a congregational "reader" (*hazan*) and a teacher. He developed a strong interest in Hebrew grammar and wrote a summary of the rules of Hebrew grammar in Ladino for the Sephardic community he was then serving. Subsequently, in 1839, he published his first book, *Darkhei Noam* (Pleasant Ways), on Hebrew grammar, with the help of a few individuals in his community.[19]

In the introduction to this book, which appeared just one year before 1840, Alkalai adds his name to the roster of those who predicted the imminent arrival of the Messiah and states that he wrote his long introduction to encourage repentance and good deeds, lest the year designated for redemption turn into a year of evil.[20] In his second book, *Shlom Yerushalayim* (The Peace of Jerusalem), published in 1840, which he wrote in response to those who were critical of his allusions to the impending redemption, he relates that for many years he had been trembling with fear, lest that year bring many evils with it, and in fact a number of them have already occurred.[21] He then attempts to pacify his fellow Jews, who may be overcome with fear and disillusionment over the absence of the Messiah, by suggesting that the calculated date, 5600, does not refer to only one year, but to the century beginning in 5600,[22] and again calls on his brethren to repent. This time he focuses on the specifics of the repentance and calls for the establishment of a tithe that will be directed toward the rebuilding of Jerusalem: "The first repentance, the first correction, and the first heavenly yoke which we must accept is that of taking one-tenth of everything which the Holy One, Blessed be He, provides us with during the course of that year and to send it to Jerusalem. This matter with which we are dealing is a great *mitzvah,* and it has the power to greatly hasten the redemption in our days."[23] The remainder of the book consists of elaborations, through a multitude of midrashic and kabbalistic references, on the Messiah and redemption and the importance of implementing the tithe as the sine qua non of repentance.

In the introduction to his next book, *Minchat Yehudah* (The Offering of Judah), published in 1843, Alkalai writes lavish praises of Sir Moses Montefiore.[24] The book itself is an elaboration and further development of the basic ideas in his previous work. In this book he stresses that the redemption will not come suddenly, but in stages: "You should not imagine that the end, the redemption, the salvation, the restoration, and the arrival of our Messiah are separate terms and that all will come simultaneously and in one day. Each has its own time. . . . For its beginning is a small matter which is not sensed. . . . And anyone who says that the beginning of the redemption will come about through Messiah, the son of David, is as one who says that the sun will shine before daybreak, which is nonsense."[25]

Since the redemption will come in stages, requires preparation, and is about to commence, Alkalai called for the implementation of those preparations through his earlier plea for a tithe for the rebuilding of Jerusalem and for the beginning of a Jewish return to Eretz Israel. As a first step, he calls for the return of twenty-two thousand Jews to the Land.[26] This, of course, will require governmental support, which Alkalai was confident would be forthcoming. He then urges every Jew to send one of his children to settle in Eretz Israel.[27]

At this point Alkalai suggests that redemption involves not only the Land but the People as well: "Behold, in truth and in full faith that this matter is of great necessity for us, to gather our dispersed from the four corners of the world to be united into one, because, as a result of our many sins, we are very spread out and very disparate one from his brother, because each country has its own distinct language and customs which separate the group and prevent the redemption."[28]

Alkalai was one of the earliest advocates of a return to Hebrew as *the* language of the Jewish people, a theme he reiterated in his later works. He declares:

> I can testify that I have always been pained by the fact that our forebearers erred in that they so allowed our holy language to be forgotten. Our nation has been replaced by the seventy nations and our language replaced by the seventy languages of the nations among whom we are dispersed, to the point that several years are required before a child is able translate the Torah, and when God will perform for us all of His miracles and will gather our dispersed from

the four corners of the Earth, we will not be able to speak with one another, and this divided community will not be successful. . . . Therefore, we should not despair, but should devote our efforts to reinstate our language and to make it central. And God will cast His spirit upon the teachers and the students, on the boys and on the girls, and they will learn to speak fluently.[29]

Moreover, he argues, although the final redemption and the arrival of the Messiah, the son of David, are events whose time one can neither reckon nor hasten, earlier steps in the process of redemption, including the arrival of the Messiah, the son of Joseph, are definitely dependent on us,[30] and the appropriate era for the arrival of the first Messiah, the son of Joseph, is from the year 5601 (1841) on.[31] Therefore, we should give due recognition to the efforts of the Rothschild family and others and contribute our own funds to the settlement of the Land.

In his next book, *Kol Korei* (A Beckoning Voice), first published in 1848, Alkalai offers a somewhat radical interpretation to the *mitzvah* of *teshuvah*. In place of the traditional understanding of *teshuvah* as repentance, Alkalai interprets the term literally to mean "return," that is, to return to the Land: "It is well-known and accepted by all Israel that [the redemption] depends upon *teshuvah*. . . . Therefore, there is no greater *teshuvah* than for us to accept upon ourselves His Godliness, that is, to return to His land. . . . That is to say, when God will be our God, which is, when we return to His land, on that day will God be One and His name One."[32]

In *Kol Mevaser* (A Harbinger's Voice), written in 1852 in response to conventions of Reform Judaism, which he saw as representing total assimilation, Alkalai reaffirms the traditional Jewish ban on rebelling against the nations of the world in the effort to reestablish Jewry in Eretz Israel. Rather, he says, Jews must organize themselves and appoint leaders who will enlist the assistance of the nations of the world, and he cites many biblical, talmudic, and midrashic sources to assure that that assistance will be forthcoming.[33]

In all his later works, Alkalai embellished these themes, namely, that his times were those of the beginning of the redemptive process, that the first Messiah, the son of Joseph, would arrive and act in natural ways, and that it is incumbent upon all Jews to begin to return to the Land, initially by helping those who are now prepared to go and by supporting those who are already there. For example, in *Meikitz Nirdamim* (Awakener of the Sleeping), written in 1863, he writes: "Therefore, as a first and leading step to the redemption of our selves, every Jew . . . is obligated to oversee the income of our brethren who sit in the front row in the Kingdom of Heaven, those who dwell in Eretz Israel and to develop for them employment and work so that they will be able to support themselves."[34]

In 1871 Alkalai himself went to live in Jerusalem, where he continued his efforts to organize Jewry for the support of the rebuilding of Eretz Israel. In an article written that same year, he tells of his success in organizing Ashkenazi and Sephardi leaders of Jerusalem for the establishment of a branch of Kol Israel Chaverim (All of Israel Are Brothers), an organization founded in Paris in 1860, of which Alkalai was an enthusiastic supporter. The Jerusalem branch had as its explicit objective assisting the poor in the settling and building of the Land.[35] Likewise, he was an avid supporter of the Society for the Colonization of Palestine in Frankfurt on the Oder, and of the agricultural school Mikveh Israel. In a letter written from Jaffa in 1865, he again stresses that "the beginning of the redemption is a physical redemption . . . and the major barrier to the arrival of the Messiah is because of those physical things in this world which must be corrected, that is, to redeem the Land and to build a settlement in Eretz Israel, so that it will not stand empty and desolate."[36]

Thus, though he remained a messianist throughout his life, Alkalai came to believe, like Kalischer, that the redemption, at least in its early stages, would be realized through a natural process that required the active involvement of Jews in that process.

The third of the three "true forerunners of Zionism"[37] was Moses Hess (1812–75). Born in Bonn and a descendant of rabbis–his paternal great-grandfather was a rabbi in Mannheim and his maternal grandfather was a rabbi near Frankfurt–Hess was a secular Jew who in his youth became estranged from Jews and Judaism,[38] married a non-Jewish woman who had been a prostitute, was an editor of the *Rheinische Zeitung* and a prominent figure in the German radical movement, and was "the first German Communist."[39] He had developed a relationship with Marx, who was a regular contributor to the *Rheinische Zeitung,* through their mutual interest in the philosophy of Hegel and socialist theory and praxis,[40] and was nicknamed by his friends "the communist rabbi."[41]

According to his own account, it was Hess's reactions to the notorious blood libel in Damascus in 1840 that led him to write *Rome and Jerusalem,* first published in 1862.[42] The book was revolutionary in that it asserted that Jews are a national entity and advocated the establishment of a Jewish national home in Eretz Israel. When Herzl read the book, in 1901, he proclaimed, "Everything that we have tried is already in his book."[43] Jews are primarily a nation, Hess argues, and he is highly critical of both non-Jews and Jewish reformers who deny its national character. In contrast to Christianity, Judaism is not simply a religion: "A Jew is a Jew by birth. And even if he or his parents converted, he is still Jewish. It may be that according to modern conceptions of religion this is a paradox. However, in reality and practice, I have found this view to be true. An apostate is perforce a Jew and will remain a Jew much as he strongly resists it."[44]

As a student of modern nationalist movements with convictions of the ultimate liberation of the oppressed classes, Hess proceeds to argue for Jewish national liberation with the same passion he held for other oppressed nations. Jewish nationality, he argues, consists of "a unity which cannot be separated from the heritage of my forefathers, from the Holy Land and the Eternal City, from the birthplace of the faith in the Divine unity of life and the pact of brotherhood which will be taken between all peoples."[45]

Despite the vast differences in the backgrounds of Hess, Kalischer, and Alkalai, they shared a common belief in the dawning of the messianic era in the nineteenth century. For Hess, that century marked the "springtime" of human history and was characterized by the liberation and regeneration of oppressed nations and classes, and it was the destiny of the Jewish people, in their own liberation and regeneration, to play a pivotal role in the universal process of liberation:

> We Jews have always maintained the belief in the coming of the messianic era. This belief found expression in our historical religion through the Sabbath. The Sabbath embodies the notion which has been the pulse of our spirit in all generations, that the future will bring for us a historical Sabbath just as surely as the past brought us the natural Sabbath, and that history, just as nature, will have its epoch of completion and harmonious perfection.
>
> . . . The epoch of the maturity of the world begins, according to our historical religion, with the messianic era. That is the time when the Jewish people and all historic nations will be rejuvenated and regenerated–the time of "the resurrection of the dead," or "the coming of the Redeemer," or "the Heavenly Jerusalem," or other symbolic names whose meaning will no longer be able to be misunderstood.
>
> The messianic era–that is the present epoch which began to germinate with Spinoza and its first historical manifestation was with the great French Revolution.

. . . The narrow confines of this letter don't allow me to suffi-ciently broaden the discussion to such an encompassing discussion. Besides that, the fate of my people concerns me so at this moment that I cannot divert my attention with a problem which, although strongly interconnected with the Jewish question, will have to wait for its solution only after this finds it solution.[46]

Hess's strong belief in the coming of the Messiah, a belief he terms "the soul of Judaism,"[47] was criticized as untraditional because he believed that the Messiah would come through a natural process. In response to one critic, Leopold Leff, he wrote:

Were you not known as a talmudic scholar and a student of Jewish literature and thought, I would have assumed you to be one of those Jewish "priests" who are suitable as no one else to be Chris-tian theologians. . . . In the mouth of such a "priest," who can't read Hebrew without vowels . . . your criticisms would not have surprised me. But who as you, sir, knows that our rabbis and scholars fash-ioned Judaism, guarded it and developed it, were not capable of turning the product of their spirit into some kind of idolatry. They could not have allowed Biblical-Talmudic Judaism, with whose mes-sianic belief, free of delusion, I firmly identify, to become estranged and distorted with that uncritical orthodoxy of a later period to which I do, indeed, explicitly object. You know that the great scholars of Israel in the Talmudic period and during the Middle Ages believed that the arrival of the Messiah and the regeneration of Israel will come about in a natural way.[48]

Although Hess was unique, and most of the secular Zionist lead-ers neither adhered to nor proclaimed such messianic notions, it is nevertheless the case that a large percentage of the masses of Jews were attracted to Zionism because of their messianic beliefs, and these were fed upon by the fact that "modern [Jewish] nationalism leaned heavily on the old messianism, and derived from it much of its ide-ological and even more of its emotional appeal."[49] One manifestation of this was in the widespread perception among the masses that The-odore Herzl was the Messiah. For example, on his way to Constan-tinople in June 1896 Herzl

passed through Sofia and was able to observe at first hand what an impression his appeal had made on the Jewish masses. When he went through toward Constantinople hundreds of people waited on the railroad platform to get a glimpse of him. "There was an old man in a fur hat who resembled my grandfather Simon Herzl." The crowd called him "Lord and Leader in Israel," and shouted "Next year in

Jerusalem." On the way back to Vienna he spent a few hours in the Bulgarian capital. The crowd conducted him, amid continuous cheering, to the Zionist Society, and then to the synagogue. Hundreds of people were assembled there, as though he were the bringer of messianic tidings. They pressed forward to kiss his hand. . . . Herzl's sense of responsibility revolted from this development.[50]

Nor was it only the masses who viewed him as a messianic figure. In his diaries he relates that he read in the newspaper *Haam* earlier that year that the chief rabbi or Sofia, Dr. Bierer, "considers me the Messiah. This Passover, a lecture on my publication will be given in Bulgarian and Spanish before a large audience."[51]

Likewise when Herzl came to Vilna:

> They were careful that his arrival should not become known to the masses, because they were afraid of demonstrations which might cause problems. But Herzl's visit did become known and the masses gathered in the streets and encamped at the railway station in the middle of the night. The police intervened, and the masses gladly accepted their blows, if only to have the privilege and honor of seeing the leader. "Long live the leader," someone called. The leader heard, was stunned, and tears dripped from his eyes.[52]

And as David Ben-Gurion recalls of his childhood, Herzl came to his city: "When he appeared in Plonsk, people greeted him as the Messiah. Everyone went around saying 'The Messiah has come,' and we children were impressed."[53]

All of this, of course, should not be taken to suggest that the Zionist movement per se was a religious messianic movement. Quite the contrary. The vast majority of the founders of the Zionist movement were secularists, and most of the members were not religiously observant.[54] Zionism did, however, respond to the religious notion of messianism, which was so firmly embedded in traditional Jewish culture that it was internalized even by those who were not religiously observant and may have even been ideologically secularist.

Within the Mizrachi, the religious Zionist movement, there were two divergent approaches to Zionism in general and Herzl in particular. Rabbi Isaac Jacob Reines (1839–1915), under whose leadership the Mizrachi was organized as a faction within the World Zionist Organization in 1902, viewed Zionism solely in pragmatic terms, that is, as a movement whose objective it is to guard and enhance the physical well-being of Jews.[55]

On the other hand, Rabbi Abraham Isaac Kook (1865–1935), Reines's close colleague who subsequently became the first chief rabbi of Eretz Israel and spiritual leader of the Mizrachi, viewed the contemporary period as *ikvetah demeshikhah*, "the footsteps of the Messiah,"[56] and Herzl as a messianic figure.[57]

With the establishment of the State of Israel, the issue became more complex because it entailed, for the first time, the question of attributing sacred and messianic significance to an existing political entity that even the most ardent messianists were convinced was not the fulfillment of the messianic dream. Even among religious Zionists differences remain, for example, as to whether one should recite the prayer *Hallel* on Israel's Independence Day, Yom Haatzmaut, and whether or not to say it with a *brakhah* (blessing). Although there is less of a controversy with respect to the "Prayer for the Well-Being of the State," which was coined by the chief rabbinate and describes the state as "the first shoots of our redemption," there is no consensus on this.[58]

3

American Jewry and the Land of Israel in the Eighteenth and Nineteenth Centuries

Although America was "the New World" and the American Jewish community developed differently, in many respects, from the Jewish communities of the Old World, American Jews did, nevertheless, maintain close ties with their brethren abroad, especially those in Europe. They also retained the traditional rituals commemorating both the destruction of Jerusalem and the hope and faith in its rebirth.

The American Jewish community had its genesis in New York with the arrival of twenty-three Jewish refugees from Brazil to New Amsterdam on September 7, 1654. These Jews and most of those who followed them throughout that century and into the next were Sephardim, followers of the traditions of the Spanish center of Jewish subcultural traditions, which had been most prominent in southern Europe. In 1664 the British captured New Amsterdam from the Dutch and renamed it New York, and in 1674 the duke of York granted freedom of religion in the colony. Accordingly, in the 1690s the twenty Jewish families in New York organized an official synagogue, and by 1706 they had a formal constitution and called themselves Congregation Shearith Israel (the Remnant of Israel). In 1729 they erected a building on Mill Street that housed their synagogue for most of the following century.[1]

By the middle of the eighteenth century, the Jewish population in North American was concentrated in five major cities: New York, Newport, Philadelphia, Charleston, and Savannah. The fact that these were port cities is reflective of Jewish involvement in commerce and trade. The New York community, the oldest and largest, numbered about sixty families. The Newport community, second both chronologically and demographically, consisted of approximately thirty families. The Philadelphia and Charleston communities had about twelve families each, and the Savannah community had less than ten.

At the outbreak of the revolutionary war, the Jewish population in the country numbered between one thousand and twenty-five hundred individuals, out of a total population of between two and a half million. Because they were concentrated in five cities, however, they took on greater significance than the one-tenth of 1 percent of the total colonial population that they actually were. Both numerically and in the level and character of their service, Jews figured prominently in the military aspects of the war, as well as in its financial and economic aspects. Most Jews supported the revolution because of political and economic grievances against England and because of the growing sense of Americanism that was also rife among Jews. Those who remained loyalists did so primarily out of a sense of obligation to England or because they had economic contacts with British firms.

The outcome of the war was uniquely revolutionary for Jews in that the United States was the first country in modern times to grant complete equality of rights to Jews. The Constitution, which was ratified in 1789, proclaimed in Article VI that "no religious Test shall ever be required as Qualification to any Office or public Trust under the United States." In 1791 the first ten amendments to the Constitution, the Bill of Rights, were adopted, and the First Amendment guaranteed that "Congress shall make no law respecting an establishment of religion, or prohibiting the free exercise thereof; or abridging the freedom of speech, or of the press; or of the right of the people peaceably to assemble, and to petition the Government for a redress of grievances."

America was different for Jews in other respects as well. That President George Washington was favorably disposed toward Jews is evidenced by the responses he sent to the congratulatory letters received upon his inauguration from the various Jewish communities in the country.[2] Also, Jews enjoyed fairly wide social equality even before the Constitution guaranteed them legal equality. To many religious Christians, Jews had special privileged status. America was the "New Zion," and Jews were viewed as the descendants of the Hebrews of old.

The earliest recorded direct contact between North American Jews and the Holy Land was in the form of emissaries who, even before the Revolution, came from Eretz Israel and elsewhere to raise money for Jewish institutions abroad or for themselves while, at the same time, imparting Jewish learning among those whom they solicited. The first among these seems to have been one Rabbi Moses Malki, from Safed, who was with New York's Shearith Israel for four months at the end of 1759 and then was in Newport for a brief while. In 1761 another emissary from Safed, Chaim Muddahy, arrived in New York to raise funds for the relief of those who suffered from the earthquake in Safed on October 30, 1760.[3] Following the visits of these two emissaries, correspondence between Jews in Eretz Israel and Jewish communities in North America, in which the former solicited funds from the latter, became fairly regular.[4]

The most notable among the early emissaries from the Holy Land was Rabbi Chaim Isaac Karigal, from Hebron, who in 1772 spent a month in Philadelphia, almost a half year in New York, and then was in Newport from March through July 1773. One of his sermons, preached in Newport on the first day of the Jewish holiday of Shavuot (Pentecost), became the first Jewish sermon published in America.[5] During the course of his stay in Newport, Karigal developed a close relationship with the Reverend Ezra Stiles, a local Congregationalist minister who later became president of Yale University. Stiles was a frequent visitor at the synagogue and had close contact with quite a few Jews in Newport, with whom he engaged in discussions of theology and mysticism. In his diaries he recorded that, on August 10, 1769, a Jew told him of his calculations indicating the arrival of Messiah in 1783. Stiles also mentions a Jewish custom in Newport indicating that Jews there were ever alert to the imminent arrival of the Messiah.[6] Karigal was warmly received in Newport and was considered the rabbi of the community during his stay there.

The only other such emissary during the eighteenth century of whom a record is known to exist was Rabbi Samuel Cohen of Jerusalem. He apparently was in North America for only a brief time, since the only record of his presence, in Newport, is in the diaries of Ezra Stiles. It would appear that the Revolution brought a halt to the journeys of emissaries from Eretz Israel to the United States, not only during its duration but until well into the next century, when the relationship between American Jews and the Holy Land took on a much more actively national dimension.

Even during this interim, however, American Jews maintained their religious connection with the Holy Land. Not only did they express their hopes for restoration and the return to Zion in their prayers; it was also emphasized in many of the sermons delivered in the various congregations in the United States. A most prominent indication of the deep faith in the Jewish return to Zion and plea for its speedy realization is in the sermons of the Reverend Gershom Mendes Seixas, of New York's Shearith Israel. For example, in his Thanksgiving sermon of 1789, Seixas began with the first three verses in the Hundredth Psalm, raised the question of how human knowledge of God is possible, and then proceeded to focus on Jews in biblical times, the condition of the Jews in dispersion, the Jewish belief in the Messiah, and the return to Zion. "From that period even till now, our predecessors have been, and we are still at this time in captivity among the different nations of the earth; and though we are, through divine goodness, made equal partakers of the government by the constitution of these states, with the rest of the inhabitants, still we cannot but view ourselves as captives to what we were formerly, and what we expect to be hereafter, when the outcasts of Israel should be gathered together, as it is said in Isaiah ch. xxvii, v. 12."[7]

Seixas was not the only one to publicly profess these yearnings for the return to Zion. In 1784 New York's Congregation Shearith Israel participated in a prayer for Governor Clinton, which concluded with similar yearnings:

> As Thou has granted to these thirteen states of America everlasting freedom, so mayst Thou bring us forth once again from bondage into freedom, and mayst Thou sound the great born for our freedom. . . . May He show us wonders as in days of old, and may He the Holy One, blessed be He, restore the Presence to Zion and the order of service to Jerusalem. . . . May He send us the priest of righteousness who will lead us upright to our land. May the beauty of the Lord be upon us, and may the redeemer come speedily to Zion in our days.[8]

In his sermon on May 9, 1798, a day designated by President John Adams for national fasting and prayer following the notorious XYZ Affair, Gershom Seixas was even more explicit. He began by praying for the well-being of the country to which divine will brought them so that they may enjoy its rights and privileges and, rather than engaging in any civil or political discussion, proceeded to offer a religious explanation of the dreadful state of the world and the disdain with which America has been treated. "When we reflect on the situation and circumstances of the present wars, and the depravity and corrupt state of human nature, that prevails almost throughout the world, we must necessarily be led to believe that the glorious period of redemption is near at hand, and that our God will make manifest his intentions of again collecting the scattered remnants of Israel, and establishing them according to His divine promise."[9]

While Seixas was but a preacher who constantly kept the notion of the return to Zion alive,[10] he apparently had a strong influence on one of the foremost American Jewish personalities during the first half of the nineteenth century, Mordecai Manuel Noah.[11] He was born in Philadelphia in 1785, and when he was not quite seven years old his mother died and his father disappeared. Thereafter, he was raised by his maternal grandfather, Jonas Phillips, who had been one of the organizers of Philadelphia's Congregation Mikveh Israel. As a youth, Noah also lived in New York and Charleston, and he drew public attention due to his early career as a journalist, author, and playwright. In 1913 he was appointed American consul in Tunis, but was recalled two years later. Among the reasons given by Secretary of State James Monroe was the fact that Noah was Jewish and that this would interfere with his consular functions.[12]

Noah returned to New York and became the editor of the Democratic party's Tammany Hall newspaper, the *National Advocate,* for ten years. A deeply committed Jew, he was a central figure in New York's Jewish community and was one of the organizers, in 1925, of Congregation Bnai Jeshurun, the city's first Ashkenazi synagogue. Noah also held a number of official positions in New York City government. Subsequently, until his death in 1851, he edited several other newspapers and wrote plays, some of which were quite successful.

Noah was the first American Jew who might be called a "pre-Zionist."[13] Initially, Noah sounded like no more than a faithful follower of his teacher, Gershom Seixas. For example, in a discourse he gave at the consecration of the new synagogue building for New York's Congregation Shearith Israel, on April 17, 1818, Noah observed: "Never were prospects for the restoration of the Jewish nation to their ancient rights and dominion more brilliant than they are at present."[14] Echoing all of Seixas's sermons, Noah said that the Jewish presence in the United States is also temporary, but "until the Jews can recover their ancient rights and dominions, and take their rank among the governments of the earth, this is their chosen country."[15] As such, Noah urged the congregation to find a rabbi, to learn and perpetuate the Hebrew language, and to observe the Sabbath.[16]

Also, since education is the means by which people become aware of and come to appreciate God's blessings, he called on Jews to maintain their high standards of education. After educating their children, they should guide them toward independence by "giving them a lasting fortune, in causing them to be taught a useful branch of labor,"[17] ideally that of the patriarchs, agriculture. In this sermon Noah emphasized the cooperation Jews can anticipate from enlightened people, regardless of their religion, in bringing about a much better world, and he called on the Christian clergy to preach tolerance and benevolence toward Jews. "The light of learning has exhibited the errors of the past. The justice and mercy now established–the morality and good faith now encouraged and promoted, are sure guarantees for the future. Instead of whips and chains, blows, and contumely, we have the olive of peace extended to us; and we now have only to combat the errors of education–the prejudice of other religions. . . . From their pulpits they should call for blessings on the Jews."[18] At this point Noah sounded like a good positivist and liberal American who had complete faith in the progress of history and in salvation through education.

Less than two years later, on January 16, 1820, he presented the New York State Legislature with a petition requesting that it sell him Grand Island, an island of some 17,381 acres located in the Niagara River, Erie County, to serve as a colony for Jews around the world. The idea was certainly a novel one; it even aroused the interest of European Jews.[19] Although that sale was never finalized, after several years Noah was able to convince several fellow Jews to buy a tract of land on the island. On September 24, 1825, the cornerstone of Ararat, "A City of Refuge for the Jews," was laid. At that affair Noah gave a lengthy address in which he elaborated on his vision of the role of Ararat in the process of the regeneration of the Jewish nation. He began by emphasizing the temporary nature of the project: "In calling the Jews together under the protection of the American Constitution and laws and governed by our happy and salutary institutions, it is proper for me to state that this asylum is temporary and provisionary. The Jews never should and never will relinquish the just hope of regaining possession of their ancient heritage, and events in the neighborhood of Palestine indicate an extraordinary change of affairs."[20]

Noah indicated some of the components of this "extraordinary change of affairs," such as developments in Greece, Russia and Egypt, all of which might cause the Turks to "leave the land of

Canaan free for the occupancy of its rightful owners."[21] However, Noah averred in terms somewhat similar to those expressed by Rabbi Yehuda Alkalai several decades later,[22] Jews coming to the Holy Land from many different countries will bring with them many different languages and customs and will be united solely in certain religious doctrines to which they all adhere. The differences among them would make it impossible for them to organize under any form of government and would also likely create divisive factors among them that would be "as dangerous and difficult to allay as those fatal ones which existed in the time of the first and second Temples." Therefore, "it is in this country that the government of the Jews must be organized. Here, under the influence of perfect freedom, they may study laws–cultivate their mind, acquire liberal principles as to men and measures, and qualify themselves to direct the energies of a just and honorable government in the land of the Patriarchs."[23]

Being anything but modest–he "volunteered" himself for the highest position of authority–Noah then proceeded to detail a broad series of measures that should be undertaken by the Jews as part of their regeneration, such as the establishment of the authority of the Judges over all religious, military, and civil matters; ;the reintegration of the many dispersed segments of the people, such as Chinese and black Jews, as well as Samaritans and Karaites,[24] and the American Indians, who Noah believed to be descendants of the ten lost tribes of Israel;[25] the institution of a tax to promote emigration to the Holy Land, as well as supporting institutions of charity and seminaries in the Holy Land; the prohibition of polygamy among Jews, making literacy a precondition to marriage, as well as the strengthening of marriage and preventing the excessively loose exercise of religious divorce laws. In addition, Noah stated that "there are many subjects of great interest, which I reserve for future communication."[26]

Despite the pomp and circumstance accompanying Noah's address or, perhaps, precisely because of it and the central authoritative role Noah assumed for himself, the Ararat project was a total failure. Nothing ever came of Noah's plan, and what remains of Ararat today is the cornerstone, which is housed in the Grand Island Town Hall. Although Noah never again mentioned the city of refuge, however, he persisted in attempting to maintain Jewish faith in the restoration of the Holy Land as the homeland of the regenerated Jewish nation. In the fall of 1844 Noah delivered a two-part address to a large audience at the New York Tabernacle, on October 28 and December 2, at which many Christian clergy were present. Titled

Discourse on the Restoration of the Jews,[27] the discourse was devoted entirely to the subject of the return of the Jews to the Holy Land. Essentially, it was a lengthy appeal to Christians, based on Christian theology and liberal morality, for their support in the endeavor to have the Holy Land designated for Jewish settlement. But in it Noah also showed himself to be akin to the true forerunners of Zionism–Kalischer, Alkalai, and Hess.[28] More than halfway through the discourse, after having recapitulated the most recent historical events relating to the Ottoman empire, specified why and how Jews are in a favored position to reclaim the land of their forefathers, and called upon Christians show "take an interest in the fate of Israel to assist in their restoration by aiding to colonize the Jews in Judea,"[29] Noah momentarily turns his attention to his fellow Jews. In so doing, he strongly states one of the cardinal elements of *modern* Zionism, both religious and secular, namely, that Jews must be active participants in the process of redemption and restoration, and that they cannot sit passively and wait for God to do everything alone. As Noah put it:

> The Jews suppose that the period of the restoration, which they so ardently desire and pray for, must be determined by the will of God alone, and that their agency in bringing about this great advent is not required, and, consequently, they wait patiently, without making those preliminary efforts so essential to the consummation of that great object. We never yet have been fully sensible of our duties and obligations as agents of a higher Power. Providence has endowed us with mind, with reason, with energy; blessed us with ample means to carry out his expressed wishes, laws, and ordinances. If we do not move when he disposes events to correspond with the fulfillment of his promises and the prediction of his prophets, we leave undone that which he entails upon us as a duty to perform, and the work is not accomplished, the day of deliverance has not arrived. He has spoken–he has promised. It is our duty, if the fulfillment of that Divine promise can be secured by mortal means and human agency, to see it executed. Will the dews of heaven produce a harvest without the labour of the husbandman?[30]

The Jewish response to Noah's discourse was largely unfavorable, primarily because of his many discussions of Christian theological tenets and, especially, the positive light in which he portrayed them. One of his staunchest critics, though the two men would subsequently become colleagues, was the Reverend Isaac Leeser, the most dynamic and creative leader of traditional Judaism in the nineteenth century. Born in Westphalia, Germany, in 1806, brought to the

United States by an uncle in Richmond in 1824, Leeser became the "reader" (*hazan*) at Congregation Mikveh Israel in Philadelphia in 1829, and subsequently became involved in a long series of activities that were to have a profound impact on American Jewry for generations to come. Between 1837 and his death in 1868 Leeser wrote Hebrew textbooks for children and works on Judaism, translated the Prayer Book and Bible into English, edited and published the first national Anglo-Jewish weekly in the United States, the *Occident*, and established the first American Jewish theological seminary, Maimonides College. He was also the driving force behind the establishment of the Hebrew Educational Society, the first Jewish Publication Society, and the Jewish Hospital, all in Philadelphia, and was the first to devise a program for the national unification of American synagogues. He also established the first American Jewish defense organization, the Board of Delegates of American Israelites.[31]

Leeser objected to Noah's discourse on several grounds. He did not believe that non-Jewish nations would allow a Jewish state in the Holy Land, and he believed that individual Christians would only become involved in such a project for the purpose of converting Jews to Christianity. As far as the Jews were concerned, he believed that they were too fragmented to undertake restoration, and he maintained the traditional Jewish belief that the restoration could only come about through divine intervention.[32]

Within a few years after this incident, however, Leeser himself became a fervent supporter of the effort to create a Jewish state in Eretz Israel. He even went so far as to say that the restoration could, in fact, take place by human effort, without overt divine intervention. He continued to believe that most of world Jewry would continue to live in the Diaspora, but he also felt that a Jewish state would be beneficial to Diaspora Jewry.[33] Although Leeser did not become involved in political action on behalf of restoration, he and his fellow traditionalist who was active in distributing charity funds to the Holy Land, the English-born Samuel Myer Isaacs, did devote considerable energy to attempts to reform the system by which charitable funds were raised for institutions in Eretz Israel, specifically, by having individual messengers (*meschulachim*) from the Holy Land travel around and collect funds. He felt that this was highly inefficient and too easily abused by corrupt individuals who posed as pious representatives of institutions in the Holy Land. He, along with a small group of others, suggested the establishment of an American Jewish agency whose responsibility it would be to raise funds for institutions in Eretz Israel.[34] Although Leeser's proposal was not acted upon and the messenger system persisted, he continued until his death, in 1868, to criticize, in the *Occident*, both the manner in which funds were raised in the United States and the ways in which they were spent in the Holy Land. He strongly urged that money be spent on agricultural and other productive projects that would provide real solutions to the economic challenges in Eretz Israel.[35] The older Leeser became, the more his writings resembled those of the forerunners of Zionism.

Another episode that indicated Leeser's proto-Zionism involved his befriending and support of Michael Boaz Israel, a devout convert to Judaism who moved to Eretz Israel.[36] Israel was born to a well-known Quaker family in 1798 as Warder Cresson. A zealous Christian, he left Quakerism and went through stages in which he was a Shaker, a Mormon, and a member of several other evangelical denominations. In 1840 Cresson began an association with Leeser, and during the next four years Cresson developed a special interest in Jerusalem, decided to go there, and used the influence of a friend of his to reach the secretary of state and have himself appointed the first American consul to Jerusalem in 1844. Although he arrived in Jerusalem as a practicing Christian, Cresson was increasingly attracted to Judaism, and in March 1848 he became a convert. He returned to Philadelphia later that year to close his affairs there before permanently settling in Jerusalem. After several months his wife and son, who had remained in Philadelphia throughout, had him legally declared insane. He appealed, was granted a trial by jury, and was finally vindicated. This whole process lasted several years, during which time he was an active member of Congregation Mikveh Israel. He also renewed his relationship with Leeser, and when Cresson finally returned to Jerusalem permanently, in 1852, Leeser wrote a warm and supportive column in the *Occident*. Cresson had gained some knowledge and experience in agriculture and was planning to start an agricultural colony in Emek Rephaim, near Jerusalem, and Leeser enthusiastically supported this project.[37] As it turned out, the project was a failure, but Cresson remained in Jerusalem and continued his efforts on behalf of both the poor of Jerusalem and the economy of the Holy Land. He died in 1860 and was buried on Mount Olives with the honors usually reserved for great rabbis.[38]

Although certainly among the first American Jewish immigrants to Eretz Israel, Cresson was not the first. Evidence indicates that as early as 1834 there was a Jew from New York who went to settle there.[39] Also, Cresson himself related that shortly after his arrival in Jerusalem he set about organizing an agricultural committee, and among those who served on that committee was one Benjamin Lilienthal, an American citizen who was then living in Jerusalem.[40] These were, however, highly unusual cases. The actual immigration of American Jews to the Holy Land did not really begin in any significant way until the end of the century.[41]

Two years after Cresson left for Jerusalem, Leeser wrote an article in the *Occident* in which he strongly supported both the Jewish return to the Holy Land and its economic development, particularly through agriculture. He sounded like Noah on the matter of not waiting for the Messiah to miraculously and suddenly bring about the restoration.

> Were Palestine once more open to receive Jewish immigrants; were its agricultural wealth once more accessible to our people; were its fields once more fertile and its cities rebuilt anew: not alone that many could unite themselves to its inhabitants to cultivate the soil, sure of a speedy and rich return for their labor; but those who have the genius and tact for business, could carry on profitable commerce with all parts of the world, in exchange for the rich mineral resources which now lie unused and unknown, against whatever is raised from the soil and produced by skill and labor in every other country. This is no mere dream, the realization of which is beyond the range of possibility. . . . There is no conceivable reason why Palestine and Asia Minor should be given over to sterility and desolation, when to former ages they were not alone the nursery of mankind, but the seat whence knowledge and religion were scattered all over the earth. . . . We will not at present enter into a discussion of the prophecies bearing on this topic; nor investigate how far we should rely on a sudden development of the divine policy which is to effect the great end of the prediction of Israel's seers; but it surely cannot be wrong for us to endeavor to promote the happy future by some exertions of our own.[42]

Whereas Isaac Leeser became an advocate of restoration and the economic development of the Holy Land, during the second half of the eighteenth century an increasing number of American Jewish religious leaders took public stands against Zionism. Isaac Mayer Wise, who arrived in New York from Bohemia in 1846 and early on was an ally of Leeser's in the attempt to unify American Jewry, broke with him and went on to become the institution builder of Reform Judaism in America.[43] He was strongly opposed to Zionism,[44] as were virtually all Reform rabbis in America in the nineteenth century. In fact, among the principles adopted in the first representative statement of Reform rabbis, the Pittsburgh Platform of Reform Rabbis in 1885, is an explicit rejection not only of any of the traditional Jewish religious "laws concerning the Jewish State," but also of the very notion of Jewish nationhood and of a return to Palestine.[45] During the second half of the nineteenth century, Reform Judaism became the dominant form of American Judaism,[46] and expressions of support for Zionism were in the clear minority. In fact, as Zionism as a social movement gained in strength, the opposition of Reform Judaism became more vocal. For example, at almost the same time as the first World Zionist Congress was taking place in Basle, the rabbinic organization of American Reform Judaism, the Central Conference of American Rabbis, passed a resolution that declared:

> Resolved, That we totally disapprove of any attempts for the establishment of a Jewish state. Such attempts show a misunderstanding of Israel's mission which from the narrow political and national field has been expanded to the promotion among the whole human race of the broad and universalistic religion first proclaimed by the Jewish prophets. . . .
> We reaffirm that the object of Judaism is not political nor national, but spiritual, and addresses itself to the continuous growth of peace, justice and love in the human race, to a messianic time when all men will recognize that they form "one great brotherhood" for the establishment of God's kingdom on earth.[47]

One year later, in 1898, the synagogue organization of American Reform Judaism, the Union of American Hebrew Congregations, proclaimed: "We are unalterably opposed to political Zionism. The Jews are not a nation, but a religious community. Zion was a precious possession of the past, the early home of our faith, where our prophets uttered their world-subduing thoughts, and our psalmists sang their world-enchanting hymns. As such it is a holy memory, but it is not our hope of the future. America is our Zion. Here, in the home of religious liberty, we have aided in founding this new Zion, the fruition of the beginning laid in the old."[48]

Although there were a small number of Reform rabbis who did support Zionism, they were invariably from the larger Jewish communities in the big cities; in smaller Jewish communities they were almost nonexistent. As Malcolm H. Stern suggests for southern Jewry: "For the majority of Southern Jews and their rabbis, America was their Zion, and they wanted no other. . . . To be outspokenly Zionist before World War II in a Southern Reform congregation took courage on the part of a rabbi."[49] Several decades were yet required before the newly arrived Eastern European Jews in the United States would begin to join the ranks of Reform Judaism and encourage it, especially on the eve of the Holocaust, to alter its ideological stance on Zionism. But that was already in the twentieth century.

In the closing decades of the nineteenth century, in the large cities, there were a variety of different types of organizations involved in one way or another with the developing Jewish presence in the Holy Land. There were, for example, Hovevei Zion groups in a number of cities, as well as a small organization, called Shave Zion, whose aim was to buy land in Palestine for Jewish settlement.[50] Most of these were imported by the newly arriving Eastern European immigrants and became part of the American Zionist movement, which became institutionalized at the turn of the century.

PART II

4

Early Twentieth-Century American Zionism

With the convening of the First Zionist Congress in Basle, in 1897, Zionism as a social movement became institutionalized, and the World Zionist Organization become the official umbrella organization of Zionism.[1] As was the case with the larger movement, American Zionism initially consisted of a variety of ideologies that were able to unite only insofar as they all supported the goal of a national homeland for Jews in the Holy Land. Above and beyond all of the particular variations were two fundamentally different conceptions of Zionism that were rooted in even more basically different definitions of Jewish group identity.

It will be recalled that although the first American Jewish communities were founded by Sephardim, from the very beginning of the eighteenth century many more Ashkenazim–from England, Germany, and Poland–had immigrated to America than had Sephardim, and very few Sephardim arrived after 1760. During the nineteenth century the American Jewish population grew from approximately 2,000 at the onset to some 250,000 in 1880, most of whom were first- or second-generation immigrants from central Europe. In 1881 a tidal wave of immigration from Eastern Europe began such that between that year and 1900 more than a million Jews arrived in the country, and this wave continued until the passage of the Johnson Immigration Acts of 1921 and 1924, bringing the total number of Jewish immigrants during that forty-two-year period to more than 2.75 million.[2] In part because of the differences in the nature of their societies, Eastern

European countries being neither as ethnically homogeneous nor as religiously diverse as Germany, Eastern Europe did not develop the distinction between religion and nationality that Germany and the West had. Moreover, until the end of the nineteenth century most Eastern European Jews lived in small towns and villages, *shtetlach*, in which both the religion and the culture were Jewish. In fact, it was virtually impossible to distinguish between the two. Thus, whereas German and Western Jews were able to conceive of themselves as Jewish by religion and German, French, British, or American by nationality, Eastern European Jews conceived of themselves as simply Jewish. They defined Judaism as both a religion and a culture, and to be Jewish meant to be a member of the religious and national group.[3]

With respect to Zionism as well, German Jews and Eastern European Jews related to it from very different perspectives. At least initially, German, indeed Western, Jews initially conceived of Zionism in philanthropic terms. Even the early "German Zionist's efforts to foster emigration to Palestine were exerted largely in behalf of their less fortunate brethren to the East. . . . This philanthropic version of Zionism was humorously, and accurately, characterized as a third-person affair: one man collected money from a second in order to send a third to Palestine."[4] In Eastern Europe, Zionism, from its inception, was conceived of as a nationalist movement, one that would solve the problem of Jewish national existence by the creation of and participation in the Jewish national homeland. In Eastern Europe, the ideologists of Zionism were not solely concerned with the physical well-being of Jews but with their national well-being as well. There were, of course, differences among the Eastern European Zionists as to the extent to which they saw Zionism as concerned with "the problem of the Jews," the followers of Herzl, or "the problem of Judaism," the followers of Ahad Ha-am.[5] With all of their differences, however, both the political Zionists and the cultural Zionists saw Zionism in national terms.

In the United States at the time, the mainstay of Zionism was in the Federation of American Zionists (FAZ), which was the forerunner of the Zionist Organization of America. FAZ was founded in 1898 under the leadership of Richard Gottheil. In 1902 Jacob de Haas became secretary and also editor of its publication, the *Maccabean*. Both Gottheil and de Haas were British-born and strong supporters of Theodor Herzl. Paradoxical as it may seem, although they subscribed to Herzl's political Zionism, neither of them made strong efforts to reach out to the community of newly arrived Eastern European Jewish immigrants. Moreover, the newly arrived Eastern European Jews were highly suspicious of Gottheil and de Haas and did not accept them as leaders.[6] It was not until 1904, when Harry Friedenwald and Judah Magnes took over the leadership of the federation, that it began to develop ties with the Eastern Europeans, perhaps because Magnes himself was of Eastern European background[7] and Friedenwald had a long history of activity in Jewish communal affairs. In addition, Friedenwald was closely affiliated with Conservative Judaism and served as a trustee for its rabbinical school, the Jewish Theological Seminary. The shift in FAZ to Eastern European leadership so closely allied with Conservative Judaism[8] greatly enhanced the stature of FAZ and Zionism among the new immigrants. Not coincidentally, both Friedenwald and Magnes were cultural, rather than political, Zionists, and the chairman of the administrative committee of FAZ was Dr. Israel Friedlaender, professor of biblical literature at the Jewish Theological Seminary. Friedlaender was very familiar with the work of Ahad Ha-am and, prior to his arrival in the United States, had translated some of Ahad Ha-am's work into German.[9] The leadership of American Zionism, thus, also shifted to one that expressed the cultural Zionist ideology.

The early growth of the American Zionist movement, however, was not solely the consequence of the ideological orientation and quality of the leadership of FAZ. Sociological factors played, perhaps, an even greater role than did ideological ones. As Ben Halpern astutely points out, the Zionist societies were highly functional for the newly arriving immigrants.[10] While continuing the traditions and structures of European Zionism, the American Zionist societies served as agencies that eased the adjustment of the new immigrant to American society.

Zionist societies often took the form of lodges and fraternal orders or of landsmanshaften composed of fellow-townsmen from abroad. They adopted measures o mutual aid in sickness and need and for burial; organized picnics, balls, and lectures; and in adopting this common pattern of behavior, they became an integral part of a broader institutional network that promoted the first adjustment of the Jewish immigrant ghetto at large. In this way Zionist societies, landmanshaften, and lodges, like other similarly organized immigrant groupings, even while recreating copies of the Old Country overseas, served no less than trade unions and the ghetto settlement houses did to advance the Americanization of the immigrants as a cohesive community.[11]

Although leaders of American Zionism might have debated ideological issues such as political versus cultural Zionism, or "general" versus religious or socialist Zionism,[12] the majority of the membership was attracted less by ideology than by familiarity. Most were attracted because the Zionist societies were familiar to them and because these societies had something to offer them. Since most were not strongly committed to the ideologies of either religious or socialist Zionism, they joined the societies of FAZ. For all intents and purposes, FAZ was synonymous with American Zionism. In addition, American Zionism grew because of the same social forces that fostered the development of Conservative Judaism and because most of the leaders of Conservative Judaism gave religious legitimation and support to Zionism.

Conservative Judaism, as Marshall Sklare has keenly observed, began as a uniquely American religious movement.[13] Founded in the early twentieth century by moderate traditionalists, it grew rapidly in the early twentieth century because of its ability to respond to the changing needs and values of American Jewry and to reshape Judaism while retaining much of the tradition.[14] Many young immigrants and children of immigrants from Eastern Europe, who found Orthodoxy too confining and inhibiting in their drive for economic and social mobility, but who, nonetheless, strongly wished to retain their Jewish ethnic and religious identity, embraced Conservative Judaism as being the ideal alternative between the "too religious" Orthodox and the "nonreligious" Reform. Accordingly, the Conservative synagogue became the central institution in American Jewish community, and both the religious and secular ethnic activities of the community were centered within it.[15]

Zionism, too, and especially the general Zionism of FAZ and, as it later came to be known under the leadership of Louis D. Brandeis, the Zionist Organization of America (ZOA), had appeal for the Eastern European American Jews because of its essential ethnic premise. Given the strong ethnic self-definition of Eastern European Jews and the fact that many of them were familiar with, even if they themselves had not been members of, Zionist groups in Eastern Europe, it was natural for them to join the Zionist Organization once it was officially established. Especially after the Zionist Congress of 1907 enabled both Mizrachi and Poalei Zion to become autonomous organizations and they broke off from FAZ, of which they had previously had been factions, most American Jews who became official Zionists opted for membership in FAZ. Mizrachi was for the religious Zionists and Poalei Zion was for the socialist Zionists; but for the majority of the recently arrived American Jews who were Zionists because of their ethnic ties rather than because of ideology, the much less ideologically sophisticated general Zionism of FAZ and ZOA was the logical choice.

These tendencies were reinforced by the fact that almost all of the leaders of Conservative Judaism were self-proclaimed Zionists who defined Zionism as an integral part of Judaism. As Moshe Davis aptly put it: "Zionism was an integral part of the program of thought and action which the Historical School developed in the closing decades of the past century and which it transmitted to the Conservative Movement. Conservative Judaism and Zionism developed separately, but their interaction was constant. As a result, both were stimulated conceptually and organizationally."[16]

The particular version of Zionism that most of the leaders of Conservative Judaism expounded was very different, however, from the dominant European versions, which were centered on Eretz Israel and emphasized the doctrine of *shlilat hagolah,* the denigration of the Diaspora. Most of the leaders of Conservative Judaism and of American Zionism preferred, instead, their own versions of the cultural Zionism of Ahad Ha-am, which defined the Holy Land as the "spiritual center" of the Jewish people but not necessarily the material or demographic center, and which accepted and sought to strengthen Jewish communities in the Diaspora. This was clearly the case, for example, with Israel Friedlaender (1876–1920), who, as mentioned earlier, had translated several of Ahad Ha-am's essays and who, for American Zionism, had coined the slogan "Zionism plus Diaspora, Palestine plus America."[17]

An even more prominent leader of Conservative Judaism who espoused Zionism and whose version of it was much more of a cultural than a political Zionism was Solomon Schechter (1847–1915), who became president of the Jewish Theological Seminary in 1902 and founded the synagogue organization of Conservative Judaism, the United Synagogue. Schechter's firm attachments to Eretz Israel go back to his early childhood. He did not, however, immediately respond to Herzl's clarion and join the Zionist Organization because of his aversion to the secularism that characterized formal Zionism, especially Herzl's political Zionism. In 1904, in a letter to the noted

Anglo-Jewish author and chairman of Herzl's first Zionist conference in England, Schechter wrote: "I have spent nearly 50 years on the study of Jewish literature and Jewish history and I am convinced that you cannot sever Jewish nationality from Jewish religion."[18] Nevertheless, Schechter ultimately concluded that Zionism is "a genuine manifestation of the deeper Jewish consciousness; deeper perhaps than several of its leaders realised,"[19] and he joined FAZ in 1905. But he retained his opposition to secular political Zionism and, indeed, was much closer to Ahad Ha-am's cultural Zionism than to Herzl's political Zionism. Thus, in 1906, he wrote: "I belong to that class of Zionists that lay more stress on the religious-national aspects of Zionism than on any other feature peculiar to it. The rebirth of Israel's national consciousness, and the revival of Israel's religion, or, to use a shorter term, the revival of Judaism, are inseparable."[20] The admiration and esteem that Schechter had for Ahad Ha-am were such that, when he traveled through London in 1910, Schechter refused to even check his luggage until he first paid his respects to Ahad Ha-am.[21]

After Schechter's death in 1915, Cyrus Adler (1863–1940), a non-Zionist, presided over the Jewish Theological Seminary. He was an institutional leader, however, and did not pretend to be a religious leader. The individual to emerge as the most prominent religious leader at the seminary was Mordecai M. Kaplan (1881–1983), the ideological father of Reconstructionist Judaism.[22] Although he takes issue with Ahad Ha-am on some matters,[23] Kaplan was clearly strongly influenced by him both in terms of his own conception of Jewish "peoplehood" and "civilization," and especially in terms of his own Zionism. Thus, he argued that "a movement like spiritual Zionism, *the purpose of which is to keep the Jews of the world united and creative,* is entitled to a place in the Jewish religion. Spiritual Zionism cannot content itself merely with the rebuilding of Palestine. If the Jews throughout the world are to be united and creative, they must not only have a spiritual center in Palestine; wherever they live in considerable numbers they must organize themselves into vigorous communities" (emphasis added).[24]

In a later work, devoted to the reconstruction not of American-Jewish life but of Zionism, Kaplan asserts:

> *We can no longer afford to postpone the long-needed re-orientation of Zionism.* Otherwise the Jewish People is bound to be like a man unable to swim who is thrown into deep water, so that nearly everything he does in his struggle is the opposite of what would be effec-

tive. It will not do to persist in stubbornly ignoring the realities of human nature. *If Zionism exists for the Jews and not the Jews for Zionism, it has to adjust itself to what may reasonably be expected of them.* [emphasis in original.][25]

Thus, Kaplan urged Zionism not to dwell on aliya, since Jews in the West feel "at home," and it is unrealistic to expect they leave those countries in which they are accorded equal rights. But

> Zionism as a movement to bring about the spiritual or religious revival of all throughout the world would be fully entitled to ask the Jewish communities of the free countries to provide their quota of able-bodied and high charactered men and women to come to Israel either to live there permanently, or, at least, to devote several years to its service. Those who remain at home could then be expected to become personally involved in the fate and fortunes of Eretz Yisrael. As part of a spiritual movement, the demand for *halutzim* (pioneers) would be no more resented than the demand of the churches for missionaries to go to the ends of the earth to spread Christian gospel.[26]

Ironically, where Kaplan saw his conception of Zionism as dramatically new, it probably was and remains the dominant way in which most American Jews relate to Zionism. Most American Jews do view their Zionist activity and Israel as part of the Jewish religion; at the same time, they do not consider themselves to be "religiously observant" and, therefore, their Zionist activity is frequently limited to fund raising for Israel and Israeli institutions. American Jews do relate to their Zionist activity as being part of the Jewish social gospel, which includes the obligation to assist Israel as well as the obligation to aid less fortunate Jews wherever they may be. It is only within that context that one can explain, for example, the widespread American Jewish phenomenon of dedicating the synagogue appeal on the eve of Yom Kippur, the most sacred day in the Jewish calendar, to a campaign for Israel Bonds. Likewise, it is within that context that one can explain the presence of Israel's flag on the front walls of many American synagogues. Such things serve to reinforce the conception of Israel and activity on its behalf as religious activity. Indeed, as Charles Liebman convincingly argues, Israel has increasingly come to define the content and be the expression of American Jewish religious identity.[27] Be that as it may, Kaplan's Zionism was much closer to that of Ahad Ha-am than to that of any other of the so-called fathers of modern Zionism in that he saw the objective of Zionism as the cultural regeneration of the Jewish people, he saw a continuing vitality in American Jewry, and he perceived the role of Zionism to be the strengthening of Judaism and the Jewish people wherever they may be.[28]

One other major figure who played key roles both in American Jewish communal life and in American Zionism and who helped shape the cultural Zionism of American Jewry was Judah L. Magnes (1877–1948).[29] Although he was ordained in 1900 at Hebrew Union College and served as rabbi at the prestigious New York Reform congregation Temple Emanu-El, Magnes was much more traditional than Reform Judaism was at the time. Even as a student he was enthusiastic about Zionism. After his ordination he went to study in Berlin, where he became an "ardent disciple" of Ahad Ha-am.[30] Magnes returned to the United States in 1903, just before the Kishinev pogrom. He was deeply stirred by the pogroms in Russia in 1903 and 1905, especially after having become somewhat familiar and empathetic with the recently arrived Eastern European Jewish community in New York City, which he saw prior to his having left for Berlin, several years earlier. At almost the same time, Magnes met and was further inspired by Solomon Schechter, and he set out to synthesize the teachings of Schechter and Ahad Ha-am. By 1910 his ideas were so out of line with those of his congregants that the board of Temple Emanu-El did not recommend his reelection, and Magnes resigned. He wrote to Ahad Ha-am, who advised him to make the primary role of the synagogue that of learning, with prayer as a secondary concern, and to spread the idea of Judaism as a national religion. After postponing a pilgrimage with his wife to Eretz Israel because of the prevalent cholera and going for a trip to Europe instead, Magnes assumed the position, in 1911, of rabbi in Conservative Congregation Bnai Jeshurun, the second oldest synagogue in New York City.[31] It was at this time that he also spearheaded a unique experiment, the establishment of a formal Jewish communal structure in New York City, the *Kehillah*.[32]

As for Magnes's Zionism it was unique. Although he was committed to both the aim of securing a Jewish homeland in Eretz Israel and rejuvenating the Jewish nation and its culture, and although he himself did go on aliya, his conceptions of Zionism, in general, and aliya, in particular, were very different from those of the classical Eastern European Zionists. Magnes's Zionism and his attitude toward aliya bore an almost uniquely American imprint.

In contrast to most of the European Zionists who, as mentioned above, advocated the denigration of the Diaspora, Magnes strongly affirmed the *galut,* the Diaspora. In an address delivered in Jerusalem in 1923,[33] Magnes begins by relating a conversation about Zionism that he had had with Maxim Gorki the previous summer. At that time Magnes had stated:

> My conception of Zionism did not at all provide for the Jews being taken out of their place in the struggling world. If it were physically possible to bring all Jews here—which of course, it is not—the world would be a poorer place and the Jewish people would deprive itself of a large part of its opportunity to be of service to mankind. Zionism, Palestine, in my opinion was not an end in itself. It was a means of strengthening the Jewish people. The Jewish people of flesh and blood wherever they lived were the chief consideration, and Palestine was one of the means, perhaps a chief means, but not the only means of making the Jewish people cleaner, better, truer. The creation of a Jewish community here would thus make the Jews every-where fitter to perform their historic task in the great world.[34]

Nor did Magnes entirely agree with his mentor, Ahad Ha-am, who saw the relationship between Eretz Israel and the Dispora as one of center and periphery, with the former being the "spiritual" or cultural center. Magnes asked, rhetorically:

> Why set Eretz Israel and the Galut over against one another at all? . . . The complex Jewish people can not be explained by a simple formula. Both Eretz Israel and the Galut are manifestations of the life of the people. . . .
> Everyone who lives here in Eretz Israel and works is helping the Jewish people create spiritual values and is thus aiding the Jewish people to carry out its work in the world. The same is true of whose who live and work in the Galut. Where a man can do best for his people is an individual and private matter.[35]

Given this conception of Zionism, it follows that his attitude toward aliya was, likewise, much more liberal and accepting than that of most European Zionists and Western Zionists who had themselves immigrated to Israel. Where they, especially those who had themselves already realized aliya, defined aliya as an obligation, Magnes did not define it as obligatory for all Zionists. Whereas even Mordecai Kaplan was to subsequently call on Jews to come to Israel either permanently or for an extended period of time during which they would do service, Magnes did not even call for this. As he stated after his second visit to Eretz Israel in 1912:

> And I say to you, you who do not want to go up, you who want to stay here . . . –you who are to stay here and ought to stay here, for we Zionists have enough contended that all Jews must go up,–may you but once in your lives take it upon yourself, instead of stopping in Egypt alone, at least to cross the water to the land of the fathers. . . . And those of you who once in their lifetime wish to make a trip, save your pennies in order that once every Jew may visit the land of his fathers.[36]

Magnes defined his personal reasons for his own aliya in terms reminiscent of those given by many contemporary American Jews who have immigrated to Israel, as will be seen in later chapters, namely, as the personal realization of a dream and because of a sense of Israel as the place where one can more deeply and extensively experience Judaism and Jewish culture. As Magnes defined his own aliya in 1922, just prior to his departure from New York: "With the same mission of quiet, of study, I go also to Eretz Israel: not as a leader, a redeemer, a Messiah, but simply as a Jew, who for merits that are not his own . . . is going to a Holy Land, bound to it not through any political programs, but through Judaism, which I cannot now conceive of without its roots planted there."[37]

Nor did Magnes leave New York with a commitment of aliya. As Yohai Goell observes: "If a prerequisite of *aliyah* is a premeditated decision to make a permanent move to Palestine, then Magnes' action in that year was not, strictly speaking, *aliyah*."[38] As do many American olim today, Magnes and his family left New York with the intention of staying in Eretz Israel for a year, after which time they would decide whether or not to stay permanently. They deliberated all through the spring and summer of 1923. On August 6, 1923, Magnes wrote: "The decision is again in our hands. We are again free to choose, again masters of the situation. Whichever way we decide it will be because we want it thus, because we think it better, not because we must."[39]

Ultimately, Magnes and his family did remain in Eretz Israel, where he became the first chancellor and first president of the Hebrew University of Jerusalem, as well as a founding member of Brit Shalom and IHUD, two societies composed primarily of Jewish intellectuals that aimed at fostering Jewish-Arab understanding and cooperation.[40] Given his activity in Jerusalem and his physical absence from the United States, his role as a leader in the American Jewish community naturally declined significantly. His conceptions of Zionism, however, along with similar ones that were later developed more elaborately by Mordecai Kaplan, became the dominant ones of American Jewry. This was because in America Jews were conceived of and conceived of themselves more as a religious, rather than an ethnic, group.[41] American Jews were, by and large, totally uninterested in and unreceptive to a Zionism based on nationalism, because they did not define themselves as a national group but, rather, as a religious one. For the same reason, ideologically secular Zionism never gained a strong following within the American Jewish community. Nor did a Zionism that denigrated the Diaspora or preached that even America is *galut,* exile, and that only in Eretz Israel is the Jew at home, either or both of which were part of the religious Zionism of the Orthodox Mizrachi and socialist Zionism at the time.[42] Such notions were simply unacceptable to the masses of American Jewry, who supported the objective of the establishment of a Jewish homeland in the Holy Land and perceived it as a haven for downtrodden Jews from Europe and elsewhere but as having no direct personal relevance for themselves and other American Jews, who were becoming increasingly comfortable in the United States.

Nor, despite the fact that the cultural Zionism of Schechter, Friedlaender, Magnes, and Kaplan became the dominant mode of American Zionism, did this mean that American Jews who considered themselves Zionists were aware of and concurred with the tenets of cultural Zionism. Far from it. Indeed, as Samuel Koenig, in an early sociological study of an American Jewish community-Stamford, Connecticut–found, for most Jews Zionist activity is, above all else, a social activity.[43] His description is very revealing:

> The Zionist movement, with which most of the Stamford Jews sympathize either actively or passively, provides another field of activity. There exist several Zionist organizations for older as well as younger people. Zionism, however, to the Stamford Jew, has come to mean little more than contributing financially to the restoration of Palestine and the maintenance of its institutions. As such it may be looked upon as largely charitable or ameliorative rather than nationalistic in character, although some, particularly the older, foreign-born generation, the veterans of the Zionist movement, take a keen interest in the political and economic life of present-day Palestine. Most of the gatherings inspired by the movement are largely devoted

to fund raising, and consist of tea, bridge, and theater parties, luncheons, dinners, concerts, etc. This is particularly true of the women's organizations, which are the strongest numerically and the most active. Reports and informative and inspirational talks by local and out-of-town speakers, whereby the interest in the Zionist cause is sought to be aroused, are, as a rule, part of those gatherings, but their general character is mainly social. Individuals belong to those organizations chiefly because it is the thing to do, because they offer social opportunities, and because they serve "a good cause."[44]

The patterns observed by Koenig in Stamford were fairly representative of the general patterns within the American Jewish community at the time. What makes them even more significant is that this was at the beginning of World War II. Although the situation today is somewhat different, as the result of the establishment of the State of Israel and a series of developments both within American society and within the Jewish community during the 1960s and 1970s,[45] the general patterns, as will be seen below, remain essentially the same.

5

American Aliya Before the Six-Day War

American Aliya did not, technically, begin in the twentieth century. There is evidence, as mentioned in Chapter 3, of some aliya from the United States as early as 1834.[1] Whatever American aliya there was in the nineteenth century was invariably religiously motivated, and many of the American olim of that century lived in dire poverty, as witness a letter from the American consul in Jerusalem, written in 1867: "The number of American Jews residing in Jerusalem is very limited, a dozen altogether; but these unfortunates are the most miserable of all and do not receive pecuniary succor from any one, the German committees never having given them a cent, and those of America perhaps do not know them at all."[2]

Toward the end of the nineteenth century a new type of American aliya developed. Some American Jews joined their Eastern European brethren in Eretz Israel and became agricultural pioneers in Palestine. Although David Ben-Gurion may have been exaggerating somewhat, he was not totally in error when he stated in an address to American Zionists in Jerusalem in 1950: "Our agricultural work began some seventy years before the state. The grandest pioneers of eastern Jewry, then intact, made it possible. Thousands of American Jews were among them."[3] Nevertheless, in terms of its being a real social phenomenon, it is something that did not actually develop until the twentieth century.

The first aliya "movement" from the United States was that of a group of Jews who were recent arrivals from Russia and who were members of a small Zionist organization, Tehiya, which was founded by Russian Jews in the United States.[4] In 1904 Eliezer L. Jaffe, who later became the ideologist of the movement of moshavim, agricultural settlements in Eretz Israel,[5] immigrated to the United States from Russia and became active in Tehiya. One year later, he led a number of members of Tehiya in the formation of an aliya group called Hehalutz.[6] The programs and activities of Hahalutz were seen as in preparation for aliya, but by 1908 several of the group's activities felt a need to give it its very specific aliya focus and to actually begin to realize that goal. Calling themselves Haikar Hatzair (The Young Farmer), they precisely declared their goal to be practical agricultural preparation for those who intend to work in agriculture in the Holy Land. Haikar Hatzair never numbered more than several dozen members, but during the few years of its existence (1908–13) approximately ten of its members actually did go on aliya. They immigrated to Eretz Israel and became active in agricultural settlement there.

Despite having been founded in the United States, however, it would be incorrect to label Haikar Hatzair an American aliya organization. As Margalit Shilah points out: "All of its members were Eastern Europeans who immigrated to America; there was not one among them who was born in the United States."[7] On the other hand, to give a more complete picture, it must also be noted that Haikar Hatzair did serve as a model in that it helped pave the way for the subsequent Hehalutz olim, the bulk of whom arrived in Eretz Israel after World War I.

Precise figures on prestate, that is, pre-1948, aliya are unavailable. One estimate is that some two thousand Americans settled between 1880 and 1914.[8] Although the basis of this estimate is unknown, it is known that American aliya increased during the period of the British mandate (1919–48) and that American olim played a role in the development of Jewish agricultural settlements in Eretz Israel. Estimates on the number of American olim during this period vary. Lapide states that more than 11,000 arrived,[9] whereas Calvin Goldscheider has found statistical evidence for a total of 6,613 registered olim during the mandatory period.[10] Although their numbers were small—even according to the highest estimate they accounted for no more than 3 percent of all olim during this period—there is evidence of their contribution to the building of the Jewish settlement in the country. Records show the arrival of American olim in collective settlements, kibbutzim and moshavim, as far back as the early 1930s.[11] Indeed, in the prestate years American olim founded a number of kibbutzim, such as Ein Hashofet (1937), Kfar Menahem (1939), Hatzor (1946), and Ein Dor (1948). Also, there were Americans who settled in the cities, some of whom planned to settle later in an agricultural settlement whereas others intended to remain urban.

The American immigrants who settled during the mandatory period were, generally, quite different from earlier olim. As mentioned, these later olim were immigrants who were active in the movement of agricultural settlement. They were drawn, in the main, not by religious ideology but by the secular Zionist ideologies of the kibbutz and the moshav. The bulk of them during this period belonged to the Hashomer Hatzair movement and the first kibbutzim founded by Americans were Hashomer Hatzair kibbutzim. Although there is no evidence that their emigration from the United States was the result of push factors, that they were or felt persecuted in the United States, their involvement in Hashomer Hatzair indicates that they sought a radical change from what their lives had been like prior to their aliya. Not only did they leave the cities of the United States–Jews have always been overwhelmingly urban in the United States–they also selected the most radical kibbutz movement. As Walter Laqueur says: "The Hashomer Hatzair concept of what a collective should be was far more radical than life in the kvutzot established by the previous generation of pioneers."[12] But it was not the United States or American society and culture per se they were rejecting. Rather, they were committed to the ideology of Zionist socialism, which "was a religious surrogate. It provided meaning and purpose to individual existence by mobilizing the individual in the collective effort to establish in the Land of Israel an ideal society based on social equality, social justice, and productive labor."[13] Thus, while their lives were radically different from what they had been in the United States and they explicitly rejected capitalist society and culture, their aliya was still motivated by pull factors; Zionist socialism defined Eretz Israel as the only place Jews would be able to create the new social order.

One of the only available empirical studies of prestate American immigrants reveals that more than half of those who remained in Israel were younger than twenty-five years of age when they went on aliya, and an additional 40 percent were between twenty-five and twenty-nine years of age. A small minority of these olim were married, and most of those who were did not have children. In contrast to traditional patterns for migrants, the majority of American olim were female.[14] Antonovsky and Katz suggest the female majority at this time was reflective of the fact that, in contrast to the case in more typical migrations, opportunities were not limited in American society and American Jewish males were usually involved in studies and career. For them to undertake migration would have meant "taking time out." Women, on the other hand, were not as career-oriented and, therefore, were not losing any time by becoming involved in migration plans and activities.[15]

The prestate American immigrants were also atypical in several other and perhaps even more important ways. They were more urban than American Jews as a whole. As Antonovsky and Katz state: "American Jews are, it is true, highly metropolitan; this is, however, even more true of American immigrants to Israel."[16] Also, they appear to be unrepresentative in terms of their generational patterns. Although they were born in the United States, more than 80 percent of their fathers were born in Eastern Europe. And although the vast majority, indeed more than 80 percent, of American Jewry at this time was of Eastern European background, it is doubtful that so many were no more than second-generation Americans.

A third way in which these immigrants were atypical of American Jewry was in terms of family size. The olim tended to come from larger-than-average American Jewish families. Although a study in Detroit found that the average Jewish woman over forty had given birth to 2.07 children, more than one-third of the American olim grew up in families with four or more children.[17]

In terms of socioeconomic status, the prestate immigrants tended to come from working-class Jewish neighborhoods in New York City, such as the Lower East Side in Manhattan and Brownsville in Brooklyn, and their fathers tended to be in such lower-middle-class occupations as small business proprietors, clerical or sales workers, or self-employed artisans. Close to 50 percent of the fathers had no secular education. On the other hand, 29 percent of the immigrants themselves had at least a B.A. and only a very small minority did not complete high school.[18]

It has previously been pointed out that there was a shift in the motivations for American aliya from the pre-twentieth to the twentieth century. Prior to the this century religious motivations were the major ones, whereas in the first half of the twentieth century Zionist motivations replaced the traditional religious ones as the primary motivations for aliya. Since the establishment of the State of Israel, however, as will be shown below, the pendulum has shifted in the opposite direction; increasingly, religious motivations are replacing

Zionist ones as the primary motivations for aliya. Nevertheless, among the prestate American immigrants almost 80 percent defined themselves as having been "ardent Zionists" before their aliya, more than 75 percent had been members of a Zionist organization during their last year in America prior to aliya, and only 17 percent stated that they had belonged to no Jewish organization.[19] When asked to state the "most important reason for coming to Israel," the distribution of the types of responses was as shown in Table 1.

The same pattern emerged when the respondents were given a set of fifteen possible reasons for their having immigrated and were asked to choose the ones they considered very important. With these questions the pre-1948 American immigrants were more likely to rate "Zionist" reasons as very important than they were to so rate "Jewish" or "religious" reasons.[20]

A further indication of the primacy of "Zionist" motivations over "Jewish" or "religious" ones among pre-1948 American olim may be deduced from the fact that two-thirds of them lived, at least for some time, on a kibbutz.[21] For the vast majority of those who choose kibbutz life, the motivations appear much more likely to be of the "Zionist" type than of the "Jewish" or "religious" type. Even for those religious Zionists who might chose a religious kibbutz, it might be expected that the motivations would be more Zionist than religious.[22]

In terms of actual numbers, during the thirty years of the mandatory period, immigration from the United States was low. As mentioned earlier, even according to the highest estimates it was not more than 3 percent of the total aliya for the period. In absolute terms, using an average between the highest and lowest estimates, there were, on average, 267 American immigrants per year.

With the establishment of the State of Israel, on May 14, 1948, there was a distinct increase in American aliya. Between 1950 and 1959 there was a total of 3,610 American immigrants, which averages out to 361 per year, an increase of almost 50 percent over the yearly average during the mandatory period. During the 1960s the increase was much more dramatic. From 1960 through 1966 there was a total of 4,892 American olim, or an average of 699 per year. These increases are significant in their own right and also because of the popular notion that it was the Six-Day War alone that marked the great turning point in the rate of American aliya. Although it's true, as will be discussed in the following chapter, that there was another strong increase in American aliya after that war, it is important to note that

TABLE 1

Distribution of Most Important Reasons
Given for American Aliya, Pre-1948

Reason	%
Zionism	48
Jewishness	21
Attraction to Israel	8
Religious reasons	1
No independent decision	11
Dissatisfaction with America	6
Trial living	3
Children	1
Idiosyncratic	1
TOTAL	100

Note: N=312
Source: Adapted from Aaron Antonovsky and Abraham David Katz, From the Golden to the Promised Land (Darby, Pa.: Norwood Editions, 1979), p. 51.

TABLE 2

American Immigrants to Israel, 1950–1987

Year	Number	Year	Number	Year	Number
1950–59	3,610	1971	7,364	1980	2,312
1960–63	2,213	1972	5,515	1981	2,384
1964	1,006	1973	4,393	1982	2,693
1965	924	1974	3,089	1983	3,469
1966	749	1975	2,803	1984	2,581
1967	665	1976	2,746	1985	1,915
1968	932	1977	2,571	1986	1,968
1969	5,738	1978	2,921	1987	1,818
1970	6,882	1979	2,950		

Sources: Israel Central Bureau of Statistics, Immigration to Israel, 1948–1972, Immigration to Israel, 1973, and Monthly Bulletin of Statistics, 1974 through January 1988 issues. Figures for 1950 through 1968 include only actual immigrants, not those of "potential immigrant" status.

American aliya had already been increasing since the establishment of the state, and especially during the 1960s.

Some of the increased during the 1950s, particularly during the years immediately after Israel's War of Independence, may be attributed to those Americans who volunteered to fight in Israel's army in its foreign volunteers program, Machal, and then decided to remain in the country. There were, reportedly, some 1,770 Americans who fought in this program, more than 80 percent of whom were American-born and almost all of whom were veterans of the U.S. Armed Forces. The overwhelming majority, 95 percent, had not been affiliated with any Zionist organization prior to their volunteering; 90 percent did not know any Hebrew; and only 3 percent said that they had even considered settling in Israel after the war. In the end, some 370 of them did immigrate to Israel.[23]

Among the others who came during the 1950s were, probably, some who immigrated for push reasons. For example, it is not unreasonable to assume that some American Jews might have immigrated to escape the threatening political atmosphere in the United States under McCarthyism. Others, especially among those between eighteen and twenty-two, may have come to escape the draft during the Korean War. Still others, especially women, may have immigrated in order to avoid the problem of intermarriage. That is, they may have experienced the shortage of available Jewish males as potential spouses and did not consider intermarriage as a viable alternative. But all of this is only conjecture.

The only empirical study of American olim during those years is that of Gerald Engel. It should, however, be emphasized that his study is of native-born American and Canadian Jews, the majority of whom were second-generation North American, who immigrated to Israel. We have no way of determining how the inclusion of Canadians, who constitute 10 percent of those in the sample, changes the picture. Given this qualification, it is a study of a sample of 443 North Americans twenty years of age or older who immigrated to Israel between 1950 and 1966 and became permanent residents of Israel during the years 1962 to 1966.[24]

The most outstanding background characteristic of the immigrants in the study was Jewish education. More than 90 percent of them had at least some formal Jewish education in America and 37 percent had attended Jewish all-day schools.[25] Given that at that time the estimate of all Jewish children in the United States attending Jewish all-day schools was approximately 13 percent, the percentage among the American olim was very high. It must be added, however, that the percentage of Jewish children attending Jewish all-day schools in Canada at the time was probably higher than it was in the United States because of Canada's tradition of cultural pluralism, whereas in the United States at that time the melting pot was still the dominant ideology. Also, in the United States separation of church

83

and state was and still is defined in such a way as to preclude any public support for religious schools, whereas in Canada the situation is different. It may be, therefore, that some of the much higher proportion of day school attendees was due to the inclusion of Canadians in the sample. Even if that was the case, however, the percentage of former day school attendees among the American immigrants was still high.

As might be expected from the data on their levels of Jewish education, the American immigrants were also not representative of American Jewry as a whole in that, at the time of their immigration, they had a high level of fluency in the Hebrew language. Only about one-third, 35 percent, of them were illiterate in Hebrew at the time of their arrival; 38 percent were able to speak Hebrew and 27 percent had some knowledge of it. By the time Engel's study was conducted only 14 percent felt they needed more training in Hebrew.[26]

Engel's data manifest a pattern mentioned previously, namely, a continuing decline in the influence of formal Zionism in the aliya of Americans. Although the majority of his respondents, 56 percent, grew up in what they defined as Zionist homes, and a majority of 57 percent had belonged to Zionist youth organizations, the size of those majorities is considerably smaller than that which Antonovsky and Katz found for the pre-1948 American immigrants.[27]

Denominationally, 41 percent stated that their parents were Orthodox and 34 percent that they themselves had been Orthodox in America; 25 percent were from Conservative homes and 24 percent stated that they themselves had been Conservative in America; 7 percent were from Reform homes and stated that they themselves were Reform Jews in America; 27 percent stated that they were from either religiously unaffiliated or "other" homes, and 34 percent had themselves been either unaffiliated or "other" in America.[28] Here we begin to see a pattern that has continued and even greatly accelerated since the founding of the State of Israel, namely, a disproportionate number of American immigrants who are Orthodox and a growing Orthodox proportion. The extent to which this is so and the reasons for it will be explained in later chapters.

Engel reported that the American olim had a higher than average level of secular education, with 78 percent having had some college and 33 percent having gone to graduate or professional schools.[29] What he fails to mention, however, is that American Jews as a whole have higher than average levels of education. When a comparison is made between the American immigrants and American Jews as a whole at that time, the educational patterns of the olim are not unusual.[30] On the other hand, it should be emphasized that in comparison to the education patterns prevalent in Israel at that time, the educational status of the American olim was very high.

Given their educational patterns, it should not be surprising that the economic situation of the American immigrants prior to their leaving for Israel was found to be good. There do not, therefore, seem to be any grounds for assuming that push factors were primary in their aliya. Engel saw their "critique of America" as playing a central role in their aliya, but their critique was a specifically Jewish one, not only in the sense that it arose from Jewish sources but in that the concerns centered on the present and future well-being of Jews in American society rather than on any concerns for the well-being of American society and culture per se. As Engel interprets his findings:

> They left because they felt a growing anxiety about being part of a society in which materialism and conformity threatened the realization of their human potential. While their parents, mostly immigrants, had become part of that society which accepted them and gave them the opportunity to live decently, the would-be olim were too American to feel grateful, and too Jewish to be satisfied. Their generation rarely voiced doubts about society; but the dissatisfied left for Israel when the pressure mounted. As committed Jews, they were specifically affected by the threat of assimilation and anti-semitism to the survival of the Jewish group. Assimilation disturbed 65 percent of all respondents. For the religious it was the most disturbing problem they faced in America. Living in Israel made the questions of anti-semitism appear urgent. Though 73 percent expressed concern over it, 53 percent now were only mildly disturbed.[31]

One of the surprises of this finding is that from American olim who immigrated at this time one might have expected at least some expression of criticism of American society, and not only insofar as it affects Jews. This was, after all, the early to mid-1960s, the years when young, educated people in American society were growing increasingly critical of arrangements and patterns in their society. How is it that there were no such criticisms from among these immigrants? The answer cannot be their ages. After all, those between the ages of twenty to twenty-nine made up 40 percent of the sample, and 31 percent were between the ages of thirty to thirty-nine. Of the rest, 17 percent were forty to forty-nine; 10 percent were fifty to sixty-six; 2 percent were sixty-seven or older.[32] Given that more than 70 percent were thirty-nine or younger, and 40 percent were younger than thirty, the sample seems to indicate a generally young population of American olim, although the mode is somewhat older than that reported for the pre-1948 American olim.

Perhaps the reason for the absence of any criticism of American society per se from these immigrants is the result of both their family status and their years in Israel. Although younger than the American average and American Jewish average, the rate of marriage for these American immigrants was almost the same as that of American Jewry in general, namely, 84 percent of the respondents were married, but only 36 percent of them were married to native-born Americans. Also, 70 percent of the sample had Israeli-born children. And 56 percent had been living in Israel five years or longer.[33] Taken as a group, these immigrants were in a much different situation than were most of the young Americans who were involved in the social criticism of American society during the 1960s. These immigrants were not college students. They were all over twenty years old. Most were spouses and parents. The majority had been away from America for five years or more and were, thus, much more Israel-oriented than American-oriented. Also, they therefore left America before it became fashionable to engage in social criticism of American society.

Nor was the Jewish critique of American society the most important reason for the aliya. Once again, rather than push factors, pull factors–the attraction to Israel–was predominant. As Engel says: "Over four-fifths were attracted by the idea of living in a Jewish homeland. They desired to live a Jewish life among Jews. The concept of Israel as the land of the Bible drew three-fourths of the settlers. Seventy-one percent were attracted by Jewish education. The intensity of feeling on all aspects of Jewish life (except for Israel as the land of the Bible) was high, with almost twice as many feeling 'much' attraction as 'some' attraction."[34]

One final interesting shift in the patterns of American aliya at this time relates to how the immigrants came. During the prestate era and especially during the mandatory period, most American immigrants came to Israel in groups, as cells or *garinim* for agricultural settlements. Once the state was established, there was a distinct change in this pattern. First, there was a steady decline in the proportion of American olim who joined agricultural settlements. Whereas, as mentioned earlier, two-thirds of the pre-1948 American immigrants lived on a kibbutz for at least some time, among the 1950–66 North American immigrants the kibbutz attracted only a minority. And related to this, kibbutz pioneering encouraged cells and group aliya; nonkibbutz-motivated aliya is much more of an individual and family phenomonon than a group one. Thus, of the latter American immigrants only 7 percent migrated in groups.[35]

Despite all of the differences between the life-styles in which the American immigrants had grown up and the nature of Israeli society and culture during the 1950s to mid-1960s-Israel was truly a developing society at that time–Engel found that 75 percent of them had felt "at home" from the moment they arrived in the country. Initially, the female immigrants had been slightly more lonely than the males, but by the end of their first year the differences disappeared and the overwhelmingly majority of both males and females felt comfortable. Indeed, at the time the study was conducted, 1967, fully 95 percent of them felt comfortable with and at home in Israeli life.[36]

Socioeconomically, the American immigrants did quite well. Relative to not only Israeli but American standards as well, the percentage employed as professionals and teachers was very high and the majority of these were working in the fields for which they had been trained. More than three-quarters, 77 percent, owned their own apartments and 90 percent of the immigrants expressed satisfaction with their housing conditions. As for income, a majority of 57 percent felt that they could readily manage on their incomes.[37] The American olim, therefore, enjoy exceptionally high socioeconomic status in Israel, and in an interesting way their high status serves to keep them in Israel and prevent their return to America, where they would probably not enjoy an equally high status. In fact, when asked, 74 percent of these immigrants stated that the high status kept Americans in Israel. This, however, was not the most highly ranked reason the Americans stayed in Israel. The desire to live in a Jewish homeland was ranked highest and the religious environment of Israel was next.[38] How the backgrounds, motivations, and experiences of these North American immigrants in Israel compare with those who came after the Six-Day War of June 1967 will be analyzed in subsequent chapters.

6

American Aliya, 1967–1987

The Six-Day War of June 1967 had a dramatic impact on Israel, both internally and externally. Externally, the outcome of the war affected not only the foreign relations in Israel–that is, the ties Israel has with other countries–but also the psychologies and social psychologies of Jews and Jewish communities around the world and the relations Israel has with those communities. Some of the ways in which the American Jewish community was affected will be discussed in Chapter 7. For now, suffice it to say that, as Table 2 shows,[1] war seems to have significantly accelerated the pace of American aliya. There was an almost 50 percent increase in the rate of that aliya between 1967 and 1968. The 1968 rate, however, was only slighly higher than the 1965 rate and was lower than the 1964 rate. And what appears to be a great jump in the rate between 1968 and 1969 is more a matter of renaming and reclassification than anything else. As it happens, in 1969 Israel's Ministry of Interior decided to reclassify "temporary residents" as "potential immigrants," and the aliya figures from then on include potential as well as actual immigrants, whereas prior to 1969 the figures included only actual immigrants. In fact, when "potential immigrants" are separated from 1969 American aliya figures, it turns out that in that year there were only 671 actual immigrants, a decrease from the pre-1967 figures.[2] On the other hand, there was a marked rise in the numbers of "temporary residents" or "potential immigrants" after 1967, so that both the total combined numbers and the numbers of atual immigrants increased after 1969.

This chapter deals with demographic and motivational issues. It will be limited to two central questions: who are the American Jews who migrate to Israel today–that is, since 1967–and why do they do so? Subsequent chapters will look at their acculturation experience and their lives as Israelis of American background.

Demographic Issues

Regional Distribution

American immigrants to Israel, olim, apparently tend to be representative of the American Jewish population as a whole in terms of the regions United States from which they came. Although Antonovsky and Katz, in their study of pre-1967 American olim, reported that they disporportionately tended to be from the New York City area,[3] Goldscheider compared 1969–70 olim with the distribution of the U.S. Jewish population by region at that time and found them to be "remarkably" similar, with about 65 percent coming from the Northeast, about 12.5 percent from the North Central region, about 10 percent from the South, and about 12 percent from the West.[4] In 1976 Gerald Berman conducted a study of North Americans who had arrived in Israel between 1970 and 1974, about 8 percent of whom were Canadians, and found a significant increase in the percentage of those from the U.S. West–20 percent–and decreases from the other regions of the country.[5] Comparing his findings with those of the regional distribution of Jews in the United States in 1981, we notice that the percentages of American olim from the Northeast and North Central areas are almost exactly proportionately represented. On the other hand, the West is overrepresented, whereas the South is underrepresented. The reasons for this disparity are unknown. It can be suggested that it might be due to the fact that the West is, generally, a newer region for American Jews and, thus, those who live there are less tied to that region and more likely to contemplate and venture new moves. Also, at least in its stereotype, the South is, in general, more conservative than the West and, therefore, its Jews would be less likely to contemplate aliya. The disparity may also reflect regional differences in what Antonovsky and Katz termed Zionist and Jewish variables. All of this is, of course, speculation.

Generational Status

Data from a number of surveys suggest that the vast majority of American olim are American-born, and that the size of that majority

AMERICAN ALIYA

TABLE 3

Regional Distribution of American Olim
and Jewish Population in the U.S.

Region	Jewish Population in U.S., 1981 (%)	American Olim, 1969–70 (%)	American Olim, 1970–74 (%)
Northeast	56.9	66.2	56
North Central	11.6	12.8	10
South	16.3	9.7	6
West	15.1	11.3	20
TOTAL	99.9	100.0	92

Sources: Jewish population in U.S. figures from *American Year Book* 82 (1982): 169; American olim, 1969–70, figures from Goldscheider, "American Aliya," 359; American olim, 1976, figures from Berman, *The Experience of Alyah,* table 1, p. 19. The 1970–74 olim figures total 92 percent because they do not include the 8 percent of Berman's sample who were Canadians.

is increasing. Thus, Goldscheider found 30.4 percent of the American immigrants in his 1969–70 study to have been "first generation," that is, not native-born American.[6] Harry Jubas conducted a study of olim between the years 1967 and 1971 that had a much larger, though not necessarily more representative, sample than that of Goldscheider, and he found that 25 percent were not "native-born American men and women."[7] Kevin Avruch conducted a survey of American olim in Jerusalem between the years 1968 and 1976, and he found 14 percent were not native American.[8] Berman's study of 1970–74 olim found 9 percent were not native American.[9] According to Israel's Central Bureau of Statistics, there were 74,775 immigrants and potential immigrants between 1948 and 1986 whose last country of residence was the United States. Of those, 57,564 or about 77 percent were born in the United States. Of the North American immigrants and potential immigrants who immigrated in 1986, 84.6 percent were born in North America.[10] The high percentage of American-born among these olim is understandable, given their relatively young ages, as will be discussed shortly. Also, the increasing size of the native American group is probably a reflection of the growing percentage of the American Jewish population that is native American, especially among the young.

Age.

As Goldscheider points out, immigrants to Israel, in general, tend to be young, and there is hardly any difference between the average age of the American and other immigrants. Thus, the American olim tend to be concentrated in the under-35-year-old age group. The median age of the 1969–70 American olim was 25.9, compared to the median age of the Jewish population in the United States in 1957, which was 36.7.[11] Since then the disparity has grown considerably wider. In 1984 68.6 percent of the immigrants and potential immigrants from North American were younger than age 35, and the median age of all immigrants and potential immigrants was 23.4, as compared to the median age of the American Jewish population, which was 49 in 1982.[12]

Sex

It was mentioned in Chapter 5 that Antonovsky and Katz reported an overrepresentation of females among the pre-1967 American immigrants.[13] In Berman's survey of 1970–74 North American olim, the majority, 60.1 percent, was male.[14] Since his was a study of those who were employed full time at the time of the survey, however, it is a purposive rather than a representative sample. The special nature of his sample accounts as well for the variances in his findings with respect to other demographic characteristics. Most post-1967 studies find the pattern of an overrepresentation of females continuing, but with some qualification. Goldscheider found that within the younger age group, the one in which American immigrants tend to be concentrated, there are more women than men, but that among those in early middle age and among those age sixty-five and older, males are overrepresented. Recent data from Israel's Central Bureau of Statistics show that among all very young immigrants and potential immigrants, through age nine, there are also somewhat more males than females.[15]

The persistence of the pattern of an overrepresentation of females in all except those two age categories would seem to place considerable doubt on the explanation suggested by Antonovsky and Katz. It will be recalled that they suggested that American Jewish males are less likely to undertake aliya because they are engaged in studies and careers. But almost the same has been true for American Jewish females in recent years.[16] The educational and career activities of American Jewish males and females do not seem to be sufficiently different today to account for the overrepresentation of females among the American olim.

Alternatively, it might be suggested that the overrepresentation of females among the American immigrants to Israel may be related to the greater likelihood of American Jewish women supporting the policies of the government of Israel. As Jay Brodbar-Nemzer found in his analysis of Steven Cohen's data from the 1981–82 National Survey of American Jews:

> In groups in which we would expect this sex difference to disappear (the highly liberal, the nonobservant, the young, the highly educated, full-time participants in the labor force), we *still* find that a higher proportion of women than men profess attitudes that are consistent with current Israeli government policy. . . .
>
> The women in this sample were more likely than men to manifest a fundamental insecurity over the status of American Jewry. Women were less likely than men to agree that "there is a bright future for Jewish life in America" (66 percent versus 75 percent), and that "virtually all positions of influence in America were open to Jews" (28 percent versus 38 percent).[Emphasis in original.][17]

If American Jewish women are more supportive and less critical of Israeli government policy and less optimistic about the future of Jewish life in America, as Brodbar-Nemzer's analysis indicates, this may explain the greater receptivity of American Jewish women to aliya. If there is merit to this suggestion, it is of particular interest that Brodbar-Nemzer's findings introduce a possible push factor to American aliya, an issue that will be dealt with at greater length in the discussion of motivations for aliya later in this chapter.

Marriage and Family

As might be expected from the relative youthfulness of American olim, there is a greater proportion of singles among them than there is in the Jewish population in the United States. Even with the increasing rate of singles in the American Jewish population, they are still a relatively small minority.[18] Among the American olim, however, according to the 1986 data of the Central Bureau of Statistics, more than half of the North American immigrants and potential immigrants age twenty and older for that year were single.[19] The high proportion of young and singles among the American olim is explained by Goldscheider as part of the simple fact that young and single are two social characteristics that allow for the greatest degree of freedom of movement, and it is this same fact that explains why there is a larger proportion of widowers than widows among the American olim. Simply, widowers have a greater degree of freedom of movement than do widows.[20]

Given what we know about the American Jewish family patterns–namely, that the birthrate of American Jews is low compared to both what it was in the past and to the average birthrate in the United States[21]–it is interesting to note that the average family size of American olim is larger than the average of all olim. The average size for all olim is 3.0 whereas for North American olim it is 3.6.[22]

Education

If the educational status of the pre-1967 American olim was high as compared to that of Israeli society, as was seen in Chapter 5, the even higher educational status of the post-1967 American olim is very striking. We know that America's Jews have an unusually high educational status,[23] and it is not surprising that those who go on aliya should have higher-than-average educational status. But given what Antonovsky and Katz said about the likelihood of aliya–namely, that those who are engaged in studies and career would not be expected immigrate–it would not be expected that the olim would have as high educational status as does the overall Jewish population in the United States. Although it is true, as Goldscheider points out, that "the relatively small number of olim from the United States precludes any real quantitative impact of educational and occupational selectivity on the American Jewish community,"[24] we can nevertheless compare the educational status of the American olim to both that of the American Jewish population and that of the Jewish population in Israel, as well as to other olim during the same period. When we do so we see that, in 1970, the percentage of the adult Jewish population in Israel that graduated college was 5.6; among all adult olim it was 17.7; among the adult Jewish population in the United States it was 32.5; whereas among the adult American olim it was 41.7 percent.[25]

The reasons for the high educational status of American olim are not difficult to understand. When we compare them with those segments of the American Jewish population that are similar in age and generational status, the educational status of the American olim no longer seems surprising. Although there are no recent national Jewish educational data broken down by age and generation cohorts, such data from the Boston Jewish community in both 1965 and 1975 are available. They reveal that in 1965 the percentage of college graduates among those in the 21–25 and 25–34-year-old cohorts was extremely high, about 90 percent. Precise comparisons with 1975 are difficult since the age cohorts are not identical–in 1975 the cohort was 18–24-but the 1975 data do suggest increasing growth in the educational status.[26] Although the Boston community is probably not representative of American Jewry as a whole, the trends manifested there are most likely similar to those of the larger American Jewish population.

Occupational Distribution

Having seen the high educational status and the relative youthfulness of the American olim, it should come as no surprise to learn that they came to Israel with high occupational status. As Table 4 shows, there was a considerably higher percentage of both male and female professionals among the American olim than among all olim and among the Jewish population in the United States in 1970.

Although the figures on the American Jewish population in the 1980s are not yet available, those on the occupational distribution of all olim in 1986 are, and they indicate a continuing if not growing high percentage of professionals among the North American olim.

Political Behavior

That the majority of the American immigrants in the 1970s were Democrats is also not surprising, given the political patterns of the Jewish population in the United States.[27] The extremely small size of the Republican minority, however, is amazing. In his 1972 and 1975 studies of American olim, Zvi Gitelman found 57 percent were Democrats, about 41 percent were Independents, the majority of whom tended toward the Democrats, and only 2 percent were Republicans. Almost 40 percent stated that they participated in peace or antiwar demonstrations.[28]

Although America's Jews have had a tradition of liberal to left-wing political behavior, there is an overrepresentation of such politics among these olim. Since this is the only study available of the political beliefs and behavior of American olim, it is difficult to determine whether the patterns found here might be atypical. One possible reason for this atypicality is that they refer to olim who came to Israel in 1972 and 1975 and, therefore, probably made their aliya decisions during the 1960s, a decade in which there was widespread criticism, especially among the young, of American society. It was a decade in

TABLE 4

Occupational Distribution, 1970

Occupation	American Olim (%)		Total Olim (%)		U.S. Jewish Population (%)	
	Male	Female	Male	Female	Male	Female
Professionals	62.5	66.9	39.0	47.3	29.3	23.8
Managers and proprietors	4.1	0.7	1.8	4.7	40.7	15.5
Clerical	5.1	27.2	11.1	29.0	3.2	41.7
Sales	10.3	1.1	16.0	2.9	14.2	8.3
Blue-collar	17.9	4.1	32.1	16.1	11.0	7.6
Unknown	–	–	–	–	1.7	3.1
TOTAL	99.9	100.0	100.0	100.0	100.1	100.0

Sources: Adapted from Goldscheider, 'American Aliya," table 11, p. 372; and Sidney Goldstein, "Jews in the United Staes," American Jewish Year Book 81 (1981): table 9, p. 54.

TABLE 5

Olim Aged 15 and Over by Continent of Residence and Occupation Abroad, 1986

Occupation Abroad	Latin America	North America	Europe	Asia-Africa	Total
Scientific and academic workers	157	364	630	112	1,267
Other professional, technical, and related	147	366	458	146	1,118
Managers and clerical	81	127	283	133	627
Sales and service	82	77	136	119	414
Agricultural	2	9	18	4	33
Skilled	38	58	200	112	408
Unskilled	2	1	24	4	31
Occupation unknown	74	161	219	275	731
Total employed abroad	583	1,163	1,968	905	4,629
Total unemployed abroad	83	603	1,146	752	3,046
Unknown	1	7	9	20	43
TOTAL	1,119	1,773	3,123	1,677	7,718

Sources: Adapted from Israel Central Bureau of Statistics, Immigration to Israel 1986, special series no. 808 (Jerusalem: 1987), table 21, p. 26.

TABLE 6

Occupational Distribution of American Olim and
Israeli Jewish Labor Force

Occupation	North American Olim, 1984	Jewish Israelis, 1984
Scientific and academic workers	33.3	8.7
Other professional, technical, and related	33.4	15.9
Administrators and managers	1.5	5.1
Clerical and related	9.2	19.8
Sales workers	6.2	7.9
Service workers	1.2	12.0
Agricultural workers	1.0	4.4
Skilled blue-workers	6.1	23.3
Semiskilled and unskilled	0.3	2.9
Unknown	7.8	–
TOTAL	100.0	100.0

Sources: Adapted from Israel Central Bureau of Statistics, *Immigration to Ismel 1984*, (Jerusalem: 1985), table 18, p. 22; and *Statistical Abstract of Israel 1984*, no. 35, table XII/17, pp. 348–49.

which identification with the Republican party among young, urban, highly educated American Jews was very low.

That does not, however, explain the very low rate of affiliation with the Republican party, since most of the American olim in Gitelman's surveys were not radicals. On the contrary, they tended to have somewhat conservative political views. For example, the vast majority agreed that "blacks in America have gone too far in their demands," and most of the 1972 respondents agreed that "everything considered, life in the U.S. was better ten years ago."[29]

Also, there is some evidence that the patterns Gitelman found were not unique to those years. As will be discussed in Chapter 10, in my own study of Americans who had immigrated to Israel up to early 1984 and who settled in Judea, Samaria, or the Gaza Strip, not one stated that he or she had been a Republican; virtually all had been Democrats, Liberals, Independents, or unaffiliated.[30] It appears that American Jews affiliated with the Republican party are much less likely than Democrats to go on aliya. Why this is so, if it in fact is, remains to be explained.

Zionist Organizational Membership

In the earlier discussion of the pre-1967 American olim, it was seen that there was a decline, from prestate to early-state years, in the rate of membership in Zionist organizations while in America. Even during the early to mid-1960s, however, the majority of olim had previously been members of Zionist organizations.[31] For the post-1967 olim, there is conflicting evidence, with some studies indicating the decline continued to the point at which those who had been members of Zionist organizations were in the minority. Among those in Goldscheider's 1969–70 survey, only 50.7 percent stated that they had previously been members of Zionist organizations, 11.4 percent of whom were nonactive members, and the rate of Zionist organizational membership decreased generationally to a point where among third-generation American olim, 60.4 were nonmembers.[32] For those 1967–71 olim in the study conducted by Jubas, the decline is even sharper, with approximately 60 percent indicating that they were not previously members of Zionist organizations.[33] By the 1970s, in two surveys by Gerald Berman, one of 1970–74 North American olim and one of those who immigrated in 1976, only about one-third had been members of Zionist organizations.[34]

On the other hand, Kevin Avruch, in his study of American olim from the years 1968–1976 who were residents of Jerusalem, found 61 percent to have been either active or not-so-active members of Zionist organizations and only 39 percent to have been nonmembers.[35] It is fair to assume, however, that Americans residing in Jerusalem are not representative of all American olim in Israel. If nothing else, the Jerusalemite ones tend to be older, and one would expect a higher rate of Zionist organizational affiliation among them.

The steady decline in the rate of Zionist organizational affiliation among the American olim is probably a reflection of both their young age–there has been an overall steady decline in Jewish organizational affiliation along generational lines in the United States–and the decline of the role of and membership in Zionist organizations in the United States. Among young American olim, in particular, since they probably had been planning their aliya for some time and, thus, did not see their future as within the American Jewish community, and because they did not need the Zionist organizations for their aliya, an increasing number probably saw no reason to formally affiliate with a Zionist organization. They didn't need the organizational affiliation to act on their Zionism; they did that by planning and making aliya.

Jewish Education
A common finding in all of the studies is that American olim arrive in Israel with much more extensive Jewish education than is typical for the Jewish population in the United States. About 60 percent of American Jewish children receive no formal Jewish education, whereas less than 20 percent of the American olim had no formal Jewish education. On the other hand, 26.3 percent of *that 40 percent* of American Jewish children who did receive some formal Jewish education in 1974–75 were enrolled in day schools, whereas more than a third of all of the olim had *at least* a day school education.[36]

Denomination
In analyzing the denominational affiliations of America's Jews in 1971, Bernard Lazerwitz found that 11 percent identified with the Orthodox, 42 percent with Conservative, 33 percent with Reform, and 14 percent had no denominational affiliation. By contrast, both Goldscheider and Jubas found that between 37 and 42 percent of the American olim in their surveys identified themselves as Orthodox. The percentage of Orthodox among these American olim is also higher than among those in Engel's 1950–66 sample and much higher than among the prestate American olim. Some reasons for the increasing proportion of Orthodox among the American olim are related to the condition to Orthodox Judaism in the United States and will be discussed in the following chapters.

There is also an overrepresentation of other or religiously nonaffiliated among the American olim–20 percent, compared to the 14 percent in the Jewish population in the United States. On the other hand, there is an underrepresentation of Conservative and, especially, Reform Jews among the olim. Table 7 gives the full range of the differences in religious denominational identification.

In their study of older immigrants in Israeli society, Sheldon Lache and colleagues found that almost three-fourths of the middle-aged and retired North American olim they interviewed classified themselves as religious. These researchers, however, used the prevalent Israeli categories–"Religious," "Traditional," and "Non-Religious."[37] This categorization is inappropriate for American Jewry, among whom Orthodox, Conservative, and Reform may identify themselves as "religious" and, therefore, cannot be compared with the data on denominational distribution. On the other hand, since it is doubtful that an Israeli researcher would classify most Conservative and Reform Jews as "religious," the data of Lache and colleagues

TABLE 7

Denominational Distribution

Denomination	U.S. Jewry, 1971	U.S. Olim, 1969–70	U.S. Olim, 1967–71	North America Lim, 1970–74
Orthodox	11	42	37	37.1
Conservative	42	24	29	26.2
Reform	33	14	12	10.5
Other/nonaffiliated	14	20	20	26.1
No answer	–	–	2	–
TOTAL	100	100	100	99.9

Sources: U.S. Jewry figures are from Waxman, America's Jews in Transition, 184–85; 1969–70 figures are from Goldscheider, "American Aliya," table 14, p. 380; 1967–71 figures are from Jubas, "Adjustment Process," table 4.13, p. 105; 1970–74 figures are from Berman, Work Adjustment, table 3, p. 30. Berman's sample includes 8 percent Canadians. Also, 4.9 percent who identified themselves "traditional" are here included among "Other."

do suggest that a very disproportionately high percentage of American olim are Orthodox.

Goldscheider found that patterns among the American olim "of overconcentration and selectivity among religious and Orthodox Jews relative to the American Jewish population"[38] also manifested themselves in their patterns of synagogue attendance and ritual observance. Specifically, among the olim the rate of synagogue attendance and observance of such rituals as fasting on Yom Kippur and dietary regulations was disproportionate when compared to the Jewish population in the United States.

Data from Israel's Central Bureau of Statistics likewise indicate the disproportionate religiosity of American olim and the increasing proportion of religiously observant among them. Of the 1978–80 North American olim, a majority, 54.0 percent, identified themselves as "religious," 20.8 percent as "traditional," 11.3 percent as "not very religious," and only 13.9 percent as "not religious at all."[39]

Most recently, although the evidence is unconfirmed, it has been reported that, for the year 1986, "Of the [approximately] 1900 [olim] who arrived from the United States, more than 1200 are Orthodox Jews and the remainder defined themselves as somewhat religiously observant."[40] This report of almost two-thirds of the American olim being Orthodox conforms with the estimates conveyed to me in interviews with the assistant director of the Aliya Department of the World Zionist Organization–American Section,[41] and others connected with that department, that about 60 percent of contemporary American olim are Orthodox.[42]

In sum, what we see is that the olim are relatively young and highly educated–in terms of both Jewish and secular learning–and that the rate of Zionist organizational membership among them is decreasing, whereas the rate of Orthodox affiliation and ritual observance is increasing.

Motivations for Aliya

In examining the motivations for aliya, several important methodological qualifications must be kept in mind. This analysis is based on surveys and other types of interviews with American olim. The data, therefore, are derived from responses given by the olim themselves. It is quite possible, however, that for a variety of reasons the motivations identified by the respondents were not the actual primary motivations for the aliya. Respondents may have been unaware, may have forgotten, or may now wish to hide their actual motivations for aliya. Thus, aliya may have actually been precipitated by one set of issues, but when the olim arrived in Israel, they perceived another value in their aliya and now "realize" that that was the most important motivation. This is especially applicable to situations where the olim left their home in America because of, say, dissatisfaction with changes in the neighborhod or the place of employment. It is probably equally applicable to situations in which individuals may have left the United States because of the war in Vietnam or in reaction to the perceived excesses of the civil rights movement. Having undergone aliya, the olim may now find it much more rewarding to attribute their aliya to pull factors, attractions to Israel, than to admit that there were push factors involved.

Furthermore, rarely is there only one motive for aliya. Invariably, there are a variety of factors involved. As was discussed in the Introduction, Eisenstadt astutely maintains that "every migratory movement is motivated by the migrant's feeling of some kind of insecurity and inadequacy in his original social setting."[43] It is true, as Avruch suggests, that the very fact that individuals decided, because of their feelings of insecurity and inadequacy in the original social setting, to immigrate to Israel rather than to move elsewhere in the United States–from New York to Florida or California, for example– indicates that living in Israel did have some special meaning to them.[44] Especially when looking at American aliya rates in comparison to the size of the American Jewish population, however, it must be emphasized that what distinguishes those who go on aliya from those who do not may be *either* that the olim attach greater significance to personally living in Israel than do the Jews who remain in America, *or* that the olim experienced insecurities and inadequacies in America that the Jews who remain in America do not. Also, if the insecurities and inadequacies the olim experienced are derived subjectively, from the depth of their Jewish identity, that means something other than insecurities and inadequacies derived from objective occupational, economic, or neighborhood factors. Finally, to further point up the complexity of the issue, it is not even that simple to distinguish between subjective and objective inadequacies, because the subjective consciousness of the individual influences, if not determines, the extent to which one will be affected by "objective" factors.[45]

When the post-1967 studies are compared with the pre-1967 ones, it becomes apparent that there has been an increase in the proportion of those who attribute religious and Jewish motivations and a decrease in the proportion of those who ascribe pioneering and classical Zionist motivations to their aliya. Whereas among the pre-1948 American olim Zionism was the major motivation for aliya identified, Jewishness second, and religious reasons almost insignificant,[46] during the poststate era religious reasons became increasingly important to the point where, after the Six-Day War, they became among the most important motivations for American aliya. Thus, in a preliminary analysis of his 1969–70 data, Goldscheider suggests that the ideology that shapes the extent and type of aliya "seems much less "Zionist" in the narrow, formal sense and much more "religious" in its broadest, sociological meaning."[47] In his study of 1967–71 American olim, Jubas found: "If the motives for coming to Israel of this population were to be summed up in one word it would be unquestionably 'Jewishness.' "[48] As he and his respondents used the term, it consisted of both ethnic and religious elements and placed emphasis on religio-ethnic identity, culture, and peoplehood. Berman, Avruch, and Dashefsky and Lazerwitz[49] have all found that Jewish religious motivations play a much larger role in American aliya today, and that the classical Zionist conceptions and foci are largely irrelevant for most contemporary American olim. For example, Berman found among his 1976 olim that "the Zionists are more likely than the non-Zionists to have come from observant homes, to be more observant themselves, to have attended synagogue frequently, and to have had seven or more years of Jewish education. In addition, a higher proportion of Zionist than non-Zionist members gave Jewish religious reasons for their migration."[50]

Avruch interprets the motivation of contemporary American olim as "identities in search of a society."[51] From among its many components, he argues, they have maximized and primordialized the specifically Jewish part of their total identity. They define themselves as more Jewish than American and seek an environment in which to give the fullest expression to their identity as such. As Avruch says: "The rhetoric of classical Zionism dealt with 'the problem of Jews' or, sometimes, with 'the problem of Judaism.' The rhetoric of a large proportion of contemporary American immigrants takes its substance, self-consciously, from a different source. It deals with the individual coming to grips with '*my* problem as a Jew.' " (emphasis in original).[52]

The next chapter takes up the theme of Jewish identity and analyzes the relationship between Jewish identity and Zionism as that ideology is now defined by the representatives of the organizational structure ostensibly designed to help realize its goals, the World Zionist Organization.

PART III

7

The Centrality of Israel
in American Jewish Life

Among the aims of Zionism, as set down by the "Jerusalem Program" of the World Zionist Organization, which was unanimously adopted by the twenty-seventh Zionist Congress and has been reaffirmed by each subsequent Zionist Congress, is "the centrality of Israel in Jewish life." Having traced the development of American Zionism and then examined the nature of American aliya, this chapter will provide a sociological analysis of that Zionist goal as it pertains to American Jewry. Essentially, this chapter seeks to determine and explain the extent to which Israel has become central in American Jewish life, because through such an analysis we can better understand how different segments within the American Jewish community relate to the notion of aliya.

American Jewish life may be viewed from at least two perspectives: objectively, in terms of the communal and institutional structure of American Jewry, and subjectively, in terms of the self-identity, behavior, and values of American Jews.[1] In this chapter American Jewry will be examined from both perspectives in order to determine the role of Israel in American Jewish life.

When viewed from the objective perspective, it would appear that Israel does, in fact, play a central role in American Jewish life. For example, when one scans the listing of "National Jewish Organizations" published toward the end of each volume of the *American Jewish Year Book*, the centrality of Israel in the listed objectives and activities of the majority of them is readily apparent. Moreover, thirty-eight of the largest and most active of the national Jewish organizations are affiliated with the Conference of Presidents of Major Jewish Organizations, for which Zionist and pro-Israel activity is the major emphasis. The Conference of Presidents is housed at 515 Park Avenue in New York City, which is the American headquarters of the Jewish Agency and the World Zionist Organization, and virtually all of the chairpersons of the conference had previous records of activity on behalf of Israel.

The deep and extensive involvement American Jews have with Israel is, indeed, a unique and fascinating phenomenon, and Melvin Urofsky describes it as it probably appears to many non-Jews:

> No other ethnic group in American history has so extensive an involvement with a foreign nation; no other nation relies upon a body of private individuals who are neither residents nor citizens of their land to underwrite a major portion of their budget. American Jews buy Israel bonds, give generously to the United Jewish Appeal, lobby governmental representatives to pursue a pro-Israel policy, travel extensively to Israel (where they are greeted by "Welcome Home" signs), respond immediately to every crisis in that part of the world, and yet maintain passionately that they are Americans first and Jews afterward. It is a curious, puzzling, and yet totally logical arrangement.[2]

Insofar as the centrality of Israel in American Jewish organizational life is concerned, Daniel Elazar shows how defense activity for Israel has become a vehicle for gaining prominence within the Amercan Jewish community.

> After the establishment of the Jewish state in 1948 . . . Israel became the major focus of Jewish communal attention. Especially since the Six-Day War of 1967, insuring the survival of Israel has become the heart of the defense function of the American Jewish community. Even the community-relations agencies are now spending a high proportion of their time and resources seeking to increase support for Israel in the United States. Since as a result the most important factors in the community are persons and groups who are connected with the defense of Israel, there has been an effort on the part of many groups to climb on that particular bandwagon.[3]

Indeed, Israel has become so central to American Jewish organizational life that some observers tend to confuse symbols with substance and assume that Israel is now central to every facet of American Jewish life. For example, Yakir Eventov and Cvi Rotem, writing in the *Encyclopedia Judaica,* give a sweeping panoramic view of the extent to which Israel has become central within the American Jewish community since the Six-Day War.

> American Jews showed themselves more willing and ready to be identified as Jews, to affiliate with Jewish organizations and institutions, and to send their children to Jewish schools as a result of their ties with Israel. Israel occupies an important place in synagogue activities, sermons, and various religious celebrations, and Israel Independence Day assumes an important place in the American Jewish calendar. The Israel flag is frequently displayed in synagogues and community centers. In many synagogues, prayers for the welfare of the State of Israel and world Jewry are recited on Sabbaths and holidays following that for the welfare of the United States. Both the Conservative and Reform branches attempt to establish themselves in Israel through rabbinical schools and various educational programs.
> Another impact of Israel has been the use of the Hebrew language in contrast to the decline of Yiddish. Hebrew songs and Israel folk dances have become American Jewish popular culture: at weddings, bar mitzvot, and on many college campuses. Jewish art, which traditionally concentrated on East European themes, expanded to include Israel symbols; Israel crafts find a wide market among American Jews. Fiction on Israel life increases rapidly and an extensive periodical literature is directed from Israel institutions toward American Jewry.[4]

Although it is true that Israel plays a central role in the organizational life of the American Jewish community, this does not mean that American Jews are as interested in it and as knowledgeable about it as is frequently assumed. On the contrary, as Steven Cohen found in his survey of American Jewish attitudes toward Israel, most American Jews are ignorant about Israeli society and culture, including its language, Hebrew. For example, although two-thirds of the respondents in his national sample were aware that "most major Jewish religious holidays are also legal national holidays in Israel," only one-third knew even such elementary facts as that Menachem Begin and Shimon Peres are not from the same political party, that Conservative and Reform rabbis cannot officially marry couples in Israel, and that Arab Israeli and Jewish Israeli children do not generally go to the same schools.[5]

In order to more fully understand the attachment of American Jews to Israel it is necessary to further examine not only their organizational character but also their values, behavior, identity, and self-identification. When those become the area of focus it will be found that the role of Israel is very different from what may have been deduced from a strictly organizational analysis. When American Jewish life is viewed from a subjective perspective, it is found that while American Jews are overwhelmingly pro-Israel, they are also clearly not Zionist in either the classical sense or as Zionism is defined by the Jerusalem Program.

There has been some controversy over the question of who is a Zionist, but one need not go to the extreme of David Ben-Gurion, who argued that a Zionist is only one who actually goes on aliya,[6] to accept the distinction between Zionist and pro-Israeli. The pro-Israeli American Jew is the one who lives in the United States and supports Israel economically, politically, and emotionally, but whose primary source of Jewish identification is derived from and oriented to the American Jewish community. Moreover, the pro-Israeli American Jew perceives and accepts the legitimate cultural and religious autonomy of American Judaism. A Zionist, by contrast, is one who, while not necessarily anticipating his or her own aliya in the near future, because of any number of reasons, nevertheless does hold aliya to be an ideal and an imperative. And a Zionist would consider Israel to be the spiritual and cultural center of Jewry, at least as an ideal if not yet in fact. In essence, a Zionist is one for whom Israel plays a central role in one's own personal life, in one's sense of identity and very existence.[7]

The pioneering study of Jewish identity in a representative American Jewish community, the "Lakeville" study, was completed prior to the Six-Day War. The data there indicate variations of pro-Israeli sentiments both in generational terms and in terms of religious inheritance.[8] The vast distinction between Zionist and pro-Israeli sentiments is manifest in the fact that whereas 91 percent of the respondents approved of American Jews raising money for Israel, only 14 percent felt that Israeli financial needs take precedence over local Jewish causes and only 1 percent would even consider becoming citizens of Israel or encouraging their children to go on aliya.[9]

In conjunction with his study of reconstructionism, in 1969 Charles Liebman surveyed Orthodox, Conservative, and Reform rabbis and synagogue presidents and the presidents of local chapters of two nondenominational national Jewish organizations on a series of statements relating to Jewish religious ideology. Among the statements were several dealing with Israel, and the responses are significant. All of the groups, except the Orthodox rabbis, disagreed with the statement "A Jew who really wants to do what Judaism requires of him should move to Israel." The same basic result was found in the responses to a statement that had the opposite connotation: "While there must be a warm fraternal relation between Jews of the USA and Israel, the center of American Jewish life must be *American* Judaism rather than a Jewish culture which has developed or will develop in the State of Israel." Conservative and Reform rabbis and lay leaders agreed, but both Orthodox groups disagreed.[10] And with the statement "Israel should become the spiritual center of World Jewry," Reform rabbis and lay leaders overwhelmingly disagreed, Conservative less so, and the Orthodox least.[11]

During that same year, Arnold Dashefsky and Howard Shapiro conducted a study of the ethnic identity of middle-class Jewish males in St. Paul, Minnesota, and included in their study were a number of questions designed to measure the respondents' Zionism. According to the findings:

> There were . . . differences in the strength of Zionism between fathers and sons. . . . Fathers were more likely than sons to score higher on our Index of Zionism. This finding reflects the greater assimilation of the younger generation, who are more likely to unequivocally view America as the homeland rather than Israel. Perhaps the difference between the generations would have been greater but for the fact that the Six-Day War had occurred less than two years earlier. The crisis of the spring of 1967 had a great impact on all generations of American Jewry, generating both an outpouring of financial contributions and young volunteers.[12]

Subsequent developments turned out differently from that which was anticipated from the study by Dashefsky and Shapiro. Although the attachment of most American Jews to Israel does not include knowledge of Israel as a real society, and although Nathan Glazer may have been exaggerating when he claimed that "Israel has become *the* religion of American Jews,"[13] Israel most definitely is an important component of the religious and ethnic behavior of American Jewry, the "civil religion" of America's Jews. As Woocher writes, "It has been said that American Judaism recognizes only one heresy which subjects the perpetrator to immediate excommunication: denial of support to the State of Israel."[14] America's Jews have been and remain, through it all, highly supportive of Israel. Eytan Gilboa has extensively analyzed almost every study of American Jewish attitudes toward Israel, beginning with the 1945 public opinion poll conducted by Elmo Roper through Cohen's 1983 National Survey, and he finds that the data reveal "continuing strong support for attachment of American Jewry to Israel. American Jews overwhelmingly supported the establishment of Israel and have had highly favourable feelings towards her."[15]

Indeed, so strong is this attachment that it is able to weather severe challenges, such as the Israeli war in Lebanon and the outright Israeli rejection of President Reagan's proposals for peace between Israel and the neighboring Arab states. Nor are there indications that there is likely to be any decrease in the intensity of the American Jewish attachment to Israel in the foreseeable future. As Gilboa concludes: "The long-term trends reveal deep-seated feelings that have transcended dramatic and controversial events such as the 1982 Israeli war in Lebanon. These trends are likely to continue as long as Israel is perceived as an important vehicle for American Jews to express their Jewishness or as a means of protecting their ethnic survival."[16]

In a more recent and detailed analysis, Cohen's 1986 survey found that approximately 85 percent of American Jews consider themselves supporters of Israel. Cohen suggests that American Jewry can be divided into three different groups: the most intensely involved with or attached to Israel, constituting about a quarter to one-third of the American Jewish population; another third, consisting of people who care deeply about Israel but do not have strong personal ties with either Israel or Israelis; and a final third or more, most of whom are probably pro-Israel but do not express the kinds of deep concerns those in the other two groups do.[17]

Cohen's projections, however, are not as optimistic as are those of Gilboa. One reason for the diminished optimism of Cohen is his finding of a lower level of attachment to Israel among the young, which does not correlate with differences in religious belief and practice along age lines. Specifically, those who are age sixty-five or older had the highest percentage of those who scored high on the attachment index, whereas those who were between the ages thirty and thirty-nine had the lowest. Interestingly, the thirty to thirty-nine year age group had a lower percentage of those who scored high on the attachment index than did the below-thirty age group. Although no explanation is given for this finding, Cohen does imply that it may indicate an actual decline in the attachment of American Jews to Israel.[18]

Another revealing finding of Cohen's is that of a significant relationship between denomination and level of attachment to Israel. Specifically: "The extent of Orthodox Jews' attachment to Israel, however measured, significantly exceeded that of the other denominations, and Conservative Jews consistently scored higher than Reform or non-denominational Jews. Moreover, differences between Orthodox and non-Orthodox were sharpest on the most demanding measures of involvement–receptivity to Aliyah (settling in Israel), familiarity with several Israelis, and fluency in Hebrew."[19]

Moreover, when compared with Cohen's earlier 1983 study, he found that the Orthodox became more intensely attached between 1983 and 1986, there was virtually no change in the percentage of Conservative Jews who were highly attached, but there was an increase in the percentage of those with low levels of attachment, and among Reform Jews there was a decline in the percentage of those who were highly attached and a sharp rise in the percentage of those with only low levels of attachment. Whereas Orthodox attachments, which were intense initially, intensified even more during those years, the attachments of the Reform and some of the Conservative weakened significantly, and the latter are a much larger group than the former.[20]

One other finding of Cohen's pertains directly to one of the central arguments of this chapter. He included a series of questions dealing with aliya, if not for the respondents themselves then at least for their children. In accordance with the definition offered above, Cohen refers to this as "the acid test of Zionism." He says: "Three questions on whether and how much time respondents would want their children to spend in Israel depicted . . . the distribution of attitudes toward the State, ranging from near indifference to mildly pro-Israel, to very pro-Israel, to intensely Zionist. Three-fourths of the sample said they would want their children to 'visit Israel,' only a third wanted them to 'spend a year there,' and an even smaller 6 percent would want them to 'live there.' "[21]

All of the available data support the argument that the "Zionism" of American Jews is actually pro-Israel sentiment. One of the reasons American Jewish sentiment is so overtly pro-Israel is that this sentiment has been defined and is perceived as being compatible and consistent with the identification of American Jews *as Americans*. This was precisely the manner in which Justice Louis D. Brandeis, the "father" of American Zionism, defined Zionism. In an address delivered in June 1915, he sought to calm those who feared that their pro-

Israel (then called Palestine) actively might put their loyalty to America in question:

> Let no American imagine that Zionism is inconsistent with Patriotism. Multiple loyalties are objectionable only if they are inconsistent. A man is a better citizen of the United States for being also a loyal citizen of his state, and of his city; for being loyal to his family, and to his profession or trade; for being loyal to his college or his lodge. Every Irish American who contributed towards advancing home rule was a better man and a better American for the sacrifice he made. Every American Jew who aids in advancing the Jewish settlement in Palestine, though he feels that neither he nor his descendants will ever live there, will likewise be a better man and a better American for doing so.[22]

This was the most blatant of the formulations of what has developed as the uniquely *American* Zionism as compared to European and Israeli Zionism. Where Mordecai Kaplan only urged American Zionism not to concentrate on aliya because he believed it was futile to expect any massive aliya from the United States[23] Brandeis went much further. To him, the activity of the Zionist is analogous to the activity of the Irish American on behalf of home rule. His is not only a de facto omission of aliya from the Zionist credo; for him, aliya is de jure irrelevant to Zionism, and his conception is that which has become the dominant one in the United States.

Thus, Norman Podhoretz was essentially echoing Brandeis when, after the Yom Kippur War of October 1973, he declared the "instant Zionism" of American Jews. "If Zionism means supporting the idea of a sovereign Jewish state in Palestine," he wrote, "then most American Jews have been Zionist at least since the end of World War II."[24] After the Yom Kippur War, he argued, "many who were formerly hostile or indifferent to Israel have . . . either become Zionists or simply faded away."[25] The opposition to Jewish sovereignty to Israel has all but disappeared because the State of Israel is an accomplished fact; because American Jews remember the Holocaust and retain a "hidden apocalyptic terror"; and most important, according to Podhoretz, because the fear of a conflict between dual loyalties has never materialized since, by and large support for Israel has been consistent with American foreign policy.[26] Given his conception of Zionism, Podhoretz was basically correct, but with some qualification. He was correct in his contention that the majority of American Jews support the sovereignty of Israel, but the available data suggest that he was grossly overetimating when he wrote that "a full 99% of them have now become Zionists," and when he proclaimed "the universal need to do something, anything, for Israel."[27] Nevertheless, his argument that almost all American Jews now support Israel's sovereignty because support for Israel is consistent with American policy is well taken. That probably explains the degree to which many American Jewish spokespersons castigated Israel and assured America of their continuing loyalty at the height of the Jonathan Pollard espionage case in 1986 and early 1987.[28]

If this phenomenon were limited to political loyalties and strictly political nationalisms, it would be easy to understand why American's Jews are so overwhelmingly pro-Israel and yet such adamantly loyal Americans. But the data suggest that much more is involved. It appears that the centrality of Israel in American Jewish life is a function of the centrality of *Jewish* identity in American Jewish life; that is, the stronger the identity of the American Jew as a Jew, the greater the likelihood that Israel will play a central role in this or her life.[29] In order to more adequately understand the subject of Jewish identity in America it is fruitful to view it within the context of the initially Western processes of bureaucratization, secularization, and modernization in general, and Jewish emancipation in particular.

Following the approach of the noted sociologist of religion Peter Berger, one of the unique characteristics of modern society is that individuals do not live within one unified social world but in a "plurality of life-worlds,"[30] which manifests itself, for example, in the sharp dichotomy between individuals' public and private lives. Not only do they play different roles in these two spheres; there may even be completely different definitions of reality appropriate within each of them. Moreover, within each sphere there is an ongoing pluralization. It is important to realize that at the very same time that this pluralization of life-worlds makes individuals more "sophisticated," more "urbane," it also results in their having a less clear, less concrete, and less plausible "home world."[31] Their own definitions of reality become relativized and, as a consequence, less firm. Their identities become "peculiarly open," "peculiarly differentiated," "peculiarly reflective," and "peculiarly individuated."[32] Since the various social worlds in which they live become relativized, reality becomes subjective rather than objective, and the freedom and rights of individuals take on priority in the value system.

The pluralization of modern society and the compartmentalization of definitions of reality have contributed to secularization. It is important to understand that this secularization does not necessarily imply a disbelief in some conception of a supreme being, God; and the theory of the secularization of modern society is not refuted by the evidence of widespread belief in God and membership in churches and synagogues. Secularization, as defined by Berger, is

> the process by which sectors of society and culture are removed from the domination of religious institutions and culture. . . . When we speak of culture and symbols ... we imply that secularization is more than a social-structural process. It affects the totality of cultural life and of ideation. . . . Moreover, it is implied here that the process of secularization has a subjective side as well. As there is secularization of society and culture, so there is secularization of consciousness. Put simply, this means that the modern West has produced an increasing number of individuals who look upon the world and their own lives without the benefit of religious interpretations.[33]

On an institutional level, secularization manifests itself in the separation of religion from the spheres of the state and the economy, which even with the increases in the influence of institutionalized religion within the past decade is still not only mandated, at least as far as the state is concerned, by the Constitution, but is also deeply embedded in American culture. The very notion that "religion leaves off at the front gate," or that there is and should be separation of religion and state, would have been totally alien and incomprehensible to premodern people precisely because religion posited an all-encompassing world view with all-encompassing definitions of reality. But for modern people social life is compartmentalized and religion "has its place" within but one of those compartments or sectors. The modern state is areligious and the Western conception of nationality is conceived of as being neutral to religion even as the state pays homage to a generalized conception of religion and attempts to incorporate traditional religious notions into the civil religion. Bureaucracy and rationalization require that the criterion for evaluation in the political and, especially, in the economic spheres be efficiency. Religion and politics should not mix too closely, nor should religion and economic activity, unless, of course, it is profitable for them to so mix. Religion, essentially, is restricted to specific times and places, which, at times, can grow very narrow. This was particularly true in American society during the 1960s, the decade in which many of the American immigrants in Israel were maturing and beginning to contemplate, if not actualize, their aliya.

For the individual, the pluralization and compartmentalization of modern society result in personal problems. Anton Zijderveld says that because of pluralization individuals must develop pluralistic identities and must constantly be able to change identities, causing a gap between themselves and their roles. Society becomes "abstract," and individuals lose their sense of who they really are."[34] Berger, Berger, and Kellner summarized this condition succinctly when they wrote that "modern man has suffered from a deepening condition of 'homelessness.' "[35] This loss of "home," they suggest, is psychologically difficult and "has therefore engendered its own nostalgias–nostalgias, that is, for a condition of 'being at home' in society, with oneself and, ultimately, in the universe."[36]

This situation presents problems of identity for members of Western society in general and also results in specific problems for the Jew in terms of Jewish identity. Before dealing with those, it should be suggested that the pro-Israel sentiment of America's Jews is part of the attempt to fill the gap of homelessness as discussed, and it has several aspects to it. That is, the American Jewish identification with Israel is related to family and essentially is a nostalgic longing for "the home."

Elsewhere I have suggested that American Jews seem to hold to political positions for Israel that are very different from those to which they hold in other societies, and that the reason for this is that they do not relate to Israel in political terms. Rather, they relate to it in extended familial, ethnic terms. It is not the State of Israel, the political entity, to which American Jews are so attached. Rather, it is the Land of Israel, Eretz Israel, to which they attach so much meaning.[37] As Liebman argues, Israel has importance for American Jews as a *heim*, the Yiddish word for "home," which has all of the nostalgia that surrounds that concept. Its meaning may be captured more accurately if it is translated "the old home."[38] American Jews subscribe to political liberalism for political entities. Israel, however, I have suggested, being perceived more as a "home," what Christopher Lasch terms a "haven within a heartless world,"[39] than as a political entity, is therefore not subject to the rules that apply to political entities. Just as the family does not necessarily operate according to the rules of democratic procedure, so with Israel, which is part of the extended family. Just as the family does not necessarily function in accordance with rational or legal-rational rules and is the place where "they'll always take you in," so it is with Israel for many American (and other) Jews. And the political and other leaders of Israel frequently reinforce this perception of Israel when, for example, they speak of the obligations world Jewry has to Israel. In fact, the very existence of the Law of Return supports this notion of Israel as the home of the extended family.

What is important in terms of the distinction between pro-Israel and Zionist is that in the context of the nostalgic longing the "home" can in no way be seen as playing a central role in one's life. As Liebman argues: "Now, the characteristic of the *heim* . . . is that one doesn't live there. It is the parents' home, or in the case of Israel the surrogate parents' or surrogate grandparents' home. One visits it on occasion, one sends money . . . and one wants very much to feel that life goes on there as it always has. . . . This is the Jew who is quite certain he would be completely at home in Israel, though he knows very little about the country and makes no special effort to learn anything."[40]

Whereas Liebman attributes this nostalgic longing for the *heim* primarily to poor, elderly American Jews, I am arguing that a large segment of American Jewry is "homeless" in this sense, though obviously not in the material sense, and that their pro-Israel sentiment is rooted in their sense of extended families and nostalgia for "the home."[41] The previously cited finding in Steven Cohen's survey about American Jews' ignorance of Israeli society and culture even as they strongly support Israel is also understandable within this context.

In addition to its effects on people and society in general, modernization, through its corollary, emancipation, has had particular consequences for Jews collectively as well as for the individual Jew.[42] On the one hand, emancipation meant that Jews were relieved of their legal status as "strangers" and were accepted as full-fledged citizens with the same rights and duties as others. On the other hand, the effect of this historic achievement was to set in motion the process of pluralization and compartmentalization discussed. From the purview of the state, "religion" was now a private matter. But for Jews, the acceptance of this distinction between the public-state and private-religious spheres was a radical leap, since until that point Judaism had never considered the implication that there was a range of binding norms and values beyond those of Judaism itself. This break with tradition found expression not only among secularists but among religionists as well.[43] As Nathan Rotenstreich points out: "Even for what might be called modern Orthodox Jews, as represented by Samson Raphael Hirsch, the distinction between *Torah* and *derech eretz*–*Torah* as Jewish Law and *derech eretz* as general normative moral guidance—connotes not only a compromise, but also an acknowl-edgement that there exists, outside the Jewish boundaries, a binding and meaningful realm of human behavior."[44]

As a result of these developments, that is, the sharp division between the public and private spheres in society, Judaism too became increasingly relevant only within the private sphere. Within the larger society, this separation of spheres also led, as Berger has shown, to religious demonopolization and a situation in which religion is a mat-ter of personal preference.[45] Moreover, from an institutional perspec-tive, Judaism in the United States followed the dominant pattern of Protestant denominationalism and has produced at least three "branches" of Judaism, each with a broad Right-Left continuum. From the perspective of individual Jews, this situation provides them with the "freedom" to choose the particular legitimate brand of Jew-ish identification and expression with which they feel most comfort-able. But for institutional Judaism it has set in motion a process of religious free enterprise that Berger finds analogous to the economic market situation: "The religious tradition, which previously could be authoritatively imposed, now has to be *marketed*. It must be 'sold' to a clientele that is no longer constrained to 'buy.' The pluralistic situ-ation is, above all, a *market situation*. In it, the religious institutions become marketing agencies and the religious traditions become con-sumer commodities. And at any rate a good deal of religious activity comes to be dominated by the logic of market economics."[46]

In addition, although individuals now have the benefit of being able to choose their particular variety of Judaism, there are, at the same time, severe psychological consequences in terms of establishing a Jewish identity. A number of the problems Jewish children face have been highlighted by Isidor Chein:

> We first note that the Jewish child faces a diversification of Jewish points of view, and a fractionalization of the Jewish community to the degree that never confronted his grandparents [today great-grandparents—ed]. There are contending interpretations of the Jewish religion. . . . For better or for worse, there is no longer a sin-gle model of Judaism. It is not surprising, therefore, that even many adult Jews, to say nothing of the children, are hard pressed when asked for a more-than-glib characterization of what they mean when they say they are Jewish. . . . We next note a second aspect. . . : the reduced scope of Jewishness. There was a time when Jewishness per-meated virtually every moment of one's existence. . . . This all-pervasiveness of Jewishnes no longer exists. . . . One by-product is

the tendency for the psychological isolation of Jewishness, its restriction to an island in the personal life space. . . . Hence the more circumscribed does Jewishness become, the less meaningful does it also become. . . . And yet another aspect of the narrowed scope of Jewishness: the more it becomes identified with certain activities at certain times, the greater is the tendency to experience one's identity as a Jew only in those activities and at those times. Jewishness becomes a sort of role that one plays, and one is only a Jew while playing this role.[47]

It seems, therefore, that it is because Jewishness is a role one experiences when playing that role that there is a stronger sense of Jewish identity and that Israel plays a much more central role among Orthodox Jews. There are countless more moments in the everyday life of Orthodox Jews when they "play the role" of Jews, and a greater proportion of Orthodox wish to increase the role of Judaism in their lives. Hence, they are more likely than others to go on aliya. As was discussed in the previous chapter, indications are that a clear majority or recent American olim are Orthodox.[48] The 40 to 50 percent who are not Orthodox also have strong Jewish identities and deep affiliational ties with the structures of the American Jewish community. As Miriam Haron found in her interviews with non-Orthdox American olim, they too have very strong Jewish identities and frequently attribute their Zionism and aliya to Hebrew school, a Jewish camping experience, or a Zionist family background.[49]

But for the majority of American Jews, Jewishness and Jewish identity are limited to infrequent intervals, and their identity in general is abstract. Not surprisingly, therefore, Israel does not play a central role in their lives.

But there must be more to it than that. There are, after all, various kinds of Orthodox Judaism. Surely they, too, must have been affected by the forces of modernity. Or have they been immune? And how does all of this affect aliya? We will explore these questions in the next chapter.

8

Orthodox Judaism
in Modern American Society

The fact that Orthodox Judaism continues to survive and even thrive in American society presents us with two anomalies, one from the perspective of rabbinic leadership and one from that of the sociology of religion. It appears almost ironic that prominent Orthodox rabbis in Eastern Europe at the turn of the century and even on the eve of World War II pronounced a ban on emigration to the United States on the grounds that America is a *treifeneh medineh*, a secular society in which Judaism could not possibly survive. For example, the well-known rabbi of Slutsk, Jacob David Wilowsky (RIDVAZ), publicly proclaimed in 1900 "that anyone who emigrated to America was a sinner, since, in America, the Oral Law is trodden under foot. It was not only home that Jews left behind in Europe, he said, it was their Torah, their Talmud, their *Yeshivot*–in a word, their *Yiddishkeit*, their entire Jewish way of life."[1] It seems almost unbelievable that within a relatively short period of time America would become the major Torah center outside of Israel, with a vast network of yeshivas and thousands of students engaged in Torah learning on levels on a par with those that existed in Eastern Europe; and that from this network of yeshivas there has developed a core of American-born Torah scholars, in addition to a wider generation of native-born Orthodox Jews who have spent many years learning in those yeshivas.[2]

Not only Eastern European rabbinic leaders but many learned American students of American Jewry were, until recently, convinced that Orthodox Judaism had no future in the United States. For example, as recently as 1955 one of the foremost sociologists of American Jewry, Marshall Sklare, proclaimed: "Orthodox adherents have succeeded in achieving the goal of institutional perpetuation to only a limited extent; the history of their movement in this country can be written in terms of a case study of institutional decay."[3] Less than twenty years later Sklare himself wrote that a "renaissance of American Orthodoxy" was taking place and that Orthodoxy had "transformed itself into a growing force in American Jewish life."[4] This renaissance of American Orthodox Judaism seems to fly in the face of a significant body of research and theory in the sociology of religion, which suggests that modernity promotes secularization and that religion, especially orthodoxy, will undergo distinct change and weakening, if it will survive at all, in its confrontation with modernity.[5] The impact of modernity is seen to be so overwhelming that Peter Berger was quoted in 1968 as predicting that "by the 21st century, religious believers are likely to be found only in small sects, huddled together to resist a worldwide secular culture."[6]

How has American Orthodox Judaism managed not only to avoid virtually complete disappearance but to actually grow and become stronger in the face of modernity? To answer this question requires an examination of the impact of patterns of Jewish immigration, education, and changes in the larger American technology and culture.[7] After reviewing each of these, the analysis will then turn to a number of developments within contemporary American Orthodox Judaism that seem to suggest that the research and theory in the sociology of religion may be much more accurate than it appears to be at first glance. It will be argued that despite its growth, Orthodox Judaism in America has been forced to make a number of significant concessions in its adaptation to modernity.

Although the Orthodox rabbinic-intellectual elite remained in Eastern Europe and did not participate in large numbers of the massive immigration of Jews to the United States during the peak years of immigration, 1881–1923, both because they were opposed to immigration to the United States and because they felt that they had an obligation, as leaders, to tend to their followers in Eastern Europe, the Holocaust changed this somewhat. During the years 1937–48 an estimated 200,000–250,000 Jewish refugess from Eastern Europe arrived in the United States,[8] of which a significant proportion were Orthodox rabbis and their followers. Although they had resisted coming to the United States in earlier years, there was now no choice for them, and they decided to come and transplant their religious culture in America. This new infusion of ideologically committed Orthodox provided the numbers and the manpower for the renaissance that was to manifest itself more than a quarter of a century later.

Numbers alone, however, would not have provided for that renaissance. Obviously, there had to be some major changes in the prevalent methods of operation of American Orthodox institutions. Otherwise, the process of institutional decay that Orthodoxy was experiencing would have been, at best, slowed somewhat. Its basic prognosis, however, would not have been altered. The rabbinic and educational elite of Orthodoxy, therefore, undertook major efforts to radically alter both the system of Jewish education and the status of sacred learning in the United States.

As a first step, the National Society for Hebrew Day Schools, Torah Umesorah, was formed with the objective of encouraging and assisting in the founding of Jewish day schools–elementary and high schools that would provide intensive Jewish education along with a quality secular curriculum–in cities and neighborhoods across the country. It should be noted that instituting this type of day school was in itself an adaptation to modernity. Many of the very same rabbinic leaders who spirited the day school movement, especially Rabbi Aaron Kotler, had been adamantly opposed to this type of school, which combined both sacred and secular education, in Europe. In the United States at this time, although a number of day schools had been founded early in the twentieth century–such as the Rabbi Jacob Joseph School, Yeshiva Torah Vedaath, among others in New York City, and the Yeshiva Torah Ve-Emuna Hebrew Parochial School, now known as Yeshiva Chofetz Chaim, Talmudical Academy of Baltimore–their numbers and, hence, their impact were relatively small. With the efforts of the leadership of the new immigration, the picture changed dramatically. There was a virtual boom in the growth of the day school movement from World War II to the mid-1970s.

As Table 8 shows, the number of day schools grew from 35 to 323 and enrollment grew from 7,700 to 63,500 during the years 1940–65. By 1975 there was a total of 425 day schools and 138 yeshiva high schools with a total enrollment of 82,200. These schools were located not only in the New York metropolitan area but in 33 states across the country. By 1975 every city in the United States with a Jewish population of 7,500 had at least one day school, as did four out of five of the cities with a Jewish population of 5,000–7,500. Among cities with smaller Jewish populations, one out of four with a population of 1,000

TABLE 8

Number of Hebrew Day Schools, Types, and Enrollments

	Total Day Schools	High Schools	Total Enrollments	Number of Communities
1940	35		7,700	7
1945	69	9	10,200	31
1955	180		35,500	68
1965	323	83	63,500	117
1970			72,000	
1975	425	138	82,200	160

Source: Egon mayer and Chaim I. Waxman, "Modern Jewish Orthodoxy in America: Toward the Year 2000," *Tradition* 16, no. 3 (Spring 1977): 9.

Jews had a Jewish day school.[9] Although the total number of Jewish children enrolled in Jewish schools of all types–including not only day schools but supplementary schools that meet two or more afternoons a week and one day a week schools–had been declining in recent years, there were increases in both the absolute numbers and the percentage of the total enrolled for those enrolled in day schools between the years 1974–75 and 1978–79.[10]

The extent to which intensive formal Jewish education has an impact on adult religious behavior and attitudes is borne out by several empirical studies conducted during the early 1970s.[11] Harold Himmelfarb's study bears most directly on this issue, and he found that supplementary schools of Jewish education, such as Sunday schools and afternoon schools, do not have any long-lasting impact on Jewish involvement, whereas day schools do have an impact for those students who have had more than six years of such schooling.[12] Of course, years of schooling are not the sole determinants; other factors such as age, parents, and spouse are also important variables. But when all of these are controlled for, the intensity of the education reveals itself as a significant variable.

A number of newly arrived Orthodox leaders had been heads of advanced rabbinical seminaries, *yeshivot gedolot,* in Eastern Europe and, almost immediately upon their arrival in the United States, set about to reconstruct those yeshivas on American soil. Such leaders as Rabbi Aaron Kotler, Rabbi Abraham Kalmanowitz, and Rabbis Eliyahu Meir Bloch and Mordechai Katz reestablished their advanced yeshivas in Lakewood, Brooklyn, Cleveland, and elsewhere, in the Eastern European mold, and helped spawn a generation of knowledgeable and ideologically committed Orthodox Jews, many of whom were to subsequently establish other advanced yeshivas in dozens of American cities.[13] In addition, Yeshiva University–which was founded as Yeshivat Etz Chaim on September 15, 1886, and in 1915 merged with the Rabbi Isaac Elchanan Theological Seminary, which had been founded in 1897, to become Yeshiva College and later Yeshiva University–was also greatly affected by the new Eastern European immigration.[14] This is not the place to delineate the tremendous impact that institution has had on the development of American Orthodox Judaism, not only in training leaders but, especially in recent years, in reaching out to communities at all levels; but the stature and, therefore, impact of that institution were greatly enhanced by the fact that, under the influence of its president, Dr. Samuel Belkin, it brought some of the outstanding rabbis who arrived in the new immigration into its faculty. They, in turn, not only taught a younger generation, which has made Yeshiva University's Rabbi Isaac Elchanan Theological Seminary a major Torah center in the United States today; they also influenced in a variety of ways the entire American Jewish community, in addition to Israel and other centers of world Jewry.

Although some of the graduates of the advanced yeshivas went on to occupations and professions within the fields of the rabbinate and Jewish education, many others entered secular professions and occupations such as law, academia, government, and business, while at the same time remaining highly supportive of Orthodox institutions and retaining their own Orthodox behavior.[15] Their higher levels of secular education and their professional experience also enabled them to spearhead the growth of highly sophisticated Orthodox Jewish communal organizations and associations, such as the Union of Orthodox Jewish Congregations of America, Agudath Israel of America, and the organizations of the Lubavitch movement, each of which has many affiliates operating on a variety of levels of American society. Thus, although American Orthodox Jewry lacked a solid institutional base during the first half of the century, it has now succeeded in developing a strong network of institutions that are at least on a par with those of other segments of American Jewry. Within the organized American Jewish community, the major Orthodox rabbinic organization, the Rabbinical Council of America, is to Orthodoxy what the Rabbinical Assembly is to Conservative Jewry and what the Central Conference of American Rabbis is to Reform Jewry. All three are perceived of as equal in stature to the rabbinic authorities of their respective branches within American Judaism. Likewise, the Union of Orthodox Jewish Congregations of America is recognized as of the same status as Conservative Jewry's United Synagogue of America and Reform Jewry's Union of American Hebrew Congregations. And with respect to Jewish education and schools, the other branches have nothing that can match the network of yeshiva movements.

One other important element in the immigration of the Holocaust period was the arrival of numerous Chasidic groups who maintained deep loyalty to their respective highly traditional and charismatic leaders. Although these groups remain a distinctive component within American Orthodox Jewry,[16] they have had an important impact on the entire spectrum of American Orthodoxy, especially with respect to the kosher food industry.

As the institutional bases of American Orthodox Judaism grew stronger it has been able to maintain a much larger proportion of its affiliates within the fold. Thus, whereas for the first three generations of Eastern European Jewry in America[17] there were both increasing defections from Orthodoxy and a large percentage of "nonobservant Orthodox," that is, nonobservant Jews who, for one reason or another, nevertheless maintained their identification with the Orthodox synagogue, the situation today is very different. There is much less defection from Orthodoxy today and a much larger proportion of the memberships of Orthodox syngogues are personally observant. Not only has Orthodoxy been much more successful at retaining its youth within the fold, there is also a perceived though as yet unquantified phenomenon of a return to Orthodoxy among mature and well-established adults,[18] as well as among young adults.[19]

As the socioeconomic status of American Orthodox Jewry rose, it spread out across the country. Today one finds Orthodox Jewish communities in cities and towns across the United States, towns that until recently were almost devoid of Orthodox Jews. Now many of them have become vibrant centers with strong institutional foundations.[20] In a perceptive sociological study of the largest and still striving Orthodox Jewish community in the United States, which has grown dramatically since the 1940s, Egon Mayer analyzed how the Brooklyn community at Boro Park Jewry, which numbers more than 55,000, has in large measure reversed the assimilation process that had been characterized as "from *shtetl* to suburb,"[21] and learned to make use of the material advantages of modernization without experiencing its cultural consequences. The Jews of Boro Park were able to "avoid the magnetic pull of cultural assimilation even as their community was becoming structurally more similar to the larger society," Mayer argues, because they emphasized the values of separateness and sanctity. Their values are perpetuated through a normative structure within which the observance of the Sabbath and dietary and "family purity" laws are pervasive and concretized by a highly organized system of institutions, including the family, the yeshiva, the large and small synagogues, and a variety of youth organizations. As members of a "cognitive minority" with highly developed value and normative structures, Mayer suggests, the Jews of Boro Park do not experience the cognitive dissonance that the traditional Jew in modern society is supposed to experience.[22] Although Boro Park is clearly unique, many of those same processes are characteristic of American Orthodox communities across the country.

Other important and rarely acknowledged factors are structural changes in American society, such as the five-day work week and technological developments in the food industry. It will be recalled that one of the major factors accounting for the defection from Orthodox affiliation during the period of the second generation was the fact that Orthodoxy was felt to be too restricting. For those who strongly aspired to socioeconomic mobility, Orthodox restrictions that prohibited working on the Sabbath and demanded eating only kosher food, foods that were prepared in a ritually correct manner, were too much of a burden to bear. They inhibited both economic mobility and social intercourse with those in the larger society. By the era of the fourth generation much of that had changed. The five-day work week was the norm for the vast majority of American Jews. Thus, Orthodoxy has been able to become more assertive in its demand for Sabbath observance.[23]

Technological developments in the food-processing industry have largely removed the restricting character and, thus, stigmatizing nature of kosher food. Whereas in earlier generations the availability and selection of kosher food was limited, today there is a wide variety of kosher food available in every large supermarket, and those foods that are not readily available locally can be easily shipped anywhere in the country. Kosher meals are available on most airlines and in many hotels. To observe dietary laws, therefore, does not restrict one's geographic mobility. Moreover, the more densely populated Jewish communities have an assortment of kosher foods that was inconceivable in earlier generations; for example, kosher pizza, Chinese, French and Italian restaurants of high quality, and even nondairy cheesecake and cheeseburgers. If "you can't have your cake and eat it too," one can, at least, eat almost any type of cake and still remain loyal to traditional Jewish dietary norms.

As a result of these and other structural and technological changes, Orthodox Jews have been able to enjoy many of the comforts of the larger middle- and upper-middle class life-style while adhering to Orthodox Jewish norms. They have, thus, been able to reduce the rate of defection from Orthodoxy and to develop a sophisticated institutional power base, and this has dramatically enhanced the influence they have within the American Jewish communal structure.

It is, however, doubtful that Orthodoxy would have become as influential as it is were it not also for a number of significant changes in the larger American Jewish community and important changes in American culture. In the larger American Jewish community, there was a dramatic shift from the trend toward increasing cultural and structural assimilation of American Jewry during the first three generations of Eastern European Jewry in America, a trend that took place during the 1960s and early 1970s and has resulted in a fourth generation that, in many ways, is much more self-conscious as an ethno-religious community and is much more survival-oriented. This "shift in the pendulum" was the consequence of a series of events within both American society at large and the Jewish community, that of the United States on its own and as related to world Jewry, especially Israel. As the result of the disproportionate number of Jews involved in the leadership of the New Left during the mid-1960s; the disproportionate involvement of Jews in the civil rights movement; the "long hot summers" of racial unrest, which affected Jews more so than other whites; the black power movement, which caused many of these Jews who had been active in the civil rights movement to feel rejected by it; the unprecedented and completely unanticipated impact of the Six-Day War on American Jewry; the blatant condemnation of Israel by spokespersons of the New Left at its New Politics convention in Chicago in August 1967; the defection from the New Left of many young activists, who then turned their activism to Jewish causes; and the awakening to the significance of the Holocaust and its emergence as a central element of American Jewish "civil religion"–as a result of all these factors a new self-consciousness has grown within the American Jewish community since the 1960s.[24]

In addition, since the early 1960s there have been some important changes in the larger American culture to which that shift in the pendulum is related, as is the specific renaissance of American Orthodox Judaism. Two in particular–the rise of religious consciousness and the rise of public ethnicity–are most relevant.

Whereas much of the discussion of the secularization of American society in the mid-1960s was highly speculative, the early 1960s were years of relatively little interest and activity in religion in the country. It certainly would have been preposterous to predict, in 1965, that there would be a significant rise of religious consciousness in the country; that there would be a dramatic rise in "new religions," cults, and Eastern religions that emphasize mysticism; and that there would be a nationwide rise in church and synagogue attendance several years hence.[25] Nor did it seem even a remote probability that a presidential candidate from one of the two major political parties would, in the following decade, include conservative religious notions as part of his campaign and that he would win the election, as did Jimmy Carter in 1976. Whereas, as mentioned above, in 1968 Peter Berger was predicting that institutional religion would almost disappear in the country by the year 2,000, by 1977 he was able to foresee "a massive reaction" to secularization, "something of the nature of a great religious revival. I can't tell you when, I can't tell you what form it will take. It may well be something within the churches. This has happened before.",[26]

Various explanations of the rise of religious consciousness, including cults and "new" religions, have been suggested. Two major elements that underlie most of them are the loss of legitimacy in the dominant instituions and the loss of community in American society in the 1960s and early 1970s. According to Charles Glock, the rise of religious consciousness among youth was in response to the disenchantment of the scientific world. As he put it:

> The effect of a scientific world view is to undermine the underlying assumptions of the old imageries, the cultural values and social arrangements informed by them, and the inherent ability of these world views to give life meaning and purpose. At the same time, by virtue of its uncertainty and ambiguity, a scientific world view offers no clear alternative formula either for organizing society or for living one's life. . . . As a consequence of its ambiguity in these respects, a scientific world view, as it diffuses and becomes the lens from which increasing numbers of people view their world, has the potential for creating crises both for society and for individuals.[27]

Modernity, including utilitarian individualism and technological rationality, was repudiated by a new generation of educated youth for whom there was a loss of meaning, and the new religious conscious-ness succeeded in filling the void.[28] Neither the mainline religions nor civic values and authority figures were able to fill the void, the former because of their increasing involvement in social activism and their increasing reliance on secular rationalism, and the latter because of such debacles as the Vietnam War and the Watergate scandal.

Not only does modernity promote a crisis of meaning, it also precipitates a loss of and subsequent search for community. The impact of modernity on community forms the theme of many of the major works of the classical sociological theorists in Europe and America in the nineteenth and early twentieth centuries, and most prominently in the work of Ferdinand Tönnies. Tönnies analyzed social change in terms of the transition from *Gemeinschaft* (commu-nity) to *Gesellschaft* (society), and he foresaw efforts to recapture some of the securities of the former within the later.[29] Among the contem-porary American sociologists, Robert Nisbet and Peter Berger have both pointed to the loss of community in modern American society as the result of structural developments and public policy. Writing of "the loss of community," Nisbet argues that "in the process of modern industrial and political development, established social contexts have become weak, and fewer individuals have the secure interpersonal relations which formerly gave meaning and stability to existence."[30] Along somewhat similar lines, Berger suggests:

> Modernization brings about a novel dichotomization of social life. The dichotomy is between the huge and immensely powerful insti-tutions of the public sphere (the state, the large economic agglomer-ates that we know as corporations and labor unions, and the evergrowing bureaucracies that administer sectors of society not properly political or economic, such as education or the organized professions) and the private sphere, which is a curious interstitial area "left over," as it were, by the large institutions and indeed . . . marked by "underinstitutionalization." Put more simply, the dichot-omy is between the megastructures and private life. . . . As long as the individual can indeed find meaning and identity in his private life, he can manage to put up with the meaningless and disidentify-ing world of the megastructures.[31]

Part of the problem, according to Berger, is that social policy in America from the time of the Depression and through the 1970s tended to undermine the important structures, such as family, neigh-borhood, religious group, and ethnic group, which provided individuals with a buffer against the megastructures and gave them a sense of rootedness. As a result of the weakening of the traditional mediating structures, when youth left the confines of the nuclear family and were confronted with only large and impersonal bureaucracies, they were attracted to either the new religions or the more conservative denominations of the traditional religions because these provide clear structure, meaning, and warmth similar to that which family provides. In essence, their quest was a quest for community.[32]

Moreover, although the consequences of the search for meaning and community first became evident in the rise of new religions and the growth of very conservative churches, they may now be seen in the more general societal pattern of a return to religion, at least within certain cohorts within the American population. Thus, several years ago it would have seemed ludicrous to anticipate a pattern that has only very recently come to light, namely, a resurgence of traditional religious patterns among those who are now young adults and among those who are parents of young children. And yet, if the findings of two recent studies of the religious patterns of Americans are indeed correct, that is precisely what is happening. In one, it was found that there has recently been a dramatic rise in attendance and involvement in religious organizations and services on college campuses throughout the New York metropolitan area. If substantiated and more than just a brief fad, this might signal a return of young adults to more religiously traditional patterns of behavior.[33] In an even more recent and nationwide study, it was found that there has been a dramatic rise in the religious involvement of Americans between the ages of thirty-one and forty-two, the so-called "baby boomers" who were the rebellious generation of the 1960s. Having moved to a later stage in life, it was found, they are now seeking more stable and long-lasting values, they find traditional religious institutions supportive in this respect, and they look to those institutions provide their children with religious training.[34]

Along with the rise of religious consciousness in American society, and as a result of many of the very same forces, there was a rise in public ethnicity and an attempt to retrieve some of the qualities of the ethnic community. Once blacks had publicly rejected the ideology of the melting pot and adopted the ideology of cultural pluralism, white ethnic groups were quick to follow suit. Ethnicity burst onto the American scene with a passion. The mass media and the advertising industry soon caught on and the public was being told that "every American has two homelands," and that a certain airline has a strong desire to fly people to their other homelands. Meltable or not, ethnics were rising and flaunting their ethnicity. For many, the assertion of ethnicity in public sphere coincided with an increasing assimilation in the private sphere. Several keen observers of the American Jewish scene remarked that many American Jews were turning the Jewish enlightenment dictum to "be a Jew in the home and a gentleman in the street" on its head; in the street they were asserting their Jewish ethnicity while in their homes, in the private sphere, they were manifesting increasing cultural assimilation. But to a large degree these Jews were just reflecting patterns characteristic of American society as a whole, patterns not unique to American Jews.

It is important to understand that although there were a variety of factors that precipitated this phenomenon, including for some a "reactionary impulse,"[35] the reactionary utilization of ethnicity as a political counter to the gains of blacks, it was also another response to the loss of meaning and identity produced by modernity. It is no coincidence that the rise of religious consciousness and the rise of ethnicity occurred almost simultaneously in American society. In no small measure they were responses to the same predicaments, the loss of community, meaning, and identity. For example, initiated for blacks by Alex Haley and then diffused throughout the society, the "roots" phenomenon was a glaring example of the search for identity. Although it may have been a fetish for some, for many others it became a serious enterprise, avocation, or hobby.

It is misleading, therefore, to view the heightening of Jewish consciousness in the fourth generation as solely an American Jewish phenomenon. Although there were, as has been discussed, a variety of factors within the Jewish community that promoted the shift in the pendulum away from further assimilation and toward greater group self-consciousness, it is also important to recognize that this shift took place at a time when there was a broad, societywide heightening of both religious and ethnic consciousness. The larger structural and cultural changes made it much more acceptable for American Jews to become more Jewish conscious.

In the final analysis, then, the heightening of Jewish consciousness was not a break with the norms and values of American society. On the contrary, it was the realization or operationalization of larger American social and cultural patterns. Paradoxical as it may appear, it was not a manifestation of the rejection of cultural assimilation; in many ways it was the realization of its persistence.

The same is true with respect to the specific case of Orthodoxy. Although the renaissance was greatly enhanced by the efforts and activities of the World War II Eastern Europe immigration, it is highly doubtful that it would have reached the proportions it has were it not for developments within the larger society and culture. All of those factors, both the specifically Jewish ones and those in the larger society and culture, which promoted the shift in the pendulum, the greater self-consciousness of the American Jewish community as a whole, also facilitated the renaissance of American Orthodox Judaism. That renaissance, in turn, acted upon and played a part in the increased self-consciousness of the American Jewish community.

It would, however, be a mistake to infer from all of this either that the process of secularization has been absolutely halted or that Orthodoxy has not been affected by it. Quite the contrary. Although the impact of secularization is perceived as having been moderated in certain spheres–namely, the very public and the very private–those are the spheres that have long been theorized to be the least affected by modernization and its concomitant, secularization.[36] The process continues nevertheless. Nor has Orthodoxy been impervious to both modernization and secularization. The only way it could feasibly do so would be to withdraw almost totally from modern society, something at which even groups such as the Amish, who explicitly made that effort, have not been completely successful. Within Judaism, perhaps the closest thing to such an attempt was that of the Sadducees, and they did not survive. Mainstream traditional Judaism long ago rejected the path of total withdrawal from society. In its confrontation with modernity, therefore, it was left with the options of resistance and/or accommodation.[37] In large measure, the development of Reform and Conservative Judaism is a manifestation of varying degrees of accommodation. But it would be a mistake to presume that Orthodoxy has adopted an approach exclusively of resistance.

As Charles Liebman argues, there are several distinct wings or schools within contemporary Orthodox Judaism, and each of these represents a different response to the confrontation with modernity.[38] Although these approaches are popularly referred to as right-wing or sectarian Orthodox and modern Orthodox, Liebman analyzes them as neotraditionalism, adaptationism, compartmentalization, and expansionism. Briefly, neotraditionalism rejects modernity and attempts to construct an alternate society that would "insulate its adherents from the spirit of modernity–most especially from choice and the assertion of individualism."[39] This is the community known in the United States as the "ultra-Orthodox" or "right-wing Ortho-dox," and in Israel as the "Charedi" or "black" community, which totally subscribes to the slogan of the late eighteenth-century rabbinic authority Rabbi Moses Sofer: "The new is forbidden by the Torah."[40] At the opposite side of the Orthodox spectrum is the adaptationist approach, which explicitly affirms the intrinsic value of modernity and seeks to reinterpret Judaism in its light while remaining, as its advocates see it, true to halakhah, traditional Jewish religious law. This is essentially the approach of many of the founders of Conserv-ative Judaism[41] and that espoused by many of the contemporary Con-servative Jews in the United States who are members of the Union for Traditional Conservative Judaism. Among the Orthodox, there are few who would publicly proclaim their adherence to this approach.

The third response, and that which consciously or otherwise char-acterizes the majority of American Orthodox Jews, is compartmental-ization, in which large areas of social and cultural life have been surrendered and accepted as the religious equivalent of a "noman's land," that is, they are perceived as irrelevant to Judaism, whereas other areas have become accentuated as the foci of Judaism and are even more stringently adhered to. Especially in the United States and the rest of the Diaspora, rather than being a total world-building sys-tem,[42] the world of Orthodox Judaism has shrunk or been compressed to the exclusion of many aspects in the political, economic, and even social spheres of the larger society.

Finally, the response called expansionism is similar to adaptation-ism in that it affirms modernity, but differs from it in that, rather than seeking to reinterpret Judaism in light of modernity, it seeks to rein-terpret modernity in light of Jewish tradition. As such, it seeks to incorporate all of the spheres of modernity, all of modern social and cultural life, within traditional Jewish thought and practice. In con-trast with the compartmentalists, to the expansionists there are no realms or spheres that are irrelevant to Judaism. In a sense, it is an effort to rupture the nexus between the modern and the secular by making the secular sacred and thus accepting and even affirming the modern. This is the approach that, in the United States, is most fre-quently associated with the ideology of modern Orthodoxy, although it has remained much more within the realm of ideology than praxis, and in Israel, where it receives much wider expression among a siz-able segment of the religious nationalists.

Leaving the neotraditionalists and adaptationists aside–the latter because they are such a small minority and the former because it is not quite clear that theirs is, in fact, a distinct response that totally rejects modernity and seeks to construct a completely alternate world–certain aspects of both the expansionist and compartmentalist responses are curiously revealing. The one with the more sophisticated legitimating ideology has been less successful in establishing an explicit leadership with a large following, whereas the one with the less elaborated ideology has been much more successful in developing both leadership and a wide following within American Orthodox Judaism. Both Liebman and Norman Lamm suggest that Rabbi Sampson Raphael Hirsch (1808–88) may be seen as the ideological father of what has been called the compartmentalist response, and that Rabbi Abraham Isaac Hacohen Kook (1865–1935) may be seen as the ideological father of modern Orthodoxy, or the expansionist response.[43] It may be argued that it is precisely in the manner in which each has elected to confront modernity in American society that its relative success or failure lies.

Compartmentalism is the dominant response of American Orthodoxy to the dilemmas of modernity and secularization precisely because it has succeeded in adapting to and even attempting to legitimate, much as it might deny any intention of so doing, a most basic aspect of modernity and secularization. As we saw in the last chapter, as Berger defines it, secularization is a process that involves both society and the individual. Objectively, it means that an increasing number of sectors and spheres within the society are no longer under the domination of the religious institutions and culture, and also that, subjectively, an increasing number of individuals go about their daily lives without the benefit of religious interpretation.[44]

Those who adopt the compartmentalist approach have not only not resisted the impact of secularization; to the contrary, they have acceded to it. It is, therefore, no coincidence that it is difficult to find any explicit ideological legitimation for compartmentalism. In essence, it is anathema to traditional religion to suggest that there are any social or cultural spheres that are not integral to the religious system. There are no such things as religion-free zones or spheres. But in a modern, pluralist society and culture, the only way for a religion to survive is to adapt accordingly. The compartmentalists have succeeded in camouflaging their adaptation by insisting on the most stringent standards in those areas they continue to define as within their domain. This approach is not unique to Orthodox Judaism. As James Hunter demonstrates, this is virtually the same strategy adopted by the Evangelicals within American Protestantism,[45] and they, too, have experienced notable success with it.

the expansionist response, on the other hand, although it has achieved a much more elaborate and sophisticated level of theoretical-ideological legitimation, is unable to attract the numbers of adherents that the compartmentalist approach attracts. There are several reasons for this. One is that the latter produces adherents who are so certain as to the authenticity of its approach and so intolerant of alternative approaches that it places others on the defensive. One consequence of this is the widely observed "swing to the right" within the entire spectrum of American Orthodox Judaism. In response to the quandry of modernity, apparently, many Orthodox Jews feel that they must demand much more stringent levels of commitment and observance, even when not necessarily called for by either the letter or the spirit of halakhah. As a result, the compartmentalists have succeeded in convincing even many of those who adopt one of the other approaches that they are the more authentic representation of traditional Judaism.

Another and interrelated reason for the greater attractiveness of the compartmentalist response is due to the fact that many of its opponents within and even outside of Orthodoxy believe that ultimately Judaism has survived and will continue to survive because of the total devotion of those in the compartmentalist camp. The modern Orthodox are viewed as being too "lukewarm" in both their ideological commitment and their ritualistic practice. This reinforces the image that the compartmentalists strive to project, namely, that they are the most authentic Jews and that theirs is *the* authentic Judaism.

Finally, and most directly related to the subject of this book, an even more basic reason for the lesser attractiveness of the expansionist approach is that it simply can never become fully realized within American society. In fact, it may not be fully realizable within any modern society, even Israel, since one of the fundamental aspects of modernity is pluralism. But at least in Israel, being a Jewish society, it is much more realizable than elsewhere. It is, thus, no coincidence that one of the strongest motivations for the aliya of modern Orthodox American Jews is that there they feel they can live a much more fully Jewish life. Moreover, as will be discussed in Chapter 10, a significant number of those American olim move beyond the "Green Line," to "the Territories"–Judea, Samaria, and the Gaza Strip–because they feel that they can live more complete Jewish lives in an

Israel they define as whole and complete. Thus, although the approach of the compartmentalists has adapted to and even legitimated the existence of the Diaspora, expansionism, by definition, can never do so. For expansionists, the aliya option is the most natural.

One other aspect of the disproportionate number of Orthodox among American olim relates to the social structural setting. There are a number of factors in the social structure setting of Orthodox Jews that, even if they do not overtly encourage aliya, facilitate the process. One such factor is a Jewish educational system that encourages spending a year during the post-high school level in studying at a yeshiva in Israel. That year frequently plants the seed, and as many parents of children who have studied in Israel know, a second year of such study often determines aliya.

In addition even if we were to assume that the social-psychological factors were the same for all American Jews, it is reasonable to predict that there would be a higher rate of aliya among the Orthodox because the social structure Orthodoxy creates invariably eases many of the physical and psychological hardships and stresses associated with relocation. Specifically, Orthodoxy presupposes a religious community and, thus, Orthodox Jews need not experience what to many others is one of the most difficult aspects of relocating in modern society, the struggle to develop ties and roots in communities to which they have recently moved. For example, by virtue of the Orthodox norms of Sabbath oservance, it is a given that one will live within walking distance of the synagogue and, invariably, within walking distance of at least some, if not most or all, of the other members of the synagogue community. Orthodox Jews do not have to worry about where they will meet people in their new community; they know they will meet them in the synagogue on the very first weekday or Sabbath there. They also know that they will probably meet children with whom their own children will socialize and, in many cases, with whom they will go to school.[46] Invariably, for Orthodox Jews the possibilities or relocation are limited by those areas where at least the minimum Orthodox synagogue community already exists. Those who relocate, therefore, are able to ease themselves into an already existing community and communal structure. Although there are, obviously, great differences between internal migration, relocating within the same country, and international migration, such as aliya, it nevertheless remains true that the Orthodox will invariably have a preexisting community into which they can fit themselves. For olim, it seems reasonable to predict that their adjustment to aliya will be eased considerably because of this. The extent to which this is so is examined in the next chapter, within the context of an analysis of the acculturation of American immigrants within Israeli society.

PART IV

9

The Acculturation of American Israelis

Acculturation, in its simplest sense, is the process of acquiring a new culture. If, as George Spindler points out,[1] the acculturation process is much more complex than that, the acculturation of any single individual is also much more complex than the simple definition implies. Also, as Milton Gordon says acculturation is but one component or variable in a much more elaborate and complex process of assimilation. Another equally important variable in the process is structural assimilation, that is, the immigrants' entrance into the important institutional structure of the society.[2] This chapter explores the cultural and structural assimilation experiences of American olim, most of whom migrated to Israel in the quest for the enhancement of not the material but the religious and cultural components of their lives. What were their experiences? How do they look upon their adjustment processes? In addition to an analysis of their status within the Israeli socioeconomic structure, this chapter also considers whether they feel they have, in large measure, achieved that which they sought in their aliya.

Prior to 1956 only a minority–7 percent pre-1948 and 19 percent for those who immigrated between 1948 and 1956–of American olim had been in Israel prior to their aliya.[3] Since then, however, the picture has changed drastically. The vast majority have previously visited Israel at least once.[4] American immigrants, therefore, do not arrive in Israel totally unaware of the nature of Israeli society and culture.[5] But there is a world of difference between being someplace as a visitor and being there as a resident. The visitor may find beauty in strangeness, whereas to the resident that very same strangeness may be downright annoying. On the other hand, the visitor may be offended by certain sights, sounds, and smells, whereas the resident gets used to them. Jay Shapiro, an American who immigrated with his wife and children in 1969, vividly portrays his initial sensations upon arriving in Israel as an oleh.

> Later Naomi and I both were to recall that the strongest impressions of our arrival in Israel were, in fact, the smells. The large variety of motor vehicles which use low octane fuel and have no antipollution devices emit odors that pervade the highways. You eventually get used to it, but in the beginning it really hits you in the nose. The sea breezes, the sweaty porters, the open stands selling *felafel* and *shewarma,* and the road pollution all combine to create an olfactory atmosphere that doesn't exist in the United States. To this day, whenever I return to Israel after a trip abroad, I feel I am back home only after my nose confirms that I've arrived.
>
> Finished at the port, we now faced a two-hour journey to the Immigrant Hostel for Academics in Lod. The drive there was uneventful, except for one incident. While waiting at a traffic light on the coastal highway in Herzliya, we noticed a man on the corner of this main intersection. He was standing in full view and urinating into the street. Somehow we had expected a more dignified welcome. So we learned . . . (a very important lesson): Don't be surprised at anything–you are now in the levant.[6]

How one adjusts to the fact of being in the Levant is another matter. Some American olim attempt, as much as possible, to avoid dealing with it by living their lives almost totally within an American or "Anglo-Saxon" subculture (all those who speak English are called Anglo-Saxons by Israelis). In Jerusalem, Rechovot, Raanana, and other cities, there are communities of Americans, British, South Africans, and other English-speaking olim who interact as much as possible only with one another; who only read Israel's English-language newspaper, the *Jerusalem Post,* and English-language books and periodicals; who listen only to the few brief English-language newscasts on the radio. Television and the movies are no problem for them since most of the television shows are imported from either the United States or England and almost all of the movies are American-made.

Although precise data are unavailable, it may be assumed that this pattern is much more typical of older American olim, those who go on aliya after retirement. But not all of even those older olim who remain apart from Israeli culture do so voluntarily. As Myrna Silverman reports, some older American olim keenly feel a deep sense of frustration and isolation from much of Israeli society and culture because of the low level of proficiency in Hebrew with which they came to Israel and their inability to learn the language now.[7]

Other data, however, indicate that such frustration and isolation are not the norm for older American olim. In their sample of older North American immigrants, Lache, Teczniczek, Mann, and Lahav found that there are very few signs of social isolation among the middle-aged (fifty to sixty-four), except for women who are on pensions, among whom the problem is, indeed, "massive."[8]

As will be discussed in Chapter 11, one of the major reasons cited by American olim for their return to the United States has to do with job dissatisfaction.[9] Among middle-aged American immigrants in Israel, however, there was little indication of such dissatisfaction. As Lache and colleagues report, they are a relatively satisfied group, to a large degree because they were already fairly affluent and occupationally successful when they arrived in Israel. They have incomes from abroad, and their current earnings in Israel are additions rather than their sole means of support.[10]

In contrast with most Israelis in the labor force, irrespective of national origin, are the American pensioners in Israel. Among them, "sufficiency of current income is attested to by the great majority of pensioners."[11]

Most American olim are relatively young and come to Israel with a fairly high level of proficiency in Hebrew. Also, most are in the Israeli work force. Therefore, unless they happen to be employed in a completely American work setting, they must, to some extent, interact with Israeli society and culture as part of their daily routines. Nor is language seen as being a problem for most older Americans. Only a small percentage anticipated, before their aliya, that it would be a problem and only a minority later experience it as one.[12] Most American immigrants invariably assimilate culturally to some extent. This should not be surprising since so many of them immigrated precisely because they wanted to be part of Israeli society and culture. In America they felt that their Jewishness somehow estranged them from the mainstream of American society and culture, and they wanted to live in Israel in order to more fully live out their Jewishness.

Many American olim find, however, that the conceptions they had before their immigration of what Jewish society and culture are like are vastly different from the realities of Israeli culture and society.

They might, as a result, feel even more alien in Israeli society than they felt in American society. Ironically, their very aliya may result in their perceiving themselves as Americans in Israeli society, whereas the reason they made aliya was that they perceived themselves as more Jewish and less American in the United States. American olim tend to compare Israeli society and culture to that with which they were familiar in the United States, and at times they gain an appreciation for American social and cultural patterns they did not have prior to aliya. Even if they do not feel alien in Israeli society, American olim invariably become more conscious of their American identity as they gain this appreciation for American patterns. In addition, they tend to become more conscious of themselves as Americans because they are treated by others as Americans.[13]

For some, the inability to adjust to Israeli society and culture is so stressful that they return to the United States. As will be discussed in Chapter 11, approximately 38 percent of the American olim return to live in the United States within five years of their aliya. Among the returnees are those who, for one reason or another, could not adjust to Israeli society and culture.

But approximately 62 percent of the American olim remain in Israel. And although there are difficulties in their adjustment to Israeli life, as there invariably are in any adjustment process, there is no firm evidence that these difficulties are severe. For example, in a psychological study of American olim that used the Social Readjustment Rating Questionnaire (SRRQ), it was found that "American immigrants to Israel rated 'Moving to a new country' (MNC) as an only moderately stressful life event while reporting a high level of adjustment in Israel (GAI)."[14] On the other hand, a study by Roskin and Edleson of the emotional health of English-speaking olim in Israel, which used the Symptom Checklist (SCL-90), found that "North American Jews, with the exception of the Orthodox, had SCL-90 scores indicating that they were less emotionally healthy than were the British and South African Jews."[15] These researchers found that North Americans differed significantly from the other English-speaking immigrants on the depression, hostility, and psychotic symptoms subscales of the SCL-90.[16] The Orthodox fared better than the others, and Roskin and Edleson offer a number of suggestions for their better emotional health:

> What may be important here is the "time horizon" under which a person is operating. A time horizon is the period of time into the

future that a person projects when evaluating the possible or real consequences of actions. Many times the obstacles to successful adjustment will seem overwhelming. For the Orthodox immigrant, however, the longer time horizon of contributing to life in a Jewish homeland and of settling the "Land of Israel" may be seen as out-weighing the short-term annoyances. While such values are also held by non-Orthodox immigrants they seem less ideological about such visions. The Orthodox group has a clear religious purpose in their life-style and in their decision to move to Israel.

In addition, an almost automatic natural support group is available to Orthodox immigrants. Previously unacquainted immigrants begin to make contacts through religious activities in and related to the synagogue. As with family, fellow Orthodox immigrants become additional resistance-resources by creating ties to a new community and new roles through the synagogue.[17]

As to why the non-Orthodox North American immigrants were less emotionally healthy than their British and South African counter-parts, Roskin and Edleson offer no definitive explanation. All they can do is speculate that it may be because "Israel is closer materially, culturally and in distance to Europe and Southern Africa than to the United States and Canada. The number and degree of changes required of North American immigrants may be greater than those required of immigrants from Britain or South Africa."[18]

In contrast to the findings of Roskin and Edleson, and much more in line with those found when the Social Readjustment Rating Questionnaire was used, are the findings of Ruth Tamar Horowitz. She compared self-reported powerlessness and alienation among North American and Soviet olim who completed a twenty-nine-item I-E scale. On two of the subscales–politically responsive versus unresponsive world and friendly versus unfriendly world–there were significant differences between the responses of the North American and the Soviet olim. North Americans tended to view the world as much more politically responsive than did the Soviets, undoubtedly as a consequence of the differences between the North American and Soviet societies. Also: "The Americans . . . tend to have much more trust in people with whom they have social ties. Americans tend to expect friendly responses not only in situations of close friendship but also in those of superficial acquaintances or even accidental encounters. Thus, the underlying assumption of the American immigrants is that the social environment is basically friendly."[19]

This, of course, does not mean that American immigrants in Israel are completely satisfied with Israeli society and culture. Quite the contrary. They are highly critical of many aspects of both. For example, they are critical of the Israeli political structure, and the Association of Americans and Canadians in Israel (AACI) has been lobbying for election reform and other changes in the political structure. Some American Israelis, especially the non-Orthodox, are highly critical of what they see as the Orthodox monopolization of Judaism in Israel, and some of them have joined the small but growing number of Conservative and Reform congregations in Israel. The Conservative and Reform movements in Judaism are relatively recent phenomena in Israel, and they do not have the same legal-political status Orthodoxy has. These movements, including their American members and others who are not actual members, are struggling to gain equal recognition under the banner of religious pluralism, and their model is that of American society.[20]

Many Americans and others are highly critical of the Israeli legal system, which, because it continues to operate under procedures introduced by Britain during the mandate era, does not provide some of the fundamental rights taken for granted in most of American society. To cite just one example, the Israeli police have the right to arrest and detain someone for a lengthy period without bringing charges. Habeas corpus as Americans know it does not yet exist in Israel. Newer American olim may be unfamiliar with the nature of Israeli criminal law, and some veteran American immigrants may have grown cynical and unwittingly come to accept it, but there are relatively few who will defend it.

These complaints, however, pale in significance when compared with the problem of bureaucracy. Bureaucracy has consistently been reported as the most distinctive and common problem experienced by American olim in their adjustment to Israel[21] and, as will be discussed in Chapter 11, was found by Jubas to be the most important reason for hypothetically considering returning to the United States among American olim. It was also ranked highest in Dashefsky and Lazerwitz's preset lists of evaluated motivations for return.[22]

When Americans in particular complain about bureaucracy, they often mean not only that there is such a vast bureaucracy in Israel but also what it does to all those who come into contact with it. Avruch cites one American immigrant who has been in Israel five years, is employed as an educational administrator, and who, prior to his aliya, had worked in a municipal bureaucracy:

Look, in the States things weren't always so rational either. But at least we had the sense of being "public servants." I mean, we may have screwed over some clients in the U.S., but we felt guilty about it–we really did think we ought to be doing something called public service. There's none of that here.

Basically, in the States they go more or less by the rules, especially in the federal agencies we dealt with. They may have carried out the regulations to the letter, to your disadvantage, but they went by the regulations. Here there are regulations too, but they can be bent by persons. Let's say I'm having trouble getting a driver's license because of my disability (a war wound). Now in the U.S., even if I know some bigshot in the motor vehicle bureau, if it's a technical thing, like my disability, the odds are he won't be able to do anything for me–short of the state legislature amending the law– even if he likes me or I'm his brother. In Israel it doesn't work that way. Even if there's a technical reason, a regulation, why I shouldn't get a license, there's always some guy, if you know the right one to go to, who can get you a license. And I'm not talking about bribery. The system works on proteksia (personal influence), not on money changing hands. Proteksia is based on reciprocity; on trading favors; on personal contacts. In a way it's more primitive than bribery. We're not talking about cash credit but about social credit. Proteksia is to bribery what barter is to cash.[23]

This, of course, was the view of one American immigrant. Others would be much less moderate in their descriptions of the Israeli bureaucracy, and this immigrant's description of the American bureaucracy may be more fantasy than reality–immigrants (and others) frequently forget some of the harsh realities of what life was really like in their native country. But empirical reality is beside the point. The important thing, sociologically, is the way the American olim perceive the Israeli bureaucracy in contrast to what they now remember of what life was like in the United States. It is *their* "definition of the situation" that affects their acculturation, and the evidence indicates that they define the Israeli bureaucracy as debilitating.

As mentioned, it is not only the bureaucracy itself that evokes such a negative reaction; it is also its perceived wider social consequences. When Avruch asked the respondents in his sample to describe how doing business in Israel differs from doing business in the United States, he found that the responses dealt

with the problems of "business ethics," such as "honesty," "accountability," and the "worth of a written contract" or "someone's word."

145

Some of the other and related responses to this query were as follows:

[Israeli] business is not oriented to customer service.
It is not competitive.
Lack of standards of excellence.
The customer is always wrong.
No "go-getter" attitude.
No rational planning possible.
Americans get taken.
No one honors their word.
Too much bargaining . . . the price always depends on *who*
    you are.
Mediterranean mentality.
Businesses are not businesslike.
Lack of what we call "WASP know-how and efficiency."[24]

Nevertheless, although many, probably most, American olim despise Israeli bureaucracy, this does not mean that they are any less acculturated as a result. One does not have to be an alien to despise Israeli bureaucracy. Many native Israelis do as well. It is a fundamental aspect and problem of daily life in Israel. As S. N. Eisenstadt points out in his discussion of the development of relatively recent problems in Israel, "There was also the tendency to the extension of bureaucracy, to over-bureaucratization, the wide spread of rather inefficient bureaucratic organs, often stifling initiative in many spheres of life. While, needless to say, the problem was unevenly distributed among the different sectors of the civil service, some of which were very open and innovative, it was widespread enough to become one of the basic aspects of daily life in Israel."[25]

Especially in light of the fact that Israel is a nation of immigrants and the society as a whole is acculturating–that is, it is still in the process of developing its own culture–it would be difficult to argue that American olim are any less culturally assimilated or acculturated than the numerous other immigrant groups there. On the contrary, the available evidence strongly suggests that American immigrants acculturate relatively successfully. That they have difficulties initially is a given, just as all other immigrant groups do. It might even be speculated at this point, though the whole issue will be discussed in greater detail in Chapter 11, that problems in acculturating account for many of those American olim who return to live in the United States. But that does not necessarily mean that the acculturation of the American immigrants was any more difficult than it is for other immigrant groups in Israel. Rather, it may and probably does mean that the conditions in the country of emigration were better for the American olim than for other olim, and, therefore, it is generally easier for American immigrants to return to their country of emigration than it is for other olim.

When measured in terms of what the immigrants themselves expected, the available evidence suggests that the majority feel mostly to completely fulfilled, and that there was an increase in the percentage of those who felt so between 1972 and 1975. Thus, when Zvi Gitelman interviewed American olim in 1972 and in 1975, he found that the proportion stating that they were "not at all fulfilled" decreased from about one-third to about one-quarter, whereas the proportion stating that they were "completely fulfilled" increased from 28 to 33.3 percent (Table 9).

When it comes to the structural assimilation of American olim, the evidence is overwhelming that Americans have entered all structural spheres of Israeli society and that their rate of structural assimilation is high. We need but cite the evidence with respect to housing, education, occupation, and income to demonstrate that Americans are indeed an elite group in Israeli society.

As was mentioned in Chapter 6, whereas the prestate and early-state American olim tended to settle in agricultural settlements–kibbutzim and moshavim–this has not been the case in more recent decades. At least since 1967, American immigrants have overwhelmingly settled in urban areas, and as Pearl Katz found, they tend "to possess better housing than the average Israeli in urban areas of Israel."[26]

With respect to education, it was pointed out in Chapter 6 that American olim arrive in Israel with considerably higher educational status than is typical within Israeli society and that they have very high occupational status within Israel.[27] And according to a trinational study of status attainment of immigrant and immigrant origin categories, education remains if not the most significant, among the most significant variables influencing occupational status in Israel.[28] Presumably, therefore, American Israelis also have better-paying jobs than other Israelis.

Above and beyond the objective determinants of structural assimilation, however, is the perhaps ultimate issue of what Milton Gordon calls "identificational assimilation," the loss of identification with the ethnic group.[29] If one were to use identificational assimilation as the "acid test" of the integration of American olim into Israeli society, it

TABLE 9

Fulfillment of Expectations of American Olim
1972 and 1975 (%)

	1972	1975
Completely fulfilled	28.0	33.3
Mostly fulfilled	11.3	22.2
Somewhat fulfilled	28.2	18.5
Not at all fulfilled	32.5	25.9
TOTAL	100.0	99.9

Source: Adapted from Zvi Gitelman, *Becoming Israelis: Political Resocialization of Soviet and American Immigrants* (New York: Praeger, 1982), table 6.9, p. 225.

would definitely be concluded that they have a very low level of integration because the vast majority of them continue to identify themselves as Americans. As Gitelman found: "Despite the fact that the Americans had strong Jewish backgrounds, they clung to their American identity . . . they did not *want* to lose their identities as Americans. . . . As one put it: 'I don't have any desire to assimilate because I don't think much of the Israelis. I'm an American living in Israel–we feel we're above them culturally and socially' " (emphasis in original).[30]

This cannot be dismissed simply as the unrepresentative attitude of a single individual. The vast majority of Americans in Israel seem to be in no rush to shed their American identity. They maintain their contacts with family and friends in America, they retain their American passports, and they vote in American elections.[31] In short, they retain their American identities. In fact, Gitelman found that "not a single American agreed with the notion that 'immigrants should adopt Israeli ways as soon as possible.' "[32]

This does not mean, however, that American olim do not integrate into Israeli society or that they are deviants or pariahs in Israel. As the above discussion of their structural assimilation shows, they have integrated well. That they strongly desire to retain their American identity is not deviant or even unusual. In contrast to most of the immigrant groups that came to the United States during the nineteenth and early twentieth centuries, American olim arrived in Israel with high levels of education, occupation, and employment, and thus did not feel the great push/pull to lose their American identities in order to become Israelis. Also, Israel is a highly pluralistic society consisting of many different subcultures. Whatever may have been in the prestate and early-state years, there is no melting-pot ideology in Israel today. If anything, ethnic consciousness is encouraged. The ethnic consciousness of American Israelis as Americans, therefore, cannot be taken as a measure of the degree to which they have integrated into Israeli society.

In the next chapter, a unique subgroup of American Israelis, those living in Israeli-administered territories beyond the pre-1967 "Green Line," the unofficial border of Israel, will be explored. As will be discussed, one of the surprising findings of research on this group is that they, too, have a keen, positive sense of their American background. Indeed, most of them are proud of being *American* Israelis.

10

American Israelis in "the Territories"

Conventional wisdom has it that the Israeli settlers in the Territories—
that is, the West Bank/Judea and Samaria, and the Gaza Strip[1]–are
political extremists and religious fundamentalists who are zealously
driven by political messianism.[2] Further, the Americans among them
are widely believed to be among the most fanatically irredentist of
all.[3] That image of the settlers, in general–even if correct for the
founders of Gush Emunim, the movement for settlement of the Territories formally established after the Yom Kippur War of October
1973–is apparently inappropriate for the bulk of those in the Territories today, as has been shown by Aronoff,[4] Shafir,[5] and Benvenisti,[6]
among others. It should be emphasized that we are dealing specifically with the Americans among the settlers. This chapter is based on
research conducted between January and May 1984,[7] which sought to
explore the backgrounds, political and religious attitudes, values, and
motivations of the American Jewish settlers in the Territories. Beginning with a preponderance of evidence for the continued political
liberalism of American Jews,[8] and evidence that American Israelis
continue to retain their liberalism after immigration to Israel,[9] the
central underlying questions of the research were: what happened to
the liberalism or, at least, the basic American values of those who
settled in the Territories? What was it in their experience, either in the
United States or in Israel, that caused them to so rebel against their
American background? Were they, in their settling, acting out defi-
ance and rejection not only of American society and culture but of

TABLE 10

Distribution of American Israelis in the Territories
by Age and Sex

Age	Males	Females	% of Total
20–29	13	40	26
30–39	49	49	49
40–49	28	9	19
50–59	8	–	4
60–69	–	2	1
70+	2	–	1
TOTAL	100	100	100

TABLE 11

Number of Children in Families
of American Israelis in the Territories

Number of Children	% of Total
None	3
1–3	47
4–6	46
7+	4

TABLE 12

Distribution of American Israelis in the Territories
by Education and Sex

Education	Males	Females	% of Total
Less than bachelor's	9.43	34.04	21
Bachelor's	43.39	44.68	44
Master's	30.18	21.27	26
Doctorate	16.98	–	9
TOTAL	99.98	99.99	100

their parents as well? If so, what led to that break? The findings were very surprising and totally at variance with the preconceived stereotypes with which the research was undertaken.

The typical American settler in the Territories is married, between the ages of thirty and forty, and has a higher than average number of

TABLE 13

Distribution of American Israelis in the
Territories by Parents' affiliation

Jewish affiliation of Parents	Respondents
Orthodox	
Active	59
Nonactive	10
Conservative	
Active	10
Nonactive	18
Reform	
Active	–
Nonactive	1
Unaffiliated	2
TOTAL	100

children. Most have three or four children, and stated that they expected to have more. Since three-quarters of those interviewed were younger than forty years of age, it is reasonable to assume that many of them will, in fact, have more children (Tables 10 and 11).

One of the most striking characteristics of the sample was their exceptionally high level of education. Less than 10 percent of the males did not have a bachelor's degree, and about 17 percent had doctorates. Among the females the educational level was somewhat lower, with 34 percent having less than a bachelor's degree and none having a doctorate. But more than 21 percent of the females had a master's degree, and about 45 percent had a bachelor's degree. The level of education of the group, therefore, is very high, not only in comparison with other Israelis but also when compared to Jews in the United States, a group that has one of the highest levels of education in American society.[10] In this respect, they are similar to other American immigrants to Israel who have been found to be more highly educated than their counterparts in the United States.[11] When one considers that, as mentioned above, this group has a higher than average number of children, their high educational level is particularly remarkable, since there is usually an inverse relationship between level of education and number of children (Table 12).

The findings yielded a number of additional surprises when the data concerning their religious backgrounds and current identification were analyzed. Of particular interest is the fact that, for most of

TABLE 14

**Distribution of American Israelis in the
Territories by Jewish Education**

Type of Jewish School	Male		
	Primary	High School	Post-High School
Day school	7.54	24.52	43.39
Afternoon school	7.54	9.43	3.77
Sunday school	–	1.88	–
None	1.88	–	–
No answer	–	–	–
TOTAL			99.95

	Female		
	Primary	High School	Post-High School
Day school	6.38	25.53	25.53
Afternoon school	8.51	12.76	–
Sunday school	6.38	4.25	–
None	8.51	–	–
No answer	2.12	–	–
TOTAL			99.97

	% of Total		
	Primary	High School	Post-High School
Day school	7	25	35
Afternoon school	8	11	2
Sunday school	3	3	–
None	5	–	–
No answer	1	–	–
TOTAL			100

153

TABLE 15

Jewish Youth Group Affiliations
of American Israelis in the Territories

Jewish Youth Group	Male (%)	Female (%)	% of Total
Bnai Akiva, Mizrachi Hatzair, Noam	35.84	36.17	36
National Conference of Synagogue Youth	5.66	6.38	6
Young Israel Youth	3.77	–	2
United Synagogue Youth	7.54	10.63	9
Betar	5.66	–	3
Young Judea	3.77	–	2
Habonim	3.77	–	2
Other	9.43	10.63	10
None	24.52	34.04	29
No answer	–	2.12	1
TOTAL	99.96	99.97	100

TABLE 16

Distribution of American Israelis in the Territories
by Period of Aliya

Period of Aliya	%
Pre-1967	7
1967–73	48
1973–80	27
1980–84	17
TOTAL	100

them, their current religious behavior and identification does not manifest a break with their past. Although the overwhelming majority of the settlers are Orthodox, the findings indicate that the widely held perception of them as being recently turned Orthodox, or *baalei tshuva*, is inaccurate. When the religious behavior of those interviewed was compared with that of their parents, it was found that only about 20 percent came from religiously nonobservant homes. The majority of those interviewed were reared in either Orthodox or actively Conservative homes, and their current religious behavior is

TABLE 17

Feelings about the U.S.
among American Israelis in the Territories

Feelings about United States	Male (%)	Females (%)	% of Total
It's a great and good society	33.96	23.40	29
Generally positive	37.73	29.78	34
Strong sense of gratitude	11.32	25.53	18
Nothing against it	1.88	4.25	3
Neutral; it's where I was born and raised	7.54	6.38	7
Disappointed with foreign policy	3.77	–	2
Ambivalent	1.88	4.25	3
Negative; it's a sinking, materialistic society; no discipline; disunity.	–	6.38	3
Resent being identified as an American, though I am one	1.88	–	1
TOTAL	99.96	99.97	100

TABLE 18

Primary Motivations of American Israelis
for Moving to Territories

Primary Motivation	Male (%)	Female (%)	% of Total
Ideological—Wanted to be part of important aspect of Jewish history; want Territories to remain under Jewish control	37.73	36.17	37
Associational—Like type of community	37.73	31.91	35
Convenient; had friends here; it was available	16.98	19.14	18
Wanted to be a pioneer; wanted challenge of starting new community	1.88	8.51	5
Economic—Less expensive, housing	5.66	4.25	5
TOTAL	99.98	99.98	100

TABLE 19

Support of American Israelis in the Territories
for Democracy as a Value

Democracy as a Value	Male (%)	Female (%)	% of Total
Strongly support	49.05	51.06	50
Support, but not for enemy (Arabs)	–	4.25	2
Limited; Israel must maintain, its Jewish character	13.20	6.38	10
Support, but halakhah, comes first	11.32	12.76	12
Torah is democracy	–	2.12	1
Judaism is best form of democracy	–	2.12	1
Very important, but doesn't work in Israel	3.77	2.12	3
Not a value for me, but see no other option	1.88	–	1
In Israel I hope for a Jewish monarchy	1.88	2.12	2
Democracy fine for U.S.; in Israel would like to see military junta	1.88	–	1
Democracy not a Torah concept; want religous state in Israel	11.32	10.63	11
Don't know	1.88	–	1
No answer	3.77	6.38	5
TOTAL	99.95	99.94	100

in conformity with, rather than a break from, their parents' religious behavior (Table 13).

This pattern of conformity with parental socialization, rather than rebellion from it, was further borne out by the findings with respect to the levels of Jewish education of the interviewees.

As Table 14 shows, the vast majority of Americans among the settlers in the Territories had day-school education, that is, intensive Jewish education, with more than 43 percent of the males and more than 25 percent of the females having continued their Jewish education on the post-high school level. These figures again suggest that, in their settling, these individuals are manifesting continuity rather than a break with their past. Table 15, which shows their affiliation

TABLE 20

Ideas on Dealing with Arabs in Territories
among American Israelis There

What to Do about Arabs, in Territories	Male (%)	Female (%)	% of Total
Leave as is except for troublemakers	24.52	36.17	30
Offer citizenship; if refuse, leave or remain second-class	33.96	25.53	30
Must find way for peaceful coexistence somehow	20.75	12.76	17
Provide various economic incentives for them to leave	13.20	6.38	10
Force them out (á la Kach*)	1.88	6.38	4
Divide Territories	3.77	2.12	3
Don't know	1.88	10.63	6
TOTAL	99.96	99.97	100

TABLE 21

Attitudes toward Kach
among American Israelis in the Territories

Attitudes	Male (%)	Female (%)	% of Total
Very positive	–	2.12	1
Agree with most of Kach's points	1.88	4.25	3
Not a Kach person but see role for it	16.98	2.12	10
Agree with philosophy but not methods; no positive strategy	15.09	12.76	14
Too extreme, fanatical; takes law into own hands	20.75	23.40	22
Opposed to philosophy and methods	11.32	14.89	13
Opposed; would cause more harm than good; terrorists, a disgrace	33.96	34.04	34
No answer	–	6.38	3
TOTAL	99.98	99.96	100

with Jewish youth groups in the United States, provides further support for this conclusion.

According to these figures, 44 percent of the respondents had belonged to Orthodox Jewish youth groups that had clear Zionist ideologies, 16 percent had belonged to non-Orthodox youth groups, a small percentage had belonged to either an Orthodox non-Zionist

TABLE 22

Attitudes toward Gush Emunim
among American Israelis in the Territories

Attitude	Male (%)	Female (%)	% of Total
Positive	45.28	44.68	45
Basically positive but needs improvement; too narrow	15.09	44.68	13
Positive but sometimes too extreme; or needs better public relations	26.41	31.91	29
Positive but unfamiliar with their politics	1.88	2.12	2
Elitist; limited contribution	1.88	–	1
Too fanatical	1.88	6.38	4
Opposed; they place land before people	7.54	–	4
No answer	–	4.25	2
TOTAL	99.96	99.97	100

TABLE 23

Belief among American Israelis in the Territories
in Equal Rights for Arabs

Believe in Equal Rights for Israeli Arabs	Male (%)	Female (%)	% of Total
Yes	43.39	31.91	38
Yes, including army or national service	28.30	23.40	26
Yes, as long as not threat to Jewish character of Israel	7.54	4.25	6
Conflicted; can't decide	5.66	12.76	9
Don't know	1.88	8.51	5
No, but wouldn't disturb status quo	–	2.12	1
No	13.20	17.02	15
TOTAL	99.97	99.97	100

youth group or a relatively small Zionist one, and 29 percent were not members of any Jewish youth group. The relatively high percentage of these American Israelis who had been members of Zionist youth groups seems to contrast with Goldscheider's findings of the negligible influence of Zionist organizations on American immigrants to Israel.[12] Apparently, although such groups may not significantly relate to aliya in general, they are significant with respect to settling in the Territories, and especially for the religious Zionist groups.

TABLE 24

Belief among American Israelis in Territories that Now Is Period of Messiah

Believe	Male (%)	Female (%)	% of Total
No, don't really see it	16.98	25.43	21
Definitely	7.54	14.89	11
Always is	5.66	2.12	4
Hope so, but people always do	–	4.25	2
Yes, but could go on for centuries	22.64	10.63	17
Probably	3.77	2.12	3
Hope so	11.32	8.51	10
Yes, but it didn't affect my settling or other actions	15.09	14.98	15
Don't know	16.98	17.02	17
TOTAL	99.98	99.96	100

Nor, as is widely presumed, are most of the American settlers very new immigrants. In fact, most of them immigrated to Israel prior to the Arab-Israeli war of 1973, the Yom Kippur War (Table 16).

When asked to identify their parents' political affiliation in the United States, the overwhelming majority of those interviewed stated that their parents were Democrats. Only five respondents said that either or both of their parents were Republicans. When asked to identify their own political affiliation in the United States prior to their immigration to Israel, none stated Republican, one stated conservative, and the remainder stated that they had voted as Democrats, liberals, independents or, in a few cases, were too young at the time to identify politically. Thus, with respect to political socialization and behavior, at least until their immigration to Israel, the respondents had not broken with their past. On the contrary, they were very much continuing the American Jewish tradition of political liberalism,[13] a pattern that, as was seen in the previous chapter, is found among American Israelis within the "Green Line," as well.[14]

The responses with respect to political behavior, however, were limited to the period prior to their immigration to Israel. It was, therefore, necessary to probe further and ask the respondents about their attitudes and feelings toward American society and American values. Given the prevalent stereotype of Americans among the settlers, the findings on these questions were also surprising. As Table 17 shows, more than 80 percent of the respondents held attitudes ranging from strongly to generally positive toward the United States. The over-whelming majority were very proud of their American background, and many said they felt that the quality of Israeli society and culture would benefit from American norms and values becoming diffused in Israeli society.[15] Also, the majority saw both their aliya and their settling in the Territories as consistent with their socialization in American society. For many, both were the culmination of the synthesis of their general American values and their particular Jewish ones.

The strong feeling of pride and belief in the basic goodness of American society was clearly expressed in the response of a 40-year-old male who went on aliya in 1970 and has lived in a settlement since 1980: "The United States is the greatest country on Earth. I say it with a tremendous amount of conviction, without any hesitation. It is the greatest country on Earth. It affords the most amount of people a freedom which is unknown elsewhere on the globe. I also feel that Jews, however, belong in Israel."

Another settler, a forty-four-year-old male who left a prominent position in the United States to immigrate and settle in 1983, stated that he continued to celebrate the American holiday Thanksgiving in Israel by having a special turkey dinner, at which time he emphasized how grateful he and his family must continue to be and how exceedingly proud he remains of his American background.

Then why did the settlers leave the United States? Virtually all of them were emphatic in stating that their immigration to Israel was not the result of push factors but, instead, was due almost exclusively to pull factors. Rather than emigrating from the United States, they immigrated to Israel. Their moving from the United States was not due to feelings of discrimination or any lack of material comfort in American society. On the contrary, they felt even more comfortable materially in the United States than they do now in Israel. Their aliya, they stated, stemmed from religious and ethnic values, or because they simply felt more "at home" in Israel. As one thirty-five-year-old male who went on aliya in 1978 and settled in early 1979 put it: "I always knew I would make aliya. Israel was always central to my concerns. From a religious standpoint, it was, to me, where the action was in terms of trying to live in all spheres and not . . . the compartmentalized approach. Also, this is where I felt the Jews express themselves. It's not because of anti-Semitism or because of dislocation in the States, but simply I felt Israel to be the natural place."

Another male respondent, age thirty-five, who immigrated to Israel in 1970 and moved to one of the most recent new towns in the

Territories, stated that even though he admires American's values and achievements, he went on aliya because of two historical events that greatly affected world Jewry in this generation:

> I came of age at a time when the overwhelming Jewish event was the Six-Day War. The Six-Day War in a sense crystallized, on the one hand, the desire to return, to come on aliya, and on the other, the fear of another Holocaust. That, plus the other great event, the exodus of Jews from the Soviet Union. As someone who had had a Zionist education and a Zionist upbringing and was always sort of headed in that direction, those were the events which really pushed me to actually make aliya. In fact, when I came to Israel I felt absolutely at home, and felt a great sense of fulfillment.

If these do not sound like the expressions of political fanatics or political-messianic zealots, neither do their reasons for settling in the Territories. When asked their primary reasons for settling in the Territories, less than 40 percent said ideological factors (Table 18).

Two of the women interviewed elaborated on their ideological motivations for moving to the Territories. One, a forty-two-year-old mother of eight who went on aliya in 1971 and was a founder of a new settlement in the Territories in 1977, stated: "It was a feeling that settlement must be done and we have no right to sit in Jerusalem when work has to be done here."

The second, a forty-six-year-old mother of eleven who came on aliya in 1956 and settled in the Territories right after the Six-Day War, in 1967, assented to the religio-ideological motivation provided by her husband. As she put it: "The Six-Day War was a sign from Heaven. . . . The idea to come . . . [here] was my husband's [he is non-American], He said like this: 'God did His part and now we have to do our part. And even though people are saying there will probably be a peace agreement, so let's not do anything,' he said that we can't leave Judea and Samaria *Judenrein*."

As the figures in Table 18 show, however, the majority were not primarily motivated by ideological factors, but rather by associational and economic factors. When asked if they would have considered a new and similar type of community within the "Green Line," were such available, instead of the settlement in the Territories to which they moved, many said that they probably would have, and others said that they possibly would have. A strong minority even said that they would have preferred a community within the "Green Line."

These findings appear to support the thesis of Gershon Shafir: that the Jewish settlement of the Territories was primarily the consequence of the policies of the Israeli government rather than of the ideology and activities of Gush Emunim.[16] The findings also back up one of Meron Benvenisti's conclusions:

> The typical settler of the 1980s is a figure well known throughout the Western world: the suburbanite. The man who wants to escape his cramped apartment in the stifling, polluted center city and to make his dream of a home of his own with a bit of lawn come true is not guided by nationalistic ideology. In his social and economic characteristics, he is similar to the average Labor voter. The main demand of these settlers is to be not more than a half-hour's drive from their places of work and entertainment.[17]

Although our findings suggest that Benvenisti has grossly overstated the essentially materialistic desires of the settlers, at least as far as the Americans among them are concerned–they were much more concerned with the associational and religious quality of life and quality educational opportunities for their children than with a private home and a bit of lawn–most, nevertheless, were not guided solely by nationalistic ideology and are probably not very different from their religious and Zionist American colleagues within the formal boundaries of Israel.

The Americans differ from Benvenisti's characterization in another important respect. Although their initial motivations for settling were not, for many, based solely or even primarily on nationalistic ideology, such ideology frequently does develop for the American settlers after the fact, that is, once they have already settled. Further research would be required to determine the depth of commitment to such ex-post-facto ideologies, but it appears to be strong. On the one hand, it may be that the current expression of such ideologies is merely a superficial rationalization and legitimation for remaining in the Territories despite opposition, but that there is no really deep commitment involved. On the other hand, it is possible that sincere and deep ideological commitments do develop, perhaps in line with Festinger's theory of cognitive dissonance,[18] as a means of relieving the stress caused by living in an area over which there are such conflicting claims. According to Festinger, two elements of knowledge "are in a dissonant relation if, considering these two alone, the obverse of one element would follow from the other."[19] Dissonance is psychologically uncomfortable and motivates those experiencing it to reduce it and achieve consonance.[20] For the American settlers, the adoption and internalization of an irridentist ideology might, in fact, reduce the dissonance and ease the stress.

Although this is a matter for further research, the responses of the interviewees to a number of related questions suggest that, even after having formulated ideological attachments to the area, they retain their liberal social, political, and religious attitudes and values in that respect. For example, not only were most of the respondents positive in their attitudes and feelings about American society and culture, as shown above; they were also highly committed to and supportive of one of the basic values of American political culture–democracy. When asked for their attitudes and feelings about democracy as a basic value, 50 percent said they were strongly supportive of that value and had no qualifications, and another 29 percent stated that they support it, but with qualifications. Less than 15 percent rejected democracy for Israel, on the grounds that "democracy is not a Torah concept"; "I want a religious state in Israel"; "I hope for a Jewish monarchy in Israel"; or, as one male stated, "Democracy is fine for the United States. In Israel, I would now like to see a military junta" (Table 19).

The responses did not suggest that the interviewees were less than serious in their professed commitment to democracy. On the contrary, they took their time in responding, and what they stated suggested thoughtfulness on the parts of all and soul-searching on the parts of some who qualified their support for the value of democracy in Israel. For example, a thirty-two-year-old male who had come on aliya in 1974 and had been a member of a kibbutz in the Beit Shaan Valley until he moved to a settlement in 1981 stated:

> I hold to the value of democracy within well-defined limits. Democracy is limited in several ways. Specifically, freedom of action in a democracy is limited by another person's same freedom of action. I won't do anything that will prevent someone else from having the same rights as myself. . . . It's also limited to protection of the public. I'm not allowed to yell "fire" in a crowded theater. It's also limited to the welfare of the state. I wouldn't want every scientist to go around telling everything that he knows about every project. One of the problems in American society and others lately is that those defined limits are becoming too flexible and not defined well enough. Democracy is a luxury which you have to work very hard to attain and a luxury which certain peoples and nations can afford and others can't. Israel could and should within the limits of its security.

Another respondent, a thirty-eight-year-old male who had immigrated in 1967 and settled in 1976, thought through the implications of his initial enthusiasm for democracy during the course of his response:

> You have to define your terms. I think that the American political system, if applied here, would enable the country to implement more of its programs, would advance the country, especially economically. The small parties, the splinter parties, including Hatchiya, are just nuisances. Assuming that the policies of whatever party will rule are consistent with whatever has to be done, then I think that the way it's run now–small parties where each member of the Knesset has a voice and can bring down a government, even though he doesn't represent anybody–is a fiction. It's not democracy; it's not a republic; it's nothing. The people can't decide who their leaders can be. . . .
>
> As far as democracy for Arabs, if they want to vote, let them vote, although on the other hand, that might be a reason not to have the American-type democracy here. But, then again, there's no problem that's insurmountable. I'm not a political expert. I would say that anyone who served in the army, that should be the criterion because that's really the main thing. That's how Israel exists. If a person has served the state or, if he can't serve in the army, then in another capacity where he gives up 2 or 3 years of his private life and serves the state, then he can have the right to vote. If he doesn't, whether he's an Arab or he lives in Meah Shearim–who also don't identify with the state, then that should be the criterion.

This last opinion, indicating a preparedness to extend democratic rights to the Arabs in the Territories were they to accept citizenship with the same rights and responsibilities Israel's Jews have, was expressed by 30 percent of the respondents when asked, "What should Israel do about the Palestinian Arabs in the Territories?" The recommendation offered by the largest number of respondents (30 percent) was that Israel should offer them citizenship with all of the rights and responsibilities pertaining thereto, and that those who do not respond positively to the offer should be required to leave or remain as second-class residents (Table 20).

Although many Israelis (and others) on the political Left tend to view the proposal to offer citizenship to the Palestinian Arabs in the Territories as insincere and cynical, it should be noted that a similar proposal was part of the platform of Ezer Weizman's Yachad party during the 1984 election campaign in Israel, and Weizman is perceived as being dovish on the issues of Palestinian Arabs and the Territories.

One of the respondents, a thirty-five-year-old male who came on aliya in 1970 and settled in the Territories in 1983, formulated his approach in the following manner:

> I think that the best idea would be a canton system, a system which would ensure an overwhelming Jewish majority. It's basically to offer the people the option of Israeli citizenship or Jordanian citizenship. Those who take Israeli citizenship have to serve 3 years in national service–not in the army, of course–and to work out a plan for autonomy, internally, that is, and then to annex, but on that basis. Although, the best idea would basically be if the Palestinians took over Jordan; that would solve everything because then they would be Jordanian citizens. In other words, it would basically mean making a federation and they would be Palestinian Jordanians.

Another respondent, a female who had immigrated in 1982 and settled in 1983, had no specific proposals, but was emphatic in stating that new approaches to peaceful coexistence must be adopted. As she put it: "I don't think that Israeli policy toward the Arabs is fair. I'd like to see more cooperation between the Arabs and the Jews, and less animosity. Arabs are treated as very low class people. And it came home to me mostly here [on an agricultural settlement in the Gaza Strip], being that we use mostly Arab labor in the hot houses."

The most extreme proposal offered by any of the respondents was that of an otherwise mild-mannered twenty-nine-year-old female who came on aliya in 1981 and settled in the Territories in 1982: "I think Israel should ask them to leave or give them the right to be *gerei toshav* ["stranger-sojourners"] as the *Halakhah* defines them. I think that the ultimate and last solution if they refuse to leave or become *gerei toshav* is, I think, they should be killed. And that is absolutely the last resource if you can't get rid of them in any other way."

This respondent, however, was a minority of one even among the small group that proposed driving the Palestinian Arabs out of the Territories. Moreover, not only did the vast majority of those interviewed not propose such drastic measures; they specifically rejected the Kach movement.[21] Tables 21 and 22 show the range of attitudes toward both Kach and Gush Emunim and are based on questions involving attitudes toward a series of political parties and movements in Israel.

The extent to which the large majority of the American settlers reject both the proposals and tactics of Kach is also evident from their responses to a question concerning Israeli Arabs, that is, those within the pre-1967 borders of Israel. When asked if they believe that Israeli Arabs should have complete equal rights with Israeli Jews, 70 percent said yes. Of these, 38 percent affirmed this without qualification, and 32 percent qualified it either on the condition that Israeli Arabs serve in the armed forces or in national service, or as long as they do not threaten the Jewish character of the country. On the other side, 15 percent opposed equal rights for Israeli Arabs. In this respect, the American settlers are, apparently, less liberal than American Israelis within Israel proper, among whom Gitelman found as many as 90 percent agreeing with the statement, "Israeli Arabs should have equal rights with Jews."[22] On the other hand, the American settlers maintain a much higher level of liberalism on this issue than does the general Jewish population of Israel, among whom it is reported that perhaps even a majority oppose, in one way or another, complete equal rights for Israeli Arabs (Table 23).[23]

Whereas most analysts of the origin of Gush Emunim attribute a major part to messianic Zionism, it was not with that aspect of the movement with which the vast majority of the American settlers identify. Although almost 90 percent of them were favorably disposed toward Gush Emunim, it was not its messianic ideology with which they identified. Rather, it was for its practical results–settlement-that they credited the movement.

When asked directly, "Do you view these times as the period of the Messiah?" 11 percent stated that they definitely do, and 21 percent stated that they do not. Almost 70 percent maintained that they hope these times are the period of the Messiah, that it always is, or that it is but it could go on for centuries. Also, when specifically asked, the overwhelming majority emphasized that their views concerning the Messiah were totally unrelated or only very indirectly related to their immigration to Israel and their settling in the Territories. In this respect, there was virtually nothing in their conceptions of the Messiah that is very different from such conceptions among Orthodox Jews in general (Table 24).

Finally, although most of the interviews were conducted prior to the arrest of the so-called "Jewish Underground," the group of settlers charged and convicted of having committed violent actions directed against Palestinian Arabs in the Territories,[24] 20 percent were conducted just after the arrests. Those interviews contained additional questions probing the respondents' reactions to the alleged activities of the Underground. Virtually all of those questioned strongly condemned the Underground on legal and pragmatic grounds, and many on moral grounds as well. This was the case not only among those unaffiliated with Gush Emunim, but even among some of its strongest adherents. For example, a thirty-three-year-old mother of five who went on aliya in 1972, moved to a settlement in 1975, and is actively involved with the settlement movement responded:

> If it turns out that there is truth in all of the allegations, I am opposed to every action. . . . I am even more opposed when it comes to harming innocent people. Not only were those actions mistaken, they were bad, very, very bad. The principle is, number one, you're not allowed to harm innocent people, and number two, you're not allowed to take the law into your own hands when you have a sovereign government. . . . The danger to undercut the government by taking the law into your own hands is very serious. . . . I think, in terms of the basic ideology and principles of Gush Emunim, no reexamination is called for. With respect to actions, on the other hand, I think that there are attitudes we might have unconsciously or deliberately passed on, consciously or unconsciously, that have given messages, not just to our children but to ourselves, our neighbors, our society, that there are times when taking the law into your own hands is a good thing. And they confuse it because this country doesn't have a long tradition of democracy and what we used to call, "the legitimate limits of protest." They don't understand that. They think that if you are right, then to the end. So you can even sit in a bunker and blow yourself up if they say they're taking away Yamit, and you can throw soldiers off roofs, as some lunatic fringe said. . . . It's not that they're really lunatics. It's just that they don't understand what are the legitimate limits of protest. In a democratic system there's some point at which you say that I've come to the end. Now I've done all that I can and there's nothing more that I can do. . . . You can't hurt your own army; you can't hurt other people; you can't undercut your own government. . . . There are some things that you just can't do, and that's when you have to fold up with your tail between your legs and go home, back to the drawing board, and say, "How come I couldn't influence?"[25]

The evidence presented underscores the wide gap between the conventional wisdom and reality. Among other things, it points to the continuing strong influence of basic American political and social values on American Israelis in the settlements. If their settling seems anomalous, it suggests a lack of understanding of the sociology and social psychology of a major segment of American Orthodox Jewry. As suggested earlier, it appears that their settling is fully consistent with and, indeed, is a natural consequence of the attempted synthesis of Orthodoxy and modernity, which is one of the responses developed by American Orthodox Judaism to the confrontation of Orthodoxy with modernity.[26] In essence, it is part of a much larger and deeper struggle and quest for a more complete Jewish life within modern society, and part of that completeness and wholeness entails living within what the settlers perceive as a whole Land of Israel.[27]

The settlers' probable uniqueness, however, should not be forgotten. No claim is being made for their being representative of American Israelis. Also, there is no evidence that their political values are of long-term significance. On the contrary, prima facie evidence suggests that the values of their children who were primarily socialized in Israel are no different than those of other children growing up in the settlements. The American Israelis in the Territories, apparently, do not or are not able to transmit their American political values to their children.

Additionally, overemphasizing the significance of this group, the beliefs and values they express, and the significance they attribute to that which they are doing with their lives may tend to overshadow the realities of day-to-day life and its difficulties as faced by most American Israelis. The difficulties are very real and many, and a significant minority of American Jews who migrate to Israel with the anticipation of permanently becoming Israeli return to the United States within a few years. It is with the analysis of return migration and its implications that the next chapter deals.

11

The Return Migration of American Olim

Of the approximately sixty thousand American Jews who immigrated to Israel, "made aliya," since 1967, it is widely estimated that at least one-third, or some twenty thousand, have returned to the United States.[1] One obvious reason for this high rate of return is the very fact that American olim are free migrants, mostly of the innovative type, who retain their American citizenship and passports, and can readily pick up and return should they so decide.

Although American immigrants in Israel have been widely studied, there has been a distinct paucity of empirical research on those who have returned to the United States. Particularly since they are such a large proportion of the American olim, and they are now, once again, part of the American Jewish community, the experiences of those who have returned are of particular interest.

Previous Research

The first empirical study of return olim was by Gerald Engel.[2] He made an analysis of the responses to self-administered questionnaires sent to 443 adult American olim in Israel and 256 returnees who had lived in Israel for at least a year prior to 1967. His general conclusion was that those who stayed did so because of ideological convictions, whereas those who left did so for practical reasons. "Job opportunities, housing, and cost of living were practical considerations for leaving. The desire to live in Jewish state, experience a religious environment, and enjoy a cultural life were ideological motives for staying."[3]

In 1970–71 Harry L. Jubas conducted an extensive study of a random sample of 1,178 American olim in Israel who had immigrated between 1967 and 1971,[4] and he included a series of questions to measure the relative importance of a variety of factors in their hypothetical consideration of returning to the United States.[5] The factor that was most frequently cited as an important one, by as many as 70 percent, was "red-tape and bureaucracy in Israel."[6] From his data Jubas suggests that there is a basic distinction between the American who came to Israel with a commitment to stay and the one who came on a trial basis. Where the latter constantly compares "the efficiency of America with the seeming incompetence of Israeli bureaucracy," the former "chooses to make light of the annoyances and says as does the Israeli, 'there is no choice.' He adjusts to this aspect of the new way of life with the optimistic hope of helping to change the system someday."[7]

Jubas's study was of American olim in Israel, however, and does not provide any information on those who actually returned. It may well be that most American olim complain about Israeli bureaucracy and even imagine this to be a major consideration for American olim to return to the United States. But that does not necessarily mean that it is, in fact, a major factor in the decision-making process of those who return.

In 1978 Mario Blejer and Itzhak Goldberg analyzed a sample of Western olim in the continuous longitudinal survey that has been conducted by Israel's Central Bureau of Statistics since 1969, in which more than one-third of the sample were from North America.[8] Utilizing a theoretical framework within which return migration is caused by the failure of expectations to materialize, Blejer and Goldberg found that one of the strongest determinants of return is unexpected unemployment. Also, those unemployed workers who get discouraged and withdraw from the labor market are even more likely to return. When housing conditions are poorer than had been expected, there is also a propensity to return. Younger immigrants are more likely to return than older ones because the younger ones expect to feel the impact of the gap between expectations and reality for a longer period of time. Not surprisingly, when the cost of return is measured by family size, it has a negative effect on return. Finally, the researchers suggest that the more knowledge the olim had of Israel and its language, Hebrew, before they immigrated, the less the probability that they would return, "presumably because they reduce the gap between expectations and reality."[9]

There are, however, several limitations of this study for our purposes. Its findings are based on a sample in which Americans are only a minority and we cannot, therefore, know whether the findings would be different if the sample were only Americans. Also, the authors, being economists, began with a theoretical framework that assumed that economic variables relating to expectations and reality were the most significant ones, and they tested the data for those. But there may have been other factors at play in the decision to return that did not show up in these data because they were not explored.

The most comprehensive and systematic study of American returnees from Israel is that of Dashefsky and Lazerwitz.[10] On the basis of data from the Israel Immigrant Absorption Survey (HAS), conducted monthly by the Israel Central Bureau of Statistics, they compared the characteristics of American olim still in Israel three years after their arrival with those of olim who had already left. Their findings refine the conclusions of Engel and Jubas. At first glance, they point to the importance of the religious factor in distinguishing between the two groups. As Dashefsky and Lazerwitz put it, "Consistently, those who stayed were more religious and had more Jewish education than those who left."[11]

When subjected to numerous statistical procedures for measuring causality, however, the significance of the religious factor was found to be much weaker. In fact, analysis of the data indicated that only about 20 percent of the difference between those who stayed and those who returned could be explained by this variable. Rather, the only factor that had any significant predictive value was confidence of staying. In line with the earlier suggestion of Jubas, Dashefsky and Lazerwitz found that those who were more confident of staying after having been in Israel either two months or one year (depending on which survey was used for the sample) were more likely to still be in Israel after three years.[12] Although the data suggest that those with higher education and those with weaker or less active Jewish commitment tend to return, no meaningful causal relationship could be established between the characteristics of the returnees and their decision to return. We are, thus, still left with the problem of understanding why American olim return. It is precisely this question to which the study at hand was addressed.

This chapter presents an analysis of return aliya or, as some might call it, American yerida, based on data gathered through telephone interviews conducted for the American Jewish Committee's Institute on American Jewish-Israel Relations with a group of seventy-one return olim. A "snowball" sample was generated in the tristate New York, New Jersey, and Connecticut area during the summer of 1983. Respondents were located through personal contacts or through their responses to advertisements placed in Jewish communal newspapers. At the conclusion of each interview, respondents were asked to suggest names of others who might be contacted. Obviously, subjects selected in this manner do not constitute a random or representative sample of returning olim, nor does such a small sample allow for broad generalization of findings. Still, their responses suggest the rough profile of American Jews who stay in Israel for some time and then return to the United States. The responses also allude to some of the critical variations in their decision to return.

All of the respondents had gone to Israel in 1967 or later, had stayed there at least one year, and had seriously considered permanent settlement during their stay. Their ages at the time they arrived in Israel ranged from sixteen to fifty-seven years, with a median age of twenty-four years. Their median age at the time of their return to the United States was twenty-nine years, with a range of twenty to sixty-four years. At the time they were interviewed, their ages ranged from twenty-nine to sixty-seven years, and their median age was thirty-five years.

Upon their arrival in Israel, forty-four respondents were never married, twenty-three were married, and four were divorced. By the time they returned to the United States, only twenty-three were never married, forty-one were married, and six had been divorced. And at the time of the interviews, ten respondents were never married, fifty-two were married, and five were divorced.

Fifty respondents had no children upon arrival in Israel; at the time of return thirty-eight still had none, whereas eight respondents each had one child. Ten respondents each had two children when they left for Israel and thirteen respondents each had two children by the time they returned. Three respondents each had three children when they left for Israel, and four had families of three when they returned. Four respondents who left for Israel with four or more children returned with families of the same size.

Since the Israeli government includes in its return aliya statistics only arrivals who entered the country as new immigrants or potential immigrants, or those who change their visa status within two months of their arrival in Israel, almost half of the respondents in this survey would not be included in the return aliya figures computed by the Israel Central Bureau of Statistics. But they are included here and are

TABLE 25

Occupational Status Before, During, and After Stay in Israel

Occupation	Before Aliya	First Job in Israel	Last Job Before Return	When Interviewed
Professional*	43.6	47.9	62.0	69.0
Student	38.0	14.1	5.6	5.6
Homemaker	9.9	5.6	4.2	12.7
Clerical worker	7.0	12.7	8.5	7.0
Other	1.4	4.2	2.8	4.2
Kibbutz worker	–	12.7	9.9	–
Unemployed	–	2.8	7.0	1.4
TOTAL	99.9	100.0	100.0	99.9

Note: N =71
*Includes teaching and human services.

called olim because, despite their initial intentions and their visa status, the overwhelming majority, 84 percent, had obtained visas as immigrants or potential immigrants by the time they left the country. The mean duration of their stay in Israel was 3.9 years. Although this figure is skewed by several respondents whose stay exceeded ten years, it appeared probable that most of them actually considered aliya at some point during their residence in Israel.

A significant proportion of the respondents were oriented toward the professions, as shown in Table 25. In fact, before they went to Israel, 43.6 percent of them had held professional occupations. By the time they returned to America, however, the proportion of professionally employed individuals had risen to 62 percent, and to 69 percent at the time of the interviews. Thirty-eight percent were students at the time of their arrival in Israel; that percentage dropped dramatically by the time they returned to the United States. This change is probably related to the life-cycle process, but it also suggests that many students obtained their first professional jobs in Israel, and others completed their education there.

The structured interviews, which were conducted over the telephone, included questions about the respondents' motives for going on aliya, their reasons for returning to the United States, and the differences between their current Jewish affiliations, practices, and attitudes and those they reported for the period preceding their aliya. Questions also touched on their attitudes toward Israel.

TABLE 26

Intentions upon Arrival (%)

Aliya	47.9
Explore aliya	28.2
No aliya intention	23.9
TOTAL	100.0

Note: N=71

Findings

Aliya

As mentioned, the respondents in the sample arrived in Israel with a variety of goals. Some came for a year's study, others for temporary employment, and still others to immigrate. As Table 26 shows, less than half of the sample considered themselves olim upon their arrival in Israel.

An examination of their visa status when arriving in Israel supports their self-defined reports. As shown in Table 27, 55 percent expressed an intent to make aliya by using either an immigrant or potential immigrant visa.

All of this suggests that at least a majority of the respondents arrived in Israel with aliya as a possibility, though they did not come exclusively for that purpose. They then went through a serious decision-making process concerning aliya during an extended stay in the country. Whatever their initial plans, almost all of the respondents had at least initiated the process leading to permanent residence in Israel. Their responses indicate a pattern of motivations for aliya that differs somewhat from that found for post-1967 American

TABLE 27

Visa Status upon Arrival (%)

Immigrant	9.9
Potential immigrant	45.1
Tourist	36.6
Student	5.6
Other	2.8
TOTAL	100.0

TABLE 28

Reasons for Aliya
Rated as "Very or Somewhat Important" (%)

Potential for fuller Jewish life in Israel	85.9
Zionist convictions	81.7
Desire for change	57.7
Minority status as Jews in U.S.	53.5
Potential for fuller religious life in Israel	42.3
Assimilation in U.S.	32.4

olim in general. Jewish and Zionist considerations dominate. The respondents left for Israel with a commitment to Judaism and a desire to participate in a Jewish society. In these ways they are similar to other American olim. But the religious factor that was found to be important to increasing numbers of post-1967 American, as discussed in Chapter 6, was even less important to these respondents than their desire for general change and their minority status in the United States.

Return

In their theoretical guidelines for the sociology of migration, Mangalam and Schwarzweller suggest that "if those deprivations that led to migration persist after relocation, and if high value continues to be attached to those desired ends, then adjustment difficulties (manifested by a second migration or a 'return migration') can be anticipated."[13] It was cogent, therefore, to determine whether the return migration of our respondents was motivated by a perception that Israel did not fulfill or live up to their Jewish expectations.

The respondents in this study were presented with two different sets of questions dealing with their reasons for returning to the United States. They were first asked to name the primary and second most important reasons for their own return. Later, they were presented with a list of possible reasons for their having returned and were asked to evaluate each.

The pattern of responses is strikingly similar to those of previous studies, namely, although Jewish issues were among the most salient in the respondents' initial move to Israel, they were not salient in the decision to return. When asked to give primary and second most important motivations for return, they did not mention Jewish considerations at all (see Table 29), and when specifically asked to evaluate "Jewish life in Israel" as a reason to return, only a small minority evaluated it as very or somewhat important (see Table 30). Rather, as Tables 29 and 30 show, economic and familial considerations were strong influences, as were professional opportunities, difficulties of daily life, and criticism of or estrangement from certain aspects of Israeli society.

Other researchers who asked their respondents to list hypothetical reasons for returning report similar findings. Harry Jubas, for example, found that complaints about bureaucracy, lower living standards, lack of occupational opportunities, and separation from family were mentioned most frequently. Similarly, Engel found that job opportunities, housing, cost of living, and familial problems ranked highest. Engel also pointed out that olim who returned to the United States were more critical of certain aspects of job satisfaction, income, and standard of living than were those who remained in Israel.[14] Return, based on both past studies and the findings in this study, can indeed be described as motivated by "daily life concerns swirling around one's family and institutional needs."[15]

But a somewhat different picture emerges from a closer look at the motivations for return suggested by the respondents themselves, as shown in

Table 29. Although still among the more important reasons listed, family reunification ranks considerably lower than other factors. But the most dramatic difference lies in the degree of importance ascribed to Israeli bureaucracy. As discussed in Chapter 9, bureaucracy has been reported as the most distinctive and common problem experienced by American olim in their adjustment to Israel and as the most important reason for hypothetically considering returning to the United States among American olim; it also ranked very high in the preset lists of evaluated motivations for return (Table 30). It was, however, very low on the list of primary reasons offered by the respondents in this survey and was not mentioned at all in their list of second most important reasons (Table 29).

The discrepancy in the relative importance ascribed to Israeli bureaucracy in the two tables may result from differences in the way the questions were formulated and the responses tabulated. Table 29 summarizes the responses to open-ended questions in which the respondents were asked to identify the two most important reasons for their return, whereas Table 30 reports the respondents' evaluations of a preset list of possible reasons. Thus, Table 30 tends to

TABLE 29

Reported Reasons for Return (%)

Reason	Primary	Second Most Important
Professional opportunities	19.4	8.5
Societal criticisms	18.1	16.9
Economics	13.9	8.5
Personal	13.9	4.2
Family reunification	9.7	15.5
Educational opportunities	8.3	4.2
Housing	5.6	–
Commitment, end of immigrant rights	2.8	4.2
Social problems	2.8	2.8
Political criticisms	2.8	–
Bureaucracy	1.4	–
Desire for change	1.4	8.5
Army service	–	2.8
Children's adjustment	–	1.4
No answer	–	22.5
TOTAL	100.0	100.0
N=71	72*	71

*One respondent gave two reasons.

highlight the pervasiveness of certain problems, whereas Table 29 tends to indicate which problems were most acute.

Israeli bureaucracy and the desire for familial reunification are both chronic, widespread problems; hence their high showings in Table 30. Nevertheless, they are not acute difficulties; they are less important than those that actually prompted return, as Table 29 shows. A similar pattern was reported by Antonovsky and Katz in their study of pre-1967 American olim. Although bureaucracy was the issue about which the olim most commonly complained, it was found to be less significant than standard-of-living and health issues as the most serious problem.[16]

The respondents also distinguished between economic difficulties and professional opportunities. The latter, a reflection of the relative size and modernization of Israel, was cited by slightly more respondents than was economic difficulties. Although Engel and Jubas present similar distinctions among the important hypothetical reasons for return, the relative importance of the two factors is not consistent among the studies.

TABLE 30

Reasons for Returning to the U.S.
Rated as "Very or Somewhat Important" (%)

Familial*	
Reunification	66.2
Spouse's adjustment	44.2
Children's adjustment	16.6
	Overall mean 42.3
Instrumental*	
Income	45.1
Difficult daily life	45.1
Israeli bureaucracy	40.8
Living quarters	28.2
	Overall mean 39.8
Expressive*	
Sense of foreignness	45.1
Belonging in U.S.	31.0
Language difficulties	25.3
Size limitations of Israel	21.1
Difficulty making friends	12.7
Jewish life in Israel	12.7
	Overall mean 20.9
Security*	
General security tensions	18.3
Time commitment to Israel army	11.2
	Overall mean 14.8

*Categorization follows that of Dashefsky and Lazerwitz, "Role of Religious Identification," p. 272.

Another important discrepancy between Tables 29 and 30 concerns the impact of criticism of Israeli society on the decision to return. This emerged in Table 29 as a significant reason for returning, ranking high both in the lists of primary and second most important reason for returning. Perhaps "a sense of foreignness in Israel" (Table 30) incorporates those criticisms of Israeli society, and it ranks high even though it was classified in the expressive category among comparatively low-ranking motivations. Moreover, the reasons listed in the instrumental category may also have implied general criticisms of Israeli society. The four categories used in Table 30–familial, instrumental, expressive, and security–follow distinctions introduced by Dashefsky and Lazerwitz, who observed that among their small sample of forty-six returned olim, stated reasons for return clustered around these four themes. This pattern, with the same approximate importance attributed to each of the categories, repeated itself in the data presented here.

The shift from the Jewish concerns that seem to have inspired the respondents' aliya to the familial, economic, professional, and societal difficulties that appear to have impelled them to return was probably accompanied by a reevaluation of their lives in Israel. As shown in Table 28, among their reasons for aliya those that place the locus of motivation in the United States (minority status, assimilation) are less important than those that place the locus of motivation in Israel (Jewish life, Zionism, religious life). When it came to their return, however, the locus of motivation was in the country of emigration (Israel) rather than in that of immigration (the United States). A large plurality of the respondents (40.8 percent) stated that problems in Israel weighed more heavily in their decision to return than did attractions to the United States (21.1 percent). This is in contrast with motivations of the more typical Israeli emigres, *yordim*, for whom "whatever the range of 'push' factors . . . the 'pull' of America retains its historical efficacy and strength."[17] The finding, however, is consistent with that reported by Dashefsky and Lazerwitz in their study of American returnees.[18]

The interpretation that push factors have more significance than pull factors in the return is reinforced by comparing the preparations the respondents made prior to having left the United States for Israel with those made prior to having returned to the United States from Israel. As shown in Table 32, over 60 percent of the respondents said they had made serious arrangements for employment or study in Israel prior to leaving the United States. By contrast, nearly three-fourths (73.2 percent) reported that they had not made any arrangements for the United States at the time of their departure from Israel.

Preparations and the perceived push/pull factors highlight the different approaches the respondents took to their two moves. Since their initial migration to Israel was motivated by pull factors, they made plans for their future in Israel. Their return to the United States, on the other hand, was motivated by push factors and, therefore, there was more of an urgency in leaving and less time to plan what to do upon their return to the United States.

It may, however, be that the differences between their planning for the move to Israel and their lack of planning for their return are due to the fact that they were Americans who had been socialized in American society and culture. They may have felt that in moving to Israel, a new society and a new culture awaited them and, therefore,

179

TABLE 31

**Distribution of Push and Pull Factors
in Decision to Return**

Problems in Israel	40.8
Attraction of U.S.	21.1
Equal influence	14.1
No answer	23.9
TOTAL	99.9

they had to plan carefully for their successful integration into that environment. In contrast, they may have felt sufficiently familiar with conditions in the United States to be able to postpone planning until after they were back.

What about the considerations that played such an important role in the initial decision of many American Jews who go on aliya–the desire to fulfill their self-identities in a Jewish environment? Few of the returnees expressed dissatisfaction with Israel in this regard. How have their attitudes toward Judaism and Israel changed? Has there been a basic shift in the way they perceive and manifest their identity? Kevin Avruch has argued that American Jews who go on aliya place primary emphasis on the Jewish component of their identity, and both he and others suggest that, once in Israel, they become much more conscious of themselves as Americans.[19] Does their return to America suggest, therefore, that their experience in Israel displaced Jewishness as the primary component of their identity? If so, does this process continue after they return to the United States? How do the returnees fit into the American Jewish community?

TABLE 32

Arrangements Before Israel and Return (%)

Arrangements	Leaving for Israel	Returning to U.S.
Did nothing	35.2	73.2
Enrolled in education program	39.4	2.8
Made contacts, had job	21.1	23.9
No answer	4.2	–
TOTAL	99.9	99.9

TABLE 33

Synagogue Affiliation
Before and After Israel (%)

	Before	After
Orthodox	29.6	29.6
Conservative	28.2	32.4
Reform	5.6	1.4
Other	1.4	11.3
None	35.2	25.4
TOTAL	100.0	100.1

The data in this study indicate that the personal religious and Jewish communal commitments of the respondents increased somewhat after returning to the United States. As shown in Table 33, synagogue affiliation increased generally, particularly among the Conservative and Havurah[20] affiliates, although there was some

TABLE 34

Frequency of Synagogue Attendance
Before and After Israel (%)

	Before	After
At least weekly	25.4	36.6
At least monthly	18.3	15.5
5 to 10 times per year	19.7	14.1
High Holidays	16.9	21.1
Never	19.7	12.7
TOTAL	100.0	100.0

TABLE 35

Planned or Current Jewish Education
of Children of Returnees (%)

Day School	60.6
Supplementary school	29.6
Unsure	7.0
No answer	2.8
TOTAL	100.0

decline among the Reform affiliates. Likewise, synagogue attendance increased, most notably among those who attended services at least once a week (Table 34).

A further indication that the returnees maintained, if not intensified, their commitment to Judaism after their Israel experience can be seen in the patterns of Jewish education of their children. The high priority the returnees place on the Jewish education of their children is evident in the fact that more than 60 percent of them stated that they now, or plan to, enroll their children in Jewish day schools, and almost 30 percent stated that they now, or plan to, enroll their children in supplementary Hebrew schools (Table 35). This is in sharp contrast to the general American Jewish patterns of Jewish education in which some 60 percent of school age children receive no formal Jewish education, and of the 40 percent who do, 26.3 percent attend day schools and 49.2 percent attend supplementary schools.[21]

Although these patterns conform with the report of Dashefsky and Lazerwitz, who found that 53 percent of their respondents consider themselves more involved in the American Jewish community after their return from Israel,[22] the present survey does not provide sufficient evidence to conclude that this is the case, or that, where it is, the change was the direct result of the Israel experience. What respondents report at a later date about their previous values, beliefs, and behavior is not a reliable basis for any firm conclusions. And even if it is assumed that the respondents are accurate in their reports of their previous Jewish commitments and that, in fact, those commitments have intensified, this does not necessarily mean that they were influenced solely by their Israel experiences. These commitments may have intensified as part of the life-cycle process, as is typical for American Jews in their twenties. It is not unreasonable to assume that these same respondents might have had more intensified Jewish commitment even if they had never immigrated to Israel.

Questioned as to their relative comfort as Jews in America since their return, as compared to how they felt before their aliya, approximately 45 percent reported no change, and the other 55 percent was virtually split between those who now feel more comfortable and those who now feel less comfortable.

The same factor, Jewish identity, played a role both for those who said they now feel more comfortable and those who said they now feel less comfortable as Jews in the United States. Those who reported feeling more comfortable added that their participation in the American Jewish community was enhanced and that their pride

TABLE 36

**Jewish/Israel Activities and Feelings
Before and After Israel**

	More	Same	Less	An Answer	Total
Comfort as Jew in					
U.S.	28.2	45.1	26.8	–	100.1
Attention to Israeli news					
items	63.4	33.8	1.4	1.4	100.0
Positive attitude toward					
Israel	43.7	36.6	18.3	1.4	100.0
Centrality of Israel to					
own life	57.7	18.3	23.9	–	99.9

in their Jewishness had become more resolute. Those who reported being less comfortable said that they miss the Israeli environment and they experience more intense pressures in their effort to maintain their ethnic and religious life in America. For both groups, the apparent consequences for their Jewishness were similar: a heightened Jewish self-consciousness after their experience in Israel.

Despite the respondents' positive attitudes toward their Jewishness, it might have been expected that they had become somewhat disenchanted with Israel, as was the case with many of the *yordim,* emigres from Israel, interviewed by Zvi Sobel.[23] On the contrary, as Table 36 shows, for a majority (57.7 percent) Israel appears to have become more central to their lives than before they left for Israel, because they had made personal friends in Israel and because Israeli culture continues to influence their lives. Only a small minority (18.3 percent) indicated a less positive attitude toward Israel after their return. Respondents were also twice as likely as before to follow Israeli news closely. This may simply be the result of their familiarity with Israel, and not necessarily an affirmation of Israel's greater centrality in their lives. But in the context of all their others responses and statements, it does seem that their increased attention to Israeli news reports is part of the larger impact Israel has had on them.

The respondents said that their contributions to the United Jewish Appeal and their purchases of Israel Bonds have increased. Whereas only 57.7 percent had given to these organizations before making aliya, 73.2 percent became contributors after their return to America. Again, this may be more a function of the life cycle than a result of their experience in Israel. When queried about the extent of

TABLE 37
Zionist Self-identification
Before and After Israel (%)

	Before	After
Strong Zionist	36.6	33.8
Zionist	38.0	50.7
Non-Zionist	21.1	12.7
No opinion	4.2	2.8
TOTAL	99.9	100.0

their Zionist identification, a larger percentage than before considered themselves Zionists, though only slightly fewer viewed themselves as "strong Zionists."

An overwhelming majority (87.3 percent) believed that the American Jewish community should support aliya. And although over half disagreed with the statement "Every Jew should at least try living in Israel," the 40.8 percent who still held this view reflected a continued commitment to Israel. Asked what the chances were that they would again move to Israel in the future, 52.1 percent replied that there was either no chance or less than a fifty-fifty chance that they would do so. On the other hand, 43.7 percent stated that they were either certain of attempting aliya again or there was more than a fifty-fifty chance that they would do so.

Despite their own experiences, the vast majority of the respondents remained supportive of the value of aliya. Only a small minority (12.7 percent) stated that they would personally discourage others

TABLE 38
Probability of Reattempting Aliya

Probability	%
None	16.9
Less than 50–50	35.2
More than 50–50	26.8
Definite	16.9
Unsure	4.2
TOTAL	100.0

TABLE 39

Agreement or Disagreement with Aliya-related Statements (%)

Statement	Agree	Disagree	Not Applicable	Total
The American Jewish community should support aliya.	87.3	9.9	2.8	100.0
Every Jew should at least try living in Israel.	40.8	54.9	4.2	99.9
I would discourage a friend from making aliya.	12.7	80.3	7.0	100.0

from going on aliya. On the other hand, fully 87.3 percent stated that they felt the American Jewish community should support aliya.

The data from this survey and others suggest that there are major weaknesses in the existing organized aliya efforts. Some are related to promoting and supporting aliya within the American Jewish community, whereas others are related to the retaining of American olim in Israel, that is, reducing the return rate of American olim. These are some of the issues dealt with in Chapter 13. Before that, however, the issue of separation from family, which was cited as one of the major reasons for return migration, has another significant aspect to it, namely, that from the perspective of the parents in the United States whose children have not and may not be contemplating return migration. The plight and coping mechanisms of such parents are discussed in the next chapter.

12

Families Apart: Parents of American Olim

As was seen in the preceding chapter, family separation plays a significant role in the return of American olim to the United States. But more than 60 percent of American olim do remain in Israel. Since the majority of American olim are relatively young, it may be presumed that most have living parents who are, presumably, still in the United States. How do the parents of American olim deal with the separation between themselves and their children? What are their feelings about their children's aliya?

If there are difficulties in obtaining a representative sample of American immigrants in Israel, they pale in comparison with those involved in obtaining a representative sample of American parents of such olim. Because no study with such a sample exists, it was decided to use extant information and data, all of which is derived from members of the organization Parents of North American Israelis (PNAI), or as it was called until 1985, Association of Parents of American Israelis (APAI). This organization had its genesis with a trip to Israel by Nahum and Sylvia Weissman, a Riverdale, New York, couple whose daughter had immigrated to Israel. In August 1973, while visiting her, they contacted the Association of Americans and Canadians in Israel (AACI) to get names of other American parents in a similar situation. The AACI provided the Weissmans with a list of some thirty such parents who had, at one time or another, contacted the AACI office with requests for help for their children. When the Weissmans returned home, Nahum wrote to those thirty families and invited them to an informal meeting in his home. On Sunday, January 20, 1974, three couples with children in Israel who had responded positively to the invitation met in the Weissmans' home to discuss common experiences. From these beginnings APAI became a nationwide organization in both the United States and Canada, and within two years had a membership of more than a thousand people, the majority of whom lived in the New York metropolitan area.[1] According to Bernice Salzman of West Hartford, Connecticut, editor of PNAI's quarterly newsletter the *Bridge*, PNAI had some thirty-five hundred member families in forty-four chapters in the United States and Canada as of January 1987.[2]

The Weissmans and other spokespersons for the organization claim that PNAI is not a support group. They assert that PNAI was founded to create a big extended family for all of their children in Israel. In the words of Nahum Weissman, "If all the parents came together, we would become a huge family for all the children."[3] And as the 1984 convention chair, Barbara Entis of Boston, put it: "We don't view a parent whose child has moved to Israel as someone who needs sympathy. Our attitude is that *aliyah* is not some sort of tragedy that strikes a family. It's something that may require understanding and adjustment, but we're proud of it. We favor *aliyah*, we encourage it, and we try to help parents help their children make a success of it."[4]

Not all members of PNAI, however, feel the way Entis does, and many more did not feel that way prior to joining PNAI. As became apparent at some of the sessions of a national convention of PNAI, the aliya of children is invariably stressful and frequently traumatic for the parents. As Ruth Seligman learned, aliya "represents a different kind of separation. For some parents, it may represent rejection–of them, of America, of a value system and way of life they cherish and enjoy. Many are confused, unable to comprehend the reasons for the willingness to leave the comforts, conveniences and opportunities of America."[5]

A case in point is the reaction of Suzanne Frank of Washington to the aliya of her adult daughter: "When 26-year-old Wendy Frank first left Washington for Jerusalem . . . her mother, Suzanne, 'couldn't even think about her without bursting into tears.' Frank's support for Israel and her commitment to Zionism had its limits: 'I don't want to contribute my daughter. I can't imagine what would make a girl . . . with a comfortable life move to the other side of the world. I don't know if I will ever be able to accept that,' she laments."[6]

In order to get a better picture of the range of reactions of parents to their children's aliya, as well as the range of parental thoughts about what motivated their children's decision to immigrate to Israel, an American-Israeli sociologist, Ephraim Tabory, conducted a systematic study of PNAI members in 1984 and derived his sample from those who had preregistered for that year's convention in Jerusalem.[7] Although this is not a representative sample of all parents of North American immigrants to Israel, nor even of all PNAI members, it does indicate the range of feelings among those who came to Israel for the convention. One of Tabory's major findings was that although most stated their child immigrated because they wanted to live in Israel, 21 percent said that it was because their child's spouse wanted to. Few of the children were married to Israelis. The vast majority of the children had visited Israel before immigrating there; more than one-third stated that their children had spent at least a year in Israel prior to their aliya; and many of the parents believed that it was the previous visits and stays that attracted their children to immigrate to Israel. Tabory astutely observed:

> It is telling that visits to Israel are not seen as equivalent to visits to a European country, for example. Israel appears to be viewed by parents of North American Jews as having a special potential for attracting immigrants. Unlike the charm of any other tourist site, visits to Israel are therefore considered "risky" by parents in that they may lead to the migration of their children. . . . This even affects certain Jewish programs in the United States. Several directors of Jewish summer camps with strong Israel-oriented programs mentioned, in interviews, that they had to spend much time throughout the year convincing parents to allow their children to attend their camps. Parents were fearful that the programs might inspire their children to want to go to Israel.[8]

A perusal of past issues of the *Bridge* supports the sense that there are a significant number of parents who oppose their children's aliya. One recent issue, for example, contains an article titled "Proposal for a Program to Reduce Parental Opposition to Aliyah," written by a longtime director of the Metropolitan Detroit Jewish Community. Part of the problem, according to Irwin Shaw, is "the fact that parents who have children living in Israel are not generally looked upon with admiration or honor but rather with pity, as poor, 'unfortunate' people who have 'lost' their children or whose children have 'deserted' them. ('There must be something wrong either with the parents or with the children for this to have happened!' ")[9]

In another issue there is a summary of a lecture given at the 1984 PNAI convention in Israel titled "When Aliyah Conflicts with Parents' Wishes." Following a religio-philosophical analysis of aliya, the author, Debbie Weissman, who is a Judaic scholar and teacher living in Israel and who also happens to be the daughter of the founders of the PNAI, asserts:

> The really central question here is, why do the parents object to their child's Aliyah? If they require the assistance of the child because of their age or ill health, that is one thing. However, if they simply don't want their child to settle in Israel, but can manage without him or her (e.g., they have other children who can help them; in any case, the child would not live near them; they are in good health), then they may, in fact, be trying to exercise undue influence over their child's life. The selection from the *Shulchan Aruch* [Code of Jewish Law–ed.] shows us that Jewish law recognizes that children, too, have their own lives to lead.[10]

As a rule, Tabory found, the parents saw their children's aliya as motivated by pull factors–by attractions to Israel–rather than by push factors. But some stated that they really had no idea why their children wanted to immigrate to Israel. Tabory summarizes it:

> The impression that emanates from reading the complete set of questionnaires is that many parents are not really sure why their children decided to move. This feeling came across even more strongly during the meeting with parents in 1982. The impression, at the time, was that many of the persons who came to hear the lectures about Israeli society wanted to know what it is about Israel that attracted their children. Even though they say their children are Zionists and love Israel very much, they ask themselves why it is *their* children who actually made the move. This was dramatically stated by one parent who, in an interview at the 1984 conference, quite seriously said that he just didn't understand it. He had sent his son to Jewish schools, Jewish summer camps, and programs in Israel. So where did he go wrong, he asked, that his son later decided to leave his parents and move to Israel?[11]

There was an interesting distribution of reactions by parents to their children's aliya. Approximately one-third expressed only negative reactions, another third had ambivalent reactions–proud of and happy for their children though personally sad and lonely–and about one-third expressed no negative feelings. Thus, despite the title of Tabory's paper, the majority of the parents did not see their children's aliya as a "deviant" act. Even among those who expressed totally negative reactions–much more commonly among parents of female immigrants than of male immigrants–those reactions did not mean that they viewed their children as deviants. Some did not believe that aliya was a wise move for financial reasons, some for political reasons, and others because of a deep concern for their children's safety.[12] As strongly as they disagreed with their children's decision to immigrate and as upset as they were by it, there was no indication that they viewed their children as deviants. Nor is there any indication that these children are so viewed within the American Jewish community and within the larger American society.

Whether parents express positive, ambivalent, or negative reactions to their children's aliya, it seems reasonable to assume that they deeply feel the absence and the distance. They may be happy for and proud of their children, but they are still parents and, presumably, miss their children. Granted that it is typical for adult American Jewish children to live away from their parents.[13] But there is a very great difference between living in another city, or state, in the United States and living in another country so far away. Telephone rates are much more expensive, and it is more difficult to get through by telephone to Israel than it is to another location in the United States.

It seems reasonable to assume that it is easier for parents to accept and even be unambivalently happy about their children's aliya if the parents have the time, resources, and energy to travel to Israel and visit with their children and even to bring them back to the United States once or twice a year. But many parents cannot afford to do so. Air travel to Israel is considerably more expensive than domestic flights in the United States, even coast-to-coast flights. Flying time, New York to Israel nonstop, is a minimum of ten hours, and most flights take several hours longer, especially if one does not live in the New York metropolitan area. And it can take anywhere from a week to more than three weeks for letters between the United States and Israel to arrive, if they do at all. How do the parents and their children cope with this situation?

Despite the greater cost and inconveniences involved in telephone communication between the United States and Israel, these families do rely on the telephone, regardless of the cost. They quickly learn what the rates are for the various times and try to schedule themselves accordingly. Given the time difference between the

United States and Israel, which generally ranges between seven hours in the eastern time zone to ten hours in the Pacific time zone, the cheapest rate may require either getting up in the middle of the night or calling someone when it is the middle of the night for them. Since Israel also has different rates for overseas calls at different times–on a call from Israel to the eastern time zone in the United States the least expensive rate applies between 1:00 and 7:00 A.M. every morning–the ordeal is the same regardless of who places the call. Also, one quickly learns that precisely at those times when they most want to speak with their children in Israel, most commonly on holidays, there are many others calling there as well. Getting through at those times is usually a test of endurance. But given the circumstances, parents and children learn to adapt.

All of this assumes, of course, that the children who made aliya have telephones. But such is often not the case. Although Israel has one of the highest proportions of telephone sets per population and one of the highest ratios of residence lines per total access lines in all of Asia and Africa, it still averages only twenty to forty telephone sets per one-hundred population.[14] As an organization, PNAI aims to become an important lobby and has on its agenda, among other things, lobbying for telephones for olim.[15]

Although Tabory makes no mention of it, one of the anxieties some American parents of olim experience is that they will not intimately know their grandchildren or be able to communicate with them. In fact, it is most commonly the communication problem that causes the lack of intimacy. Also, as was seen in the last chapter, the desire for family reunification plays a large role in the return of American olim. Not infrequently, young adults immigrate to Israel anticipating no serious personal problems because of the distance between themselves and their parents in the United States. Later, however, especially after they have children, they may strongly feel the absence of close contact between their parents and their children. They may regret that their children are growing up not really knowing grandparents. Many American olim, therefore, for this and other reasons make a determined effort to teach their children to become fluent in English. It does not guarantee that the children will be close to their grandparents, but it does increase the possibilities.

Many parents of olim have also adapted to the fact that air travel between the United States and Israel comes at considerable financial and physical expense. They rearrange their budgets in such a way as to make it possible for them to visit their children or else bring their children on a visit to them. Accordingly, PNAI has been actively involved in obtaining various related benefits for their members, such as airline discounts and the "third bag privilege" on El Al Israel Airlines, a benefit that became effective in June 1983, which entitled members to take one additional piece of luggage per flight ticket, the assumption being that they were bringing goods to their children who had immigrated to Israel.[16] Although this privilege was canceled as of June 1984, allegedly due to airline industry regulations, the organization promised to try to have it reinstated.[17] PNAI has also actively been involved in a campaign to rescind the exit travel tax imposed by the government of Israel. It argues that such a tax is an unfair burden on the families of immigrants who wish to visit relatives who are outside of Israel and thus also serves as a further hindrance to aliya.[18]

Another effort by PNAI to help parents of olim spend time with their children in Israel is the publication of short-term rentals in Israel. An up-to-date listing of such rentals is published fairly regularly in the *Bridge*, as are bread and breakfast services and HOMTEL, a home and hotel network in Israel.

PNAI has also established an emergency loan fund that is available to children of PNAI members. One of the purposes of this fund is to enable immigrants to visit their parents in the United States for health or injury-related reasons. The loan, which is limited to the cost of one round-trip airline ticket to the United States or Canada, is interest free and repayable in dollar equivalents within up to three years.

Aside from the more formal network of PNAI, many parents of olim, whether or not they are members of that organization, have developed their own informal networks of communication and, when necessary, moral support. They find out who is flying to Israel and attempt to send letters and small packages for their children with that person. The regular postal service is relatively slow and unreliable; thus if someone flying to Israel mails a letter upon landing in Israel, it will usually arrive at its destination much quicker than if sent through international post. It is even quicker and more reliable to have the traveler call the children in Israel and have them pick up the letter or small package. This, obviously, can only be done if the traveler will be in the same city in which the children live and if the children can be reached by telephone, both of which are frequently the case. Thus, it is quite common for American parents of olim to have on hand a sufficient supply of Israeli stamps–those without the monetary denomination printed on them are best since they automatically increase in value with inflation–and tokens for the public telephones in Israel, which also automatically increase in value with inflation. The less the inconvenience travelers will have in delivering the letter or small package in Israel, the greater the likelihood that they will agree to take it. Parenthetically, it should be noted that the olim, too, frequently develop the same type of informal delivery networks. Indeed, some of them have even been formalized. For example, there is a North American letter drop at the Jerusalem office of the Association of Americans and Canadians in Israel. It should also be pointed out that the reliability of this informal postal system is as good as the people taking the mail, and one is not infrequently disappointed to learn that the designated traveler either did not mail the letters or did so only after a long delay, in which case the formal international postal service may have been better.

Although the majority of the recent American olim are Orthodox, few of PNAI's three thousand member families are. According to Tabory and journalist Matthew Nesvisky, the reasons for this are rooted in the different perspectives toward aliya of those who are Orthodox and those who are not. In his report of the organization's tenth anniversary convention, held in Jerusalem in 1984, Nesvisky wrote: "It was generally agreed that Orthodox parents are less inclined to feelings of 'betrayal' when their children make *aliyah,* since they understand this as fulfillment of a *mitzvah,* and the Orthodox children themselves have less of an 'adjustment' problem since they are still moving in a familiar pattern of life."[19]

Tabory makes a similar point when he suggests: "The social circle of parents of migrants who are themselves Orthodox Jews may not view migration to Israel as a 'deviant' act. Orthodox Jews mention the return to Zion in their regular prayers, and settlement in Israel, according to some theological authorities, is a religious commandment. Their primary reference groups, ostensibly other Orthodox persons, may view migration to Israel not only as not deviant, but as almost normative."[20]

It should be added that, even if the Orthodox parents do feel betrayed and that their children's aliya is deviant, they would still be less likely to join PNAI because that would be seen as a public statement of something that runs counter to Orthodox ideology. Those parents, therefore, would tend to keep their hurt to themselves rather than risk provoking the indignation and condemnation of their primary reference group and their closest friends, their fellow Orthodox Jews.

Although separation from family is a significant issue–as was discussed in Chapter 11, it is often cited as a reason for the return migration of American olim–and is probably one of the reasons the American aliya rate is not higher, there is no evidence that it plays a major role in determining the aliya rate. As has been stressed throughout this work, there are many complex push and pull factors involved, and although Jewish identity as measured by religiosity appears to be most significant, even it is not a sufficient cause for aliya.

The final chapter of this book considers aliya not from the individual but from the communal perspective. It looks at the communal impact of aliya, evaluates existing communal aliya efforts, and speculates on the prospects for strengthening those efforts and improving the results.

13

Aliya and the Priorities
of the American Jewish Community

There seems no reason to doubt that the major determinants of the
size of American Jewish immigration to Israel are conditions both in
the United States and in Israel. Put simply, American Jews, individu-
ally and collectively, are comfortable in the United States materially,
physically, and in their ability to express their Jewishness, and they
do not feel impelled to sacrifice their comfort by immigrating to
Israel, where material conditions are obviously much more restricted.
American Jews are undoubtedly aware of both the significant rate of
American Jews who went on aliya only to return to America and the
relatively high rate of Israelis who emigrate from Israel, many of
whom settle in the United States. Nevertheless, it seems reasonable
to assume that there would be an increase in American aliya if there
were some fundamental changes in the ways in which organized aliya
efforts function both institutionally and interpersonally.

Institutionally, aliya policies and efforts are designed and oper-
ated by the Aliya Department of the World Zionist Organization
(WZO). Although it may be argued that that organization represents
the collective will of affiliated Zionists both in Israel and the world
over, the fact is that the headquarters of the WZO are in Jerusalem,
the Zionist congresses and other bureaucratically important meetings
take place in Jerusalem, Israelis are disproportionately represented in
decision-making positions, and the heads of the organization's various departments are all Israelis. Much has been argued about the
validity of this structure, but the point here is simply to clarify the

structure, not to debate its validity. The Aliya Department of the WZO appoints directors for its aliya departments in various countries and emissaries, *shlichim,* to service aliya needs on the regional and local levels. All of these appointees are Israelis who volunteer to serve in Diaspora communities for two or three years. One consequence of this arrangement is that, essentially, all of the policies and programs designed to stimulate and foster aliya from the Diaspora to Israel are designed and implemented not by the communities of potential olim but by Israelis who, by definition, are outsiders.

The origins of this arrangement are to be found both in Israel and in the Diaspora communities of Western countries. On the one hand, both before the establishment of the State of Israel and during its early years, Jewish leaders in the Diaspora communities of the West were more than happy to leave the task of aliya promotion to the WZO and Israelis. After all, they were comfortable in their Diaspora communities and did not want to become involved in activities that might put their loyalty to their own countries and communities in question. Although there was greater receptivity to aliya after the Six-Day War, the situation concerning aliya promotion did not change because, by then, the WZO had grown suspicious of Diaspora leaders, did not believe that they would sincerely promote aliya, and became very protective over the domain of what they deemed to be the heart of Zionism, aliya. The WZO came to believe that it had a rightful monopoly over aliya promotion. All of this presented problems and complications on several levels.

Beginning with the emissary, or *shaliach,* him or herself, the very fact that this person is an outsider presents difficulties in his or her ability to carry out the assignment productively. Israel and the United States are very different countries, and Jewishness, including Judaism, is institutionalized and organized differently in Israel than it is in the United States. All too often, the shaliach arrives in the United States with little knowledge about American culture and even less knowledge of and more disdain for the American Jewish community. It frequently takes about a year to acquire a sufficient working understanding of the culture and institutions and another year to become acclimated to working within the American Jewish sphere; by then, the shaliach is already looking forward to a return to Israel and beginning to wind down activities here. Obviously this is not always the case and, when feasible, the Aliya Department does attempt to recruit American olim as shlichim; but such instances are the exception rather than the rule.

Not only are the shlichim often unfamiliar with important aspects of American culture and the American Jewish community, they are also frequently unfamiliar with important aspects of Israeli society and culture, such as specific regulations, procedures, and patterns dealing with housing, employment, and education.[1] As Gerald Berman found in his study of experiences with and opinions about shlichim:

> A full one-half of the respondents complained about the information they received as being vague, inaccurate, insufficient, etc., and one-fourth referred to the indifferent attitude of the shaliach regarding the respondent's aliyah. Other areas of dissatisfaction mentioned somewhat frequently were poor handling of various types of arrangements (visas, housing, shipping, loans, and others), availability and inaccessibility of the shaliach, and personal qualities of the shaliach.[2]

Aliya is not the only area in which the WZO utilizes shlichim. Some are sent by the Youth and Hechalutz Department to service local Zionist youth movements; others are sent by that department as community shlichim to provide the Israel dimension in the various programs of the local Jewish community; and teacher-shlichim are sent by the WZO religious and secular educational departments to serve in local Jewish schools. All told, the WZO sends some 277 shlichim to North America for two-or three-year assignments. In addition, the WZO sends another 455 shlichim to other countries. And providing shlichim is only one of the many functions of the WZO both outside of Israel and within. Inside Israel, the activities and programs of the WZO are carried out by an arm called the Jewish Agency for Israel.

In February 1981 the Board of Governors of the Jewish Agency met at the Dan Caesaria Hotel and wrestled with the slow pace of progress being made in resolving a number of serious organizational problems that had been plaguing the agency for years. These problems were felt to be particularly acute by the agency's "non-zionist" partners, that is, the heads of Jewish community federations and other fund-raising institutions in the Diaspora, especially in the United States. Among the problems experienced by the Diaspora partners was that they were not true partners. They expressed a sense of powerlessness and decried the Israeli domination over the agency and their own inability to determine policy and programs in areas over which they officially had decision-making powers. As a result of this meeting, the Board of Governors undertook an form of internal review that came to be known as the "Caesaria Process." The board was mandated to carefully review the operation of the agency and to arrive at a systematic method of changes with respect to its overall governance, management, and budget, as well as with the ways in which it performs its functions of education and aliya.[3]

One of the commissions established within the context of the Caesaria Process, and the one that most directly bears on the subject of this work, was the Commission on Aliya. Co-chaired by Irwin Field, who had served as general chairman and president of the United Jewish appeal before becoming chairman of the United Israel Appeal, and Yosef ("Yoske") Shapiro of the WZO Aliya Department, who was also political activist from Israel's National Religious Party, the commission declared that aliya from all countries, free or not, "is of equal importance to individuals, to Diaspora Jewish communities and to Israel."[4] In order to improve the effectiveness of the WZO aliya efforts, the commission recommended what might be paraphrased as the "maximum feasible participation" of Diaspora communities, in the form of Jewish federations, in those efforts.[5] Within the agency itself, the Commission on Aliya recommended that an interdepartmental committee be established to streamline aliya efforts by coordinating all aliya resources and activities. But the major recommendation was the one mentioned above, which called on the Jewish communities in the United States and elsewhere in the free Diaspora to take upon themselves greater responsibility in promoting aliya and in providing assistance to olim from their respective communities. Within that context, the Council of Jewish Federations undertook to help establish five aliya pilot projects–in Atlanta, Los Angeles, Miami, Milwaukee, and Toronto–with the active participation of the Jewish federation leaders in those communities. How much the WZO and Jewish federations will actually cooperate and the impact of these pilot projects remain to be seen. At the very least, the principle of mutual responsibility for aliya has been established.

The Caesaria Process was not the only recent critique of the Jewish Agency and the WZO. Stemming from the tremendous expense incurred in maintaining the vast framework within which the shlichim function, and the growing number of complaints from both the United States and Israel about the WZO system of shlichim, in September 1984 the chairman of the WZO Executive, Arye Dulzin, appointed a commission, headed by the former chief justice of the Israeli Supreme Court, Moshe Landau, to study the system and to recommend changes. Slightly more than a year later, in December 1985, the Landau Commission submitted its report, which called for sweeping changes to clean up what it found to be the crisis situation in which the institution of Zionist *shlichut* ("emissaryism") finds itself.[6] Many of the specified weaknesses in the system are related to issues other than aliya shlichim. With respect to aliya shlichim, the commission was critical of political pressures that are frequently brought in order to have a particular candidate sent as a shaliach. The Americans on the WZO Executive related the most common complaints of the system as it functions in the United States, along with their recommendations. According to Bernice Tannenbaum, chairman of the WZO–American Section, there was a consensus on nine points:

1. There are too many shlichim based at 515 Park Avenue (the headquarters of the WZO–American Section, in New York City), and some of them do clerical work rather than being out in the field.

2. Each shaliach may cost between $75,000 and $100,000 annually. Local personnel might be able to perform much of their activity at least as effectively and at less cost.

3. Most shlichim are not sufficiently fluent in English when they arrive, and it takes many of them a full year before they can become effective linguistically. Fluency in English should be a basic criterion of selection.

4. Shlichim are not adequately briefed prior to their arrival and frequently have no chance to meet with their predecessors. They often have to start learning the job from scratch.

5. Appointment by political party affiliation is an ineffective selection basis. Appointments should be made on the basis of personal and professional qualifications.

6. Whenever possible, shlichim should represent all of WZO's interests within a community, rather than serving as compartmentalized, single-function appointees.

7. Shlichim often manifest lack of knowledge about the structure and style of the American Jewish community, and about the religious and cultural pluralism that exists in the United States. They come with religious and political biases that limit their effectiveness to only those who believe as they do. Shlichim should be intensively educated about totality of life in the United States prior to their arrival.

8. Meetings in Israel with American olim from the community to be served would help the shaliach better understand the problems of that particular community.

9. Frequently, the number of shlichim is out of proportion to the number of people they will be serving.[7]

As of this writing, it is still too early to determine whether the recommendations of the Landau Commission will actually be implemented by the WZO. But even if one were to forget the long history of that organization and assume that they will be implemented, it is doubtful that any or all of the changes will have an impact on the rate of American aliya. The reality is that even many of the constituent organizations of the American Zionist Federation (AZF), the regional branch of the WZO, do not actively promote aliya. Most pay only lip service to it, and some don't do even that much. It is, thus, not mere coincidence that in conjunction with the AZF's First Zionist Assembly, in January 1987, the AZF produced a button that read: "Real Zionists Pay Dues." Manifestly, this slogan was part of the rhetoric involved in the campaign to enlist new members to Zionist organizations, which was one facet of the political struggle that played itself out in the subsequent World Zionist Congress. But the slogan also revealed a basic truth of American Zionism, namely, to be a "real Zionist," one need not go on aliya or even be committed to aliya as an imperative; one need only pay dues to an American Zionist organization. As that assembly turned out, the direct involvement of such aliya activist organizations as Tehillah, Telem, Hamagshimim, Tagar, the North American Aliya Movement, as well as the leadership of the Israel Aliya Center, resulted in the AZF's coordinating one of the largest and most explicitly aliya-oriented national conferences in its history. If it takes such pressure to move official Zionist organizations to clearly affirm and support aliya, it would indeed be surprising if those that are not officially Zionist were to support aliya.

It is difficult to imagine that aliya will ever be a high-priority item on the American Jewish communal agenda, and for the same reasons it seems highly improbable that there will be any radical increases in the numbers of American Jews who go on aliya. Most American Jews probably agree that to be strongly aliya-oriented entails, as Eisenstadt said of immigration in general, the sense of some measure of inadequacy in the present setting, the United States. They do not feel any inadequacies in the United States or, at least, any that would not be at least equally present in Israel. Moreover, the heads of most American Jewish organizations probably resist publicly professing support for aliya, lest they be accused of being less than completely loyal to the United States and lest their organization lose its tax-exempt status. Until recently, the lack of communal involvement in aliya promotion was legitimated on the grounds of not wishing to weaken American Jewry by helping Israel siphon off the best of the future leadership of the American Jewish community. Explicitly or implicitly, American aliya was depicted as potentially helping Israel drain off many of the most promising potential leaders of the American Jewish community, especially in light of data showing that those who go on aliya invariably have high levels of Jewish and secular education and strong Jewish commitments. The fears of the communal leadership were, thus, analogous to the perceived "brain drain" of British doctors by the United States during the 1950s and 1960s,[8] and the more recently discussed brain drain of Israelis who travel to study in the United States.[9] The fact that the available empirical evidence suggested that the impact of the so-called brain drain on England and other European countries was much less than initially anticipated[10] did not cause the leaders of American Jewry to be any more supportive of American aliya.

With the Caesaria Process and the launching of the five pilot aliya projects by the Council of Jewish Federations, the fears about the negative impact of American aliya on the American Jewish community were laid to rest. For the first time aliya was officially defined as strengthening rather than weakening American Jewry. And as the evidence presented throughout this book suggests, this new official definition of aliya as a factor that strengthens, rather than weakens, the Americans Jewish community is in fact correct. American Jews who go on aliya constitute a unique migratory movement of the free and innovative type who tend to retain their ties with friends and relatives in the United States. They also tend to retain and even strengthen their self-identification as Americans. As an elite group in Israel, they have the potential for introducing American norms and values into Israeli society and thereby reducing the culture gap between American Jewry and Israel. In a variety of other ways, they increase the ties between American Jews and Israel, which in turn tends to increase the Jewish identification and communal involvement of those American Jews. And as was discussed in Chapter 11, if and when American olim undergo return migration to the United States, they become assets to the Jewish community within which they dwell. Whether the intentions of American Jewish communal leaders, in their new expressions of support for aliya, were in fact sincere remains to be seen. If the past is any indication, it may well be that their pronouncements of support for increased American aliya are little more than the consequence of their strong reality-based awareness that aliya from the United States will probably remain small in any event, so there is nothing to fear in supporting it.

Even with the most sincere of intentions and the strongest moral and material support for aliya, however, it seems reasonable to predict that there will not be any dramatic changes in the patterns of American aliya. American Jewish communal support will not convince anyone without the strong desire to do so to undertake aliya. And most American Jews do not have that strong desire, both because of their structural and cultural ties to American society and because of the structural and cultural realities in Israeli society. But if nothing else, communal aliya supports enable those who wish to undertake aliya to realize their dreams.

Notes

Introduction

1. William Petersen, "A General Typology of Immigration," *American Sociological Review* 23, no. 3 (June 1958):258.

2. Dennis H. Wrong, *Population and Society*, 3rd ed. (New York: Random House, 1967), p. 88.

3. G. Beijer, "Modern Patterns of International Migratory Movements," in *Migration*, ed. J. A. Jackson (Cambridge: Cambridge University Press, 1969), p. 48.

4. Petersen, "A General Typology of Immigration," pp. 256–66.

5. Ibid., p. 258.

6. Ibid., pp. 263–64.

7. Ada W. Finifter, "American Emigration," *Society* 13, no. 5 (July–August 1976):30–36.

8. I have discussed all of this at length in my book *America's Jews in Transition* (Philadelphia: Temple University Press, 1983).

9. S. N. Eisenstadt, *The Absorption of Immigrants* (London: Routledge & Kegan Paul, 1954), pp. 1–2.

10. Martin Mayer, *Teachers' Strike: New York, 1968* (New York: Harper & Row, 1969).

11. Sergio DellaPergola, "On the Differential Frequency of Western Migration to Israel," in *Studies in Contemporary Jewry*, ed. Jonathan Frankel (Bloomington: Indiana University Press, 1984), 1:292–315; Albert I. Goldberg, "A New Look at Aliyah Influences among North American Jews," *Jewish Journal of Sociology* 27, no. 2 (December 1985):81–102; Yitzhak Berman, "Immigration to Israel: Ideology vs. Reality," *Forum* no. 50 (Winter 1983–84):25–30.

12. J. A. Jackson, "Migration–Editorial Introduction," in Jackson, *Migration*, p. 5.

13. E. G. Ravenstein, "The Laws of Migration," *Journal of the Royal Statistical Society* 48, no. 2 (June 1885): 167–227; and 52, no. 2 (June 1889):241–301.

14. Frank Bovenkerk, *The Sociology of Return Migration: A Bibliographic Essay* (The Hague: Martinus Nijhoff, 1974), p. 8.

15. Ibid.

16. Ibid., pp. 33–35.

17. P. Neal Ritchey, "Explanations of Migration," *Annual Review of Sociology* 2 (1976): 363–404.

18. Ibid., p. 399.

Chapter 1

1. Babylonian Talmud, *Ketubot,* 110b. This passage, in and of itself, was not taken to be a statement of religious law, and there is some disagreement among the classic medieval codifiers of traditional Jewish law, halakhah, as to whether there is now a religious obligation to leave the Diaspora and relocate to the Holy Land. Nachmanides (1194–1270) lists this obligation in his enumeration of the prescriptive and proscriptive laws in the Pentateuch; Maimonides (1135–1204) does not list it in his enumeration, and there is some question as to whether he considered it a biblically derived or rabbinically derived obligation; the Tosafist rabbi Chaim Cohen (ca. 1150–1200) claims that today there is no binding obligation to live in Eretz Israel. For an in-depth analysis, from the perspective of halakhah, of the contemporary obligation of aliya, see Zvi Glatt, *Meafar Kumi* (From the Dust Arise) (Jerusalem: Keren Zvi Menachem, n.d. [ca. 1986]).

2. A compendium of homiletic passages in the Talmud, collected and edited by the medieval rabbi Shimon Hadarshan. The passage cited is found in the section on Deuteronomy 12:29.

3. Abraham Joshua Heschel, *Israel: An Echo of Eternity* (New York: Farrar, Straus & Giroux, 1969), pp. 54–55.

4. Yitzhak F. Baer, *Galut* (New York: Schocken Books, 1947). See also Arnold M. Eisen, *Galut: Modern Jewish Reflection on Homelessness and Homecoming* (Bloomington: Indiana University Press, 1986).

5. The father of the opponents of Chasidism, the Gaon, Rabbi Elijah of Vilna, will be discussed in Chapter 2, below, since his beliefs with respect to messianism and Eretz Israel fostered an actual movement of settlement in the land.

6. A people of Mongolian origin who occupied territory in the vicinity of the Ukraine and who, according to lore, ultimately converted to Judaism.

7. Judah Halevi, *The Kuzari: An Argument for the Faith of Israel*, trans. Hartwig Hirschfeld (New York: Schocken Books, 1964), pp. 88–101.

8. Ibid., pp. 99–100.

9. Ibid., p. 293.

10. Ibid., pp. 293–95.

11. Ibid., p. 295.

12. "My Heart is in the East," in Heinrich Brody, ed., *Selected Poems of Jehudah Halevi* (Philadelphia: Jewish Publication Society of America, 1952), p. 2.

13. Ibid., p. 3. The entire poem is on pages 3–7.

14. Yitzhak Baer, *A History of the Jews in Christian Spain* (Philadelphia: Jewish Publication Society of America, 1961), 1:67–77.

15. For a discussion of some of the philosophical differences between Maimonides and Rabbi Yehuda Halevi, see David Hartman, *Maimonides: Torah and Philsophic Quest* (Philadelphia: Jewish Publication Society of America, 1976), p. 264, n. 57, and p. 267, n. 73.

16. Maimonides, *The Commandments,* vol. 1, *The Positive Commandments,* trans. and ed. Charles B. Chavel (New York: Soncino Press, 1967), pp. 159–62.

17. Ibid., pp. 160–61.

18. Ibid., p. 161.

19. *Tshuvot Chatam Sofer: Yoreh Deah* (Chatam Sofer, *Responsa: Yoreh Deah*), responsum 234 (New York: M. P. Press, 1958), p. 95a. See also Yaacov Halevi Filber, *Ayelet Hashachar* (Jerusalem: privately published, 5736 [1976]), p. 28.

20. See, e.g., in *The Code of Maimonides,* book 3, *The Book of Seasons,* trans. Solomon Gandz and Hyman Klein (New Haven, Conn.: Yale University Press, 1961), "The Sabbath," VI:11, p. 35; book 4, *The Book of Women,* trans. Isaac Klein (1971), "Marriage," XIII:19, 20, p. 86; book 8, *The Book of Temple Service,* trans. Mendell Lewittes (1957), "The Temple," I:3, p. 5, II:1, p. 10, and VII:7, pp. 30–31; book 12, *The Book of Acquisition,* trans. Isaac Klein (1951), "Slaves," VIII:9–11, p. 276; book 14, *The Book of Judges,* trans. Abraham M. Hershman (1949), "Kings and Wars," V:6–12, pp. 217–19.

21. The exact nature of that obligation, according to Maimonides, is debated. See Glatt, *Meafar Kumij* and Yaacov Halevi Filber, *Ayelet Hashachar.*

22. Gershom G. Scholem, *On Kabbalah and Its Symbolism* (New York: Schocken Books, 1965), pp. 158–204; idem, *The Messianic Idea in Judaism, and Other Essays on Jewish Spirituality* (New York: Schocken Books, 1971), pp. 335–40; Arnold L. Goldsmith, *The Golem Remembered, 1909–1980: Variations of a Jewish Legend* (Detroit: Wayne State University Press, 1981).

23. On the Maharal and his thought, see Byron L. Sherwin, *Mystical Theology and Social Dissent: The Life and Works of Judah Loew of Prague* (Rutherford, N.J.: Fairleigh Dickinson University Press and Associated University Presses, 1982); Aaron Mauskopf, *The Religious Philosophy of the Maharal of Prague,* 2d ed. (New York: Bernard Morgenstern, 1966).

24. Gershom Scholem, *Kabbalah* (New York: New York Times Books, Quadrangle, 1974), p. 77.

25. The book was translated into English as *The Mitzvah Candle* (Jerusalem: Ben-Aryeh International, 1977).

26. Ibid., pp. 3–82.

27. Ibid., pp. 85–93.

28. Judah Loew ben Bezalel, *Netzach Israel* (Tel Aviv: Pardes, 1955), p. 4.

29. Ibid., pp. 7–23.

30. Ibid., p. 24.

31. The best, most comprehensive biography of Rabbi Nachman is Arthur Green, *Tormented Master: A Life of Rabbi Nahman of Bratslav* (New York: Schocken Books, 1981). For a detailed analysis of that journey, see pp. 63–93.

32. Ibid., esp. pp. 94–134.

33. Quoted in Simcha Raz, *Hasidic Sayings of R. Nachman of Bratslav* (in Hebrew) (Jerusalem: Keter, 1986), p. 51.

34. Ibid., p. 53.

35. Ibid., p. 50.

36. Ibid., p. 58.

37. Ibid., p. 54.

38. Ibid., pp. 58–59.

39. For descriptions of Eretz Israel at that time, see Benjamin of Tudela, *The Itinerary of Benjamin of Tudela*, trans. Marcus Nathan Adler (London, 1907; reprint, New York: Phillip Feldheim, n.d. [ca. 1965]), pp. 18–29; Petachia of Ratisbon, "The Travels of Rabbi Petachia of Ratisbon," in *Jewish Travellers: A Treasury of Travelogues from 9 Centuries*, ed. Elkan Nathan Adler, 2d ed. (New York: Hermon Press, 1966), pp. 64–91.

40. Judah Al-Harizi, *Tahkemoni*, trans. Victor Emanuel Reichert (Jerusalem: R. H. Hacohen Press, 1973), 2:147–48.

41. The entire episode of the Tosafist aliya is systematically analyzed in Ephraim Kanarfogel, "The Aliyah of 'Three Hundred Rabbis' in 1211: Tosafist Attitudes toward Settling in the Land of Israel," *Jewish Quarterly Review* 76, no. 3 (January 1986): 191–215.

42. Yitzhak Baer, *A History of the Jews in Christian Spain*, (Philadelphia: Jewish Publication Society of America, 1961), 2:158–62. The impact of messianism on aliya and Zionism in the nineteenth and twentieth centuries will be analyzed in Chapter 2, below.

43. Ibid., p. 310.

44. Martin Gilbert, *Atlas of Jewish History*, 3rd ed. (New York: Dorset Press, 1985), p. 29.

45. Scholem, *Kabbalah*, p. 67.

46. Ibid., p. 74.

47. Max L. Margolis and Alexander Marx, *A History of the Jewish People* (Philadelphia: Jewish Publication Society of America, 1927), pp. 570–71.

48. Israel Heilprin, *Haaliyot Harishonot shel Hachasidim Leeretz Israel* (The First Immigrations of the Chasidim to Eretz Israel) (Jerusalem: Schocken, 1946), pp. 16–18. The extent to which the rise of Chasidism was influenced by messianism and Chasidism emphasized Eretz Israel has been widely discussed and debated. See, e.g., Isaiah Tishby, "The Messianic Idea and the Messianic Trends in the Growth of Hasidism" (in Hebrew), *Zion* 32, nos. 1–2 (1967):1–45; Martin Buber, *The Origin and Meaning of Hasidism*, ed. and trans. Maurice Friedman (New York: Harper Torchbooks, 1966), pp. 202–18; Rivka Shatz-Oppenheimer, *Quietistic Elements in Eighteenth Century Hasidic Thought (in Hebrew) (Jerusalem: Magnes Press, 1980), pp. 168–77*; Scholem, *The Messianic Idea in Judaism*, pp. 176–202.

49. Heilprin, *Haaliyot*, pp. 13–16.

50. Ibid., pp. 20–37.

51. Ibid., p. 37.

52. Note that in the 1830s Rabbi Moses Sofer dealt with a four-part question regarding the request of the Prushim that all Jews in the Holy Land, including the Chasidim, tax themselves for the support of the Prushim. See *Tshuvot Chatam*

Sofer: Choshen Mishpat (Chatam Sofer, *Responsa: Choshen Mishpat*), responsum 12 (New York: M. P. Press, 1958), pp. 8b–9b (18–20).

Chapter 2

1. See, e.g., *Babylonian Talmud, Tractate Sanhedrin,* 97a–99a.

2. Ibid., 97b.

3. Maimonides, *Mishneh Torah, Hilkhot Melakhim* 12:2.

4. Abba Hillel Silver, *A History of Messianic Speculation in Israel: From the First through the Seventeenth Centuries* (New York: Macmillan, 1927); Julius H. Greenstone, *The Messiah Idea in Jewish History* (Philadelphia: Jewish Publication Society of America, 1943), esp. chap. 6; Yoseph Shapiro, *Bishvilei Hageulah* (In the Paths of the Redemption) (Tel Aviv: Lewin-Epstein, 1946), vol. 2, chap. 17.

5. In addition to the works cited in n. 4, above, see Gershom Scholem, *The Messianic Idea in Judaism, and Other Essays on Jewish Spirituality* (New York: Schocken Books, 1971); R. J. Zwi Werblowsky, "Messianism in Jewish History," in *Jewish Society through the Ages,* ed. H. H. Ben-Sasson and S. Ettinger (New York: Schocken Books, 1971), pp. 30–45. Yeshayahu Leibowitz argues that Maimonides only placed belief in the Messiah among the essential creeds of Judaism for the masses, in order that they remain loyal to Judaism's religious obligations. Yeshayahu Leibowitz, *Faith, History, and Values* (in Hebrew) (Jerusalem: Akademon, 1982), p. 95. Many of Leibowitz's interpretations, along with his politics, are highly unique and controversial. Some of the best critiques of his work appear in Ch. Ben-Yeroucham and Chaim E. Kolitz, eds., *Negation for Negation's Sake: Versus Yeshayahu Leibowitz* (in Hebrew) (Jerusalem: El Hashorashim, 1983). Even if Leibowitz is correct, the fact remains that the people–scholars and the masses–retained a strong belief in the Messiah; messianism was an integral part of Jewish religio-culture.

6. Jacob Katz, *Jewish Nationalism: Essays and Studies* (in Hebrew) (Jerusalem: Zionist Library, 1983), p. 310. For an account of the strong messianic anticipation among Yemenite Jewry during the nineteenth century, see Yehuda Nini, *Yemen and Zion* (in Hebrew) (Jerusalem: Zionist Library, 1982), pp. 142–59.

7. *Tractate Sanhedrin* 99a.

8. *Zohar* I:117a.

9. Arye Morgenstern, *Messianism and the Settlement of Eretz-Israel* (in Hebrew) (Jerusalem: Yad Izhak Ben-Zvi, 1985), chap. 2, pp. 38–65.

10. Morgenstern, *Messianism.* For an earlier and briefer version of Morgenstern's thesis, together with comments and critiques by Jacob Katz, Menachem Friedman, Isaiah Tishby, and Israel Bartal, see the symposium "Messianic Concepts and Settlement in the Land of Israel," in *Vision and Conflict in the Holy Land,* ed. Richard I. Cohen (New York: St. Martin's Press, 1985), pp. 140–89. This symposium was originally published in Hebrew in *Cathedra,* no. 23 (April 1982). Further support for Morgenstern's thesis is found in Rabbi Hillel of Shklov, *Kol Hator* (Sound of the Turtledove), ed. Shlomo Zalman Rivlin (Jerusalem: Torah Shelemah Institute, 1968). The author was the son of a first cousin and close disciple of the Rabbi Elijah, the Gaon of Vilna, and was himself, a close disciple of the Gaon. The

book purports to be the thoughts and beliefs of the Gaon on the impending redemption, which were orally transmitted to his student Rabbi Hillel.

11. Katz, *Jewish Nationalism*, pp. 285–307. Katz demonstrates that although Kalischer was receptive to developments in his time, his underlying theological approach remained traditional, and that it is a mistake to view him as an espouser of the modern conception of nationalism.

12. Zvi Hirsch Kalischer, *Drishat Zion* (Quest for Zion) (Jerusalem: Mossad Harav Kook, 1964), pp. 211–12. In a footnote, Kalischer cites Nachmanides's comment on the verse in the Song of Songs 8:12, which suggests the same sequence of stages in the process of the redemption.

13. Ibid., pp. 221–22.

14. See Israel Klausner's introduction to Kalischer's *Drishat Zion*, p. 15.

15. Ibid., n. 1.

16. Ibid., p. 173, n. 1. Lurie's organization never developed into a significant one, even though it enlisted among its members such notables as David Gordon, one of the editors of the Hebrew journal *Hamagid*, and Moses Hess, author of *Rome and Jerusalem* and a major forerunner of Zionism. A letter from Lurie to Kalischer, along with Kalischer's notes to that letter, appear in the Klausner edition of Kalischer's *Drishat Zion*, pp. 173–78.

17. Moses Hess, *Rome and Jerusalem, and Other Jewish Writings* (in Hebrew), trans. Yeshurun Keshet (Jerusalem: Zionist Library, 1983), pp. 105–6. Hess's book was first published in 1862, the same year that *Drishat Zion* appeared. Hess made other references to Kalischer, especially his messianic notions, which will be discussed below.

18. Several works claim that Alkalai spent his early years in Jerusalem. Jacob Katz, however, refutes this on several grounds. See Katz, *Jewish Nationalism*, pp. 309 and 343, n. 13.

19. Ibid.

20. Yehuda Ben Shlomo Chai Alkalai, *Darkhei Noam*, in *Kitvei Harav Yehuda Alkalai* (The Writings of Rabbi Yehuda Alkalai), ed. Yitzchak Raphael (Jerusalem: Mossad Harav Kook, 1974, 1:27–28. According to Jacob Katz, Alkalai underwent a significant transformation from his early to his later years with respect to his views on messianism and in the nature of his nationalism. Katz argues that whereas in his early writings Alkalai was an adherent of the view of the imminent arrival of the Messiah and his activity derived from his messianism, in his later writings Alkalai ceased to refer to the Messiah and based his activity of settling Eretz Israel on a conception of Jewish nationalism essentially the same as the prevalent secular conception of Jewish nationalism (*Jewish Nationalism*, pp. 311–41). Whether or not he ultimately came to reject messianism will be discussed later. In any case, there was definitely a major departure from his early messianic views.

21. He mentions the great fire on the eve of Rosh Hashanah of that year in the large Jewish community of Solonica in which many lives were lost, and the death of Rabbi Moshe Sofer, the Chatam Sofer, less than a month later. *Shlom Yerushalayim* in *Kitvei Harav Yehuda Halevi*, p. 33.

22. Ibid., pp. 34–35.

23. Ibid., p. 92.

24. *Minchat Yehudah,* in *Kitvei Harav Yehudah Alkalai,* pp. 210–11.

25. Ibid., p. 254–55.

26. Ibid., p. 237. The figure twenty-two thousand is based on the Talmudic statement that the *Shekhinah* does not rest in a place that has less than twenty-two thousand Jews. See ibid., n. 389.

27. Ibid., p. 243.

28. Ibid., p. 246.

29. Ibid., p. 247.

30. Ibid., p. 256.

31. Ibid., p. 264.

32. Ibid., p. 278.

33. Ibid., pp. 302–11.

34. Ibid., 2:579.

35. Ibid., pp. 718–19.

36. Ibid., p. 757.

37. Jacob Katz, *Jewish Emancipation and Self-emancipation* (Philadelphia: Jewish Publication Society, 1986), pp. 104–15.

38. At the beginning of *Rome and Jerusalem,* Hess wrote, "Now I have returned, after a twenty-year estrangement, and I am amidst my people" (p. 29).

39. David McLellan, *The Thought of Karl Marx* (New York: Harper & Row, 1971), p. 4.

40. See Sidney Hook, *From Hegel to Marx: Studies in the Intellectual Development of Karl Marx* (Ann Arbor: University of Michigan Press, 1962), pp. 186–219; Shlomo Avineri, *The Social and Political Thought of Karl Marx* (Cambridge: Cambridge University Press, 1970), pp. 124–25; John Weiss, *Moses Hess: Utopian Socialist* (Detroit: Wayne State University Press, 1960). For one of the issues on which Marx disagreed with Hess, see "The Centralization Question," in, *Writings of the Young Marx on Philosophy and Society,* ed. Lloyd D. Easton and Kurt H. Guddat (Garden City, N.Y.: Doubleday, Anchor Books, 1967), pp. 106–8. The best study of Hess is the intellectual biography by Shlomo Avineri, *Moses Hess: Prophet of Communism and Zionism* (New York: New York University Press, 1985).

41. Hook, *From Hegel to Marx,* p. 187.

42. In his words: "Twenty years ago, when a refuted libel which emanated from Damascus and reached us Europeans justly stirred in the heart of every Jew bitter and stinging pain due to this vulgarity. . . . Then, when I was in the middle of my socialistic aspirations, came an incident which painfully remalnded me for the first time that I am a son of this unfortunate and wrongly accused people . . . already then, even though I was distant from Judaism, I wanted to give expression to the patriotically Jewish feelings within me and to scream a loud and bitter scream. However, this scream was immediately stifled in my throat by the even greater pain which the plight of the European proletarian caused me" (Hess, *Rome and Jerusalem,* pp. 42–43). That blood libel had profound effects upon Jews around the world. Alkalai wrote his book *Minchat Yehudah* in response to it, and in the United States it was the source of the first rallying point of American Jewry and contributed to the subsequent communal organization of American Jewry. See

Chaim I. Waxman, *America's Jews in Transition* (Philadelphia: Temple University Press, 1983), pp. 17–19.

43. *The Complete Diaries of Theodor Herzl,* ed. Raphael Patai, trans. Harry Zohn (New York: Herzl Press and Thomas Yoseloff, 1960), 3:1090.

44. Hess, *Rome and Jerusalem,* p. 60. It is interesting to speculate on whether he had Marx in mind at this point, though marx was certainly not the only apostate Hess knew. Earlier, Hess wrote of other Jews who tried to hide their Judaism: "It didn't help Meyerbeer that he was always careful not to, Heaven forbid, use any Jewish theme in his operas–this did not protect him from German anti-Semitism. The respected newspaper, *Augsburg Allgemeine,* whenever it mentions his name, is careful to clarify, 'actually, Jacob Meyer Lipman Ber.' Nor did it help the German patriot, Boerne, that he changed his Jewish family-name, Barukh. He himself admits, 'Whenever my opponents run aground of "Boerne",' he says in one of his writings, 'they throw their saving anchor, "Barukh".'

"I, myself, have experienced, not only with my opponents but also with my colleagues, that the weapon of Jew-baiting, which never misses its mark in Germany, will be used in every personal argument. I have decided to assist them in their use of this weapon and to make it even easier for them, by returning to call myself from now on by my Hebrew name, Moses–and I only regret that my name is not 'Itzik' " (p. 56).

45. Ibid., p. 29.

46. Ibid., pp. 80–85.

47. Ibid., p. 59n.

48. Moses Hess, "My Belief in Messiah," in ibid., p. 166.

49. Katz, *Jewish Emancipation and Self-emancipation* p. 91.

50. Alex Bein, *Theodore Herzl* (New York: Atheneum, 1970), pp. 201–2. Although Herzl may have been revolted by the demonstrations, it is interesting to note that, at an early age, he had a dream in which the Messiah came and took him up to the clouds, where he met Moses, and "the Messiah called to Moses: It is for this child that I have prayed. But to me he said: Go, declare to the Jews that I shall come soon and perform great wonders and great deeds for my people and for the whole world" (pp. 13–14).

51. *The Complete Diaries of Theodor Herzl,* 1:310.

52. Yoseph Shapiro, *Bishvilei Hageulah,* p. 215.

53. David Ben-Gurion, *Memoirs* (New York: World Publishing, 1970), p. 34. On Ben-Gurion's own messianic convictions, see Moshe Pearlman, *Ben Gurion Looks Back* (New York: Schocken Books, 1970), pp. 224–34; see also Michael Keren, *Ben-Gurion and the Intellectuals: Power, Knowledge, and Charisma* (DeKalb: Northern Illinois University Press, 1983).

54. On this, see David Vital, *The Origins of Modern Zionism* (Oxford: Oxford University Press, 1975); and Shlomo Avineri, *The Making of Modem Zionism* (New York: Basic Books, 1981).

55. There is surprisingly little literature in English on Rabbi Reines, the best being Joseph Wanefsky, *Rabbi Isaac Jacob Reines: His Life and Thought* (New York: Philosophical Library, 1970). In Hebrew, see the biography of Reines by Geulah Bat Yehudah, *Ish Hameorot* (Jerusalem: Mossad Harav Kook, 1985). See also Eliezer

Don-Yehiya, "Ideology and Policy Formation in Religious Zionism: the Ideology of Rabbi Reines and Mizrachi Policy Under His Leadership" (in Hebrew), *Hazionut* 8 (1983):103–46.

56. It should be noted, though this is not the place for elaboration, that some prominent rabbis who were not sympathetic to the Zionist movement, and even some who were wholly antagonistic toward it, also viewed the contemporary period as *ikvetah demeshikhah*. For example, the Satmar Rav, Rabbi Joel Teitlebaum, who was an archenemy of Zionism, was convinced this is the period of the Messiah and saw Zionism as a tool of Satan. Also Rabbi Israel Meir Kahan, the Chafetz Chaim, while hardly a Zionist, was so convinced of the imminent arrived of the Messiah that he urged his students to study the laws of the priesthood so that the priests would be prepared to carry out their duties when the Temple in Jerusalem was rebuilt. See *Kol Kitvei Hachafetz Chaim Hashalem* (The Complete Writings of the Chafetz Chaim), vol. 3, *Michtavim* (Letters) (New York: A. I. Friedman, n.d.), pp. 43–44.

57. A bibliography of works in English on Rav Kook and selections of his writings in English translation appear in *Morasha 2*, no. 1 (Fall-Winter 1985):35–37. See also Abraham Isaac Kook, *The Lights of Penitence: The Moral Principles, Lights of Holiness, Essays, Letters, and Poems*, trans, and intro. Ben Zion Bokser (New York: Paulist Press, 1978). The collected works of Rav Kook were published in a uniform set by Mossad Harav Kook, Jerusalem, in 1985. For a comprehensive analysis of his thought, see Zvi Yaron, *The Philosophy of Rabbi Kook* (in Hebrew) (Jerusalem: World Zionist Organization, 1974). On Rav Kook's view of Herzl as a messianic figure, see his eulogy of Herzl, "The Eulogy in Jerusalem" (in Hebrew), *Sinai* 47, no. 12 (September 1960):327–31, reprinted in *Maamarei HaRAl"H* (Essays of RAI"H) (Jerusalem: privately printed, 5740 [1980]), 1:94–99. For his views on messianism, see Rivka Shatz-Oppenheimer, "Utopianism and Messianism in the Philosophy of Rav Kook" (in Hebrew), *Kivunim*, no. 1 (November 1978):15–27. On the influence of Moses Hess on Rav Kook, see Eliezer Goldman, "Secular Zionism, Israel's Mission, and the Objective of the Torah" (in Hebrew), *Daat*, no. 11 (Summer 1983):103–26, esp. 115ff. Parenthetically, in the home of his son, Rabbi Zvi Yehudah Kook, I saw that there were three pictures hanging next to each other on his wall: one of the Rambam, one of Rav (A. I.) Kook, and one of Herzl.

58. For a concise analytical discussion of this issue, see Walter S. Wurzburger, "Theological Implications of the State of Israel: The Jewish View–Messianic Perspectives," *Encyclopedia Judiaca, 1974 Year Book* (Jerusalem: Keter, 1975), pp. 148–51.

Chapter 3

1. Jews from northern and central Europe typically followed the subcultural traditions of the other great Jewish center, Germany, and were known as Ashkenazim. A more detailed discussion on the origins of the American Jewish community is found in Chaim I. Waxman, *America's Jews in Transition* (Philadelphia: Temple University Press, 1983), chap. 1.

2. See ibid., p. 9, for the texts of these letters.

3. David de Sola Pool, "Early Relations between Palestine and American Jewry," in *Brandeis Avukah Annual of 1932*, ed. Joseph Shalom Shubow (New York: American Student Zionist Federation, 1932), pp. 537–39. See also Salo Wittmayer Baron, *Steeled by Adversity: Essays and Addresses on American Jewish Life* (Philadelphia: Jewish Publication Society, 1971), pp. 158–266, for a detailed discussion of "Palestinian Messengers in America, 1849–1879."

4. For evidence of such activity in New York and Newport, see de Sola Pool, "Early Relations," p. 540. For Philadelphia, see Maxwell Whiteman, "Zionism Comes to Philadelphia," in *Early History of Zionism in America*, ed. Isadore S. Meyer (New York: American Jewish Historical Society and Theodor Herzl Foundation, 1958), p. 191.

5. For a facsimile of that sermon, see Abraham J. Karp, *Beginnings: Early American Judaica* (Philadelphia: Jewish Publication Society, 1975).

6. Morris A. Gutstein, *To Bigotry No Sanction* (New York: Bloch, 1958), pp. 78–79. See also Lee M. Friedman, *Rabbi Haim Isaac Carigal* (Boston: privately printed, 1940); Arthur A. Chiel, "The Rabbis and Ezra Stiles," *American Jewish Historical Quarterly* 61, no. 4 (June 1972):294–312; idem, "The Mystery of the Rabbi's Lost Portrait," *Judaism* 22, no. 4 (Fall 1973):482–89; Jacob Rader Marcus, *Early American Jewry* (Philadelphia: Jewish Publication Society, 1951), 1:193–96.

7. Gershom Mendes Seixas, *A Religious Discourse: Thanksgiving Day Sermon, November 26, 1789*, facsimile ed. (New York: Jewish Historical Society of New York, 1977), p. 12.

8. The prayer, rendered in Hebrew by Jacob Cohen, acting in place of the Hazan, was written by Rabbi Hendla-Iehochanan Van OEttingen. The translation appears in *Publications of the American Jewish Historical Society* no. 27 (1920):34–37.

9. *Discourse, Delivered in the Synagogue in New York on the Ninth of May, 1798*, facsimile ed., in Karp, *Beginnings*, p. 10.

10. There is some disagreement among historians as to the extent to which Seixas may be properly viewed as pre-Zionist. The foremost proponent that he was is Raphael Mahler. See, e.g., his essay "The Historical Background of Pre-Zionism in America and Its Continuity," in *A Bicentennial Festschrift for Jacob Rader Marcus*, ed. Bertram Wallace Korn (New York: Ktav, 1976), pp. 341–58, and his more detailed essay "American Jewry and the Idea of Return to Zion in the Era of the American Revolution" (in Hebrew), *Zion* 15 (5710 [1949–50]):107–34. On the other hand, Bernard Weinryb argues that Mahler's "attempt to make Seixas almost a modern Zionist is the result of a misunderstanding of the character of the traditional Jewish sermon beset as it was with the motif of 'return' and with the doctrines of the Sephardim." See Bernard D. Weinryb, "Jewish Immigration and Accommodation to America: Research, Trends, Problems," *Publications of the American Jewish Historical Society* 46, no. 3 (March 1957):383, n. 61. Although Weinryb is correct that the motif of return was an integral part of the traditional Jewish sermon and that Mahler exaggerated somewhat in portraying Seixas as almost a modern Zionist, it is nevertheless true that Seixas continued to stress this traditional Jewish notion even as Jews were directly experiencing the impact of the revolution by achieving equality and integration into American society. That, in itself, indicates how deeply embedded this belief and hope was.

11. The most thorough and analytic biography of Noah is Jonathan D. Sarna, *Jacksonian Jew: The Two Worlds of Mordecai Noah* (New York: Holmes & Meier, 1981). See also Isaac Goldberg, *Major Noah: American-Jewish Pioneer* (Philadelphia: Jewish Publication Society, 1936); Robert Gordis, "Mordecai Manual Noah: A Centenary Evaluation," *Publications of the American Jewish Historical Society* 41, no. 1 (1951):1–26.

12. A copy of that letter appears in Sarna, *Jacksonian Jew*, p. 26.

13. Cf. Mahler, "The Historical Background of Pre-Zionism"; Gordis, "Mordecai Manuel Noah"; Hyman B. Grinstein, *The Rise of the Jewish Community of New York, 1654–1860* (Philadelphia: Jewish Publication Society, 1945), p. 460; Louis Ruchames, "Mordecai Manuel Noah and Early American Zionism," *American Jewish Historical Quarterly* 64, no. 3 (March 1975): 195–223. Sarna accurately points out that it is technically incorrect to refer to Noah as a "forerunner of Zion," since he did not lead a movement to Palestine. In fact, he had virtually no followers. It is, therefore, more proper to view him as a "restorationist." See Sarna, *Jacksonian Jew*, pp. 152–57. See also Bernard D. Weinryb, "Noah's Ararat Jewish State in Its Historical Setting," *Publications of the American Jewish Historical Society* 43 (1954):170–91; Jacob Katz, *Jewish Emancipation and Self-emancipation* (Philadelphia: Jewish Publication Society, 1986), p. 109.

14. Mordecai M. Noah, *Discourse Delivered at the Consecration of the Synagogue of K. K. Shearith Israel in the City of New York, on Friday, the 10th of Nisan, 5578, Corresponding with the 17th of April, 1818* (New York: C. S. Van Winkle, 1818), p. 27.

15. Ibid., p. 19.

16. Ibid., pp. 30–31.

17. Ibid., p. 16.

18. Ibid., pp. 23–24.

19. See "A European Inquiry to Mordecai M. Noah, 1822," in *The Jews of the United States, 1790–1840: A Documentary History,* ed. Joseph L. Blau and Salo W. Baron (New York: Columbia University Press, 1963), 3:891–93.

20. "Address by Mordecai M. Noah," *Publications of the American Jewish Historical Society* 21 (1913):232.

21. Ibid.

22. See Chapter 2, above.

23. "Address by Mordecai M. Noah," pp. 232–33.

24. Noah incorrectly assumed that "there is no essential difference between their doctrines" and those of the Jews, and therefore "the distinction between them should cease" (ibid, pp. 236–37). In fact, there are very basic differences between the Samaritans and the Karaites themselves, as well as between them and Jews.

25. Ibid., pp. 248–49.

26. Ibid., p. 252.

27. The discourse was subsequently published, with a map of the Land of Israel and a preface by Noah, by Harper & Brothers. A facsimile of that edition of the discourse is in Karp, *Beginnings.*

28. See Chapter 2, above.

29. Noah, *Discourse*, p. 37.

30. Ibid., pp. 39–40.

31. See Maxwell Whiteman, "The Legacy of Issac Leeser," in *Jewish Life in Philadelphia, 1830–1940*, ed. Murray Friedman (Philadelphia: ISHI Publications, 1983), pp. 26–47; Bertram Wallace Korn, "Isaac Leeser: Centennial Reflections," *American Jewish Archives* 19, no. 2 (November 1967):127–41. Two unpublished doctoral dissertations on Leeser are Maxine Seller, "Isaac Leeser: Architect of the American Jewish Community" (University of Pennsylvania, 1965); and Emanuel Bennet, "An Evaluation of the Life of Isaac Leeser" (Yeshiva University, 1955).

32. *Occident* 2, no. 12 (March 1845):600–606.

33. Maxine S. Seller, "Isaac Leeser's Views on the Restoration of a Jewish Palestine," *American Jewish Historical Quarterly* 58, no. 1 (September 1968):126.

34. Baron, *Steeled by Adversity*. See also Moshe Davis, *The Emergence of Conservative Judaism* (Philadelphia: Jewish Publication Society of America, 1963), pp. 78–89. It is interesting that in 1940 an institution, the Federated Council of Israel Institutions (FCII), was founded with an objective very similar to that suggested by Leeser almost a century earlier. But the FCII has remained small, in part because it represents only Orthodox institutions, primarily yeshivot, in Israel, and in part because the United Jewish Appeal has become the major American Jewish fund raiser on behalf of projects in Israel and elsewhere. In contrast to Leeser's criticisms of the uncoordinated and inefficient manner in which funds were raised for institutions in the Holy Land, there are, today, increasing criticisms of the overcentralized manner in which such funds are raised and that, in essence, those who donate funds have virtually no control over how and to whom the funds are disbursed. See many of the articles in Marc Lee Raphael, ed., *Understanding American Jewish Philanthropy* (New York: Ktav, 1979). See also Eliezer D. Jaffe, *Giving Wisely* (Jerusalem: Koren, 1982).

35. Seller, "Isaac Leeser's Views."

36. Abraham J. Karp, "The Zionism of Warder Cresson," in Meyer, *Early History of Zionism in America*, pp. 1–20.

37. One of Cresson's major financial supporters was Judah Touro, a wealthy Sephardi from New Orleans who was a prominent Jewish philanthropist. Touro also made a large charitable contribution to Sir Moses Montefiore for poor Jews in the Holy Land. See Max J. Kohler, "Judah Touro, Merchant and Philanthropist," *Publications of the American Jewish Historical Society*, no. 13 (1905):96–103; Leon Huhner, *The Life of Judah Touro* (Philadelphia: Jewish Publication Society, 1946).

38. Karp, "The Life of Warder Cresson," p. 15.

39. Grinstein, *The Rise of the Jewish Community of New York*, p. 451.

40. "Relief by Agriculture for Palestine," *Occident* 12, no. 7 (October 1854):351–55.

41. On the founding of two American religious communities, *kollelim*, in Jerusalem, one in 1879 and the other in 1896, see Moshe Davis, "The Holy Land Idea in American Spiritual History," in *With Eyes toward Zion*, ed. Moshe Davis (New York: Arno Press, 1977), pp. 16–17; Simcha Fishbane, "The Founding of Kollel America Tifereth Yerushalyim," *American Jewish Historical Quarterly* 64, no. 2 (December 1974):120–36.

42. *Occident* 11, no. 10 (January 1854):477–83.
43. James G. Heller, *Isaac M. Wise: His Life, Work and Thought* (New York: Union of American Hebrew Congregations, 1965); Isaac Mayer Wise, *Reminiscences*, trans. and ed. David Philipson (1901; New York; Arno Press, 1973).
44. Melvin Weinman, "The Attitude of Isaac Mayer Wise toward Zionism and Palestine," *American Jewish Archives* 3, no. 2 (January 1951):3–23. Weinman and David Polish disagree over Wise's attitude toward the colonization of Palestine. Whereas Weinman maintains that Wise's opposition to that notion grew stronger (ibid., pp. 18–19), Polish argues that, especially in the early years of the twentieth century, Wise became much more supportive of colonization and that he was even ready to work with Zionists toward that end. See David Polish, *Renew Our Days: The Zionist Issue in Reform Judaism* (Jerusalem: Zionist Library, 1976), pp. 93–94.
45. W. Gunther Plaut, ed., *The Growth of Reform Judaism* (New York: World Union for Progressive Judaism, 1965), pp. 33–34. It was not until Zionism had become a major movement, Hitler had come to power, and the ethnic composition of Reform Judaism in the United States had undergone considerable change that its principles, including the anti-Zionist ones, were altered in the Columbus Platform of 1937.
46. Leon A. Jick, *The Americanization of the Synagogue, 1820–1870* (Hanover, N.H.: University Press of New England and Brandeis University Press, 1976).
47. Quoted in Plaut, *The Growth of Reform Judaism,* pp. 153–54.
48. Union of American Hebrew Congregations, *Proceedings* 25th Annual Report (1898):4002.
49. Malcolm H. Stern, "The Role of the Rabbi in the South," in *"Turn to the South": Essays on Southern Jewry,* ed. Nathan M. Kaganoff and Melvin I. Irofsky (Waltham, Mass., and Charlottesville, Va.: American Jewish Historical Society and University Press of Virginia, 1979), p. 28.
50. Hyman B. Grinstein, "The Memories and Scrapbooks of the Late Dr. Joseph Isaac Bluestone of New York City," *Publications of the American Jewish Historical Society* 35 (September 1939):53–64; Israel Klausner, "Adam Rosenberg," in *Herzl Year Book* (New York: Herzl Press, 1958), 1:232–80; Marnin Feinstein, *American Zionism: 1884–1904* (New York: Herzl Press, 1965). On the formation of Hevras Zion in Baltimore, see Alexandra Lee Levin, *Vision: A Biography of Harry Friedenwald* (Philadelphia: Jewish Publication Society, 1964), pp. 147–48.

Chapter 4
1. Actually, it was called the Zionist Organization until 1960. Since then, it has been the World Zionist Organization.
2. Chaim I. Waxman, *America's Jews in Transition* (Philadelphia: Temple University Press, 1983), pp. 29–30.
3. Ibid., pp. 32–35.
4. Stephen M. Poppel, *Zionism in Germany, 1897–1933* (Philadelphia: Jewish Publication Society, 1977), p. 27.
5. Ben Halpern, "The United States," in *Zionism in Transition,* ed. Moshe Davis (New York: Herzl Press, 1980), p. 45.

6. Evyatar Friesel, *The Zionist Movement in the United States, 1897–1914* (in Hebrew) (Tel Aviv: Tel Aviv University, Institute for Zionist Research, and Hakibbutz Hameuchad, 1970), pp. 49–51.

7. Magnes himself was born in San Francisco, but his father was born in Poland.

8. Yonathan Shapiro, *Leadership of the American Zionist Organization, 1897–1930* (Urbana: University of Illinois Press, 1971), pp. 37–46.

9. Leon Simon, *Ahad Ha-am* (Philadelphia: Jewish Publication Society, 1960), p. 336, n. 2. See also the essay on Ahad Ha-am, written in 1906, in Israel Friedlaender, *Past and Present: Selected Essays* (New York: Burning Bush Press, 1961), pp. 275–98.

10. Halpern, "The United States." See also Ben Halpern, "The Americanization of Zionism, 1880–1930," *American Jewish History* 69, no. 1 (September 1972): 15–33.

11. Ibid., p. 17.

12. General Zionism was initially the designation of the vast majority of Zionists. It included all those who did not belong to either of two political parties within the movement, the religious Mizrachi or the socialist Poalei Zion. Subsequently, the general Zionists themselves became a faction and, indeed, a party within the World Zionist Organization.

13. Marshall Sklare, *Conservative Judaism: An American Religious Movement* (New York: Schocken Books, 1972).

14. For a Conservative ideological perspective, see Mordecai Waxman, ed., *Tradition and Change: The Development of Conservative Judaism* (New York: Burning Bush Press, 1958).

15. Sklare, *Conservative Judaism.*

16. Moshe Davis, *The Emergence of Conservative Judaism* (Philadelphia: Jewish Publication Society of America, 1963), p. 268.

17. Friedlaender, *Past and Present*, p. xxiii; in that same book see his essay, originally written in 1907, "The Problem of Judaism in America," pp. 159–84. For a recent biographical study of Friedlaender, see Baila Round Shargel, *Practical Dreamer: Israel Friedlaender and the Shaping of American Judaism* (New York: Jewish Theological Seminary, 1985). Ahad Ha-am's essay "A Spiritual Centre," written in 1907, appears in *Ahad Ha-am: Essays, Letters, Memoirs*, trans. and ed. Leon Simon (Oxford: East and West Library, 1946), pp. 201–8. It should be noted that although Ahad Ha-am wrote this essay "with the object of putting an end to all misunderstanding" (p. 201) about his conception of the spiritual center, it did not achieve its intended goal. Particularly with respect to his notion of "spiritual," it is interesting to note that almost all of the American religious leaders who were (and are) Zionists were cultural Zionists and saw themselves as Ahad Ha-amists. They defined (and continue to define) Ahad Ha-am's term "spiritual" to mean religious and pointed to his support for the retention of Jewish tradition as proof of his support for a religious base to Zionism. For example, in his essay *"Shabbat Vezionut"* (Ahad Ha-am, *Al Parashat Drachim* [Tel Aviv: Dvir and Hozaah Ivrit, 1948], 2:139–42), Ahad Ha-am argued for the maintenance of the traditional Sabbath and its observances because "more than Israel kept the Sabbath, the Sabbath

kept them" (p. 139). Many secular Zionists, and especially Israeli ones, on the other hand, point out that Ahad Ha-am himself was a secularist who used the term "spiritual" in its modern Hebrew sense, "cultural," and that religion is simply one form of culture. Thus, his argument regarding the Sabbath was explicitly not formulated on religious grounds but on sociological ones. See also Ahad Ha-am, "Torah Shebalev," in *Al Parashat Drachim*, 1:78–87, for a formulation of his traditionalist secularism.

18. Quoted in Norman Bentwich, *Solomon Schechter* (New York: Burning Bush Press, 1938), p. 312.

19. Ibid., p. 316.

20. Solomon Schechter, *Seminary Addresses and Other Papers* (New York: Burning Bush Press, 1959), p. 97.

21. Bentwich, *Solomon Schechter*, p. 244.

22. Kaplan's magnum opus, originally published in 1934, is *Judaism as a Civilization: Toward a Reconstruction of American-Jewish Life* (Jew York: Schocken Books, 1967). His major thoughts on Zionism are contained in *A New Zionism*, 2d ed. (New York: Herzl Press and Jewish Reconstructionist Press, 1959).

23. See, e.g., Kaplan, *Judaism as a Civilization*, pp. 282–85.

24. Ibid., p. 328.

25. Kaplan, *A New Zionism*, p. 21.

26. Ibid., p. 22.

27. Charles S. Liebman, *The Ambivalent American Jew* (Philadelphia: Jewish Publication Society of America, 1973), pp. 88–108.

28. For a cogent overview of Kaplan's major themes, see Arthur Hertzberg, "Tfisato Hayehudit Shel Mordecai Kaplan" (The Jewish Perception of Mordecai Kaplan), *Yahadut Zemanenu* 3 (1986):19–24.

29. Herbert Parzen also considers Magnes, along with Schechter, Friedlaender, and Kaplan, among those who exerted major qualitative influence on American Zionism in the early part of the century, and he too argues that, despite his having been ordained at Hebrew Union College, Magnes not only served as rabbi in a Conservative congregation but he ultimately adopted the Friedlaender and Kaplan versions of Conservative Judaism. See Herbert Parzen, "Conservative Judaism and Zionism (1896–1922)," *Jewish Social Studies* 23, no. 4 (October 1961):235–64.

30. Norman Bentwich, *For Zion's Sake: A Biography of Judah L. Magnes* (Philadelphia: Jewish Publication Society of America, 1954), pp. 22–26.

31. Ibid., pp. 37–48.

32. The most complete analysis of the *Kehillah* is Arthur A. Goren, *New York Jews and the Quest for Community* (New York: Columbia University Press, 1970).

33. Arthur A. Goren, ed., *Dissenter in Zion* (Cambridge, Mass.: Harvard University Press, 1982), document no. 41, "Eretz Israel and the Galut," pp. 208–14.

34. Ibid., p. 208.

35. Ibid., pp. 209, 214.

36. Quoted in Yohai Goell, "Aliya in the Zionism of an American Oleh: Judah L. Magnes," *American Jewish Historical Quarterly* 65, no. 2 (December 1975): 108. It should, of course, be pointed out that is contrast to Mordecai Kaplan, who wrote

his work after the establishment of the State of Israel, Magnes's comments were made in 1912, even before the Balfour Declaration and during a time when physical conditions in the land were extremely difficult.

37. Quoted in Bentwich, *For Zion's Sake*, pp. 126–27.

38. Goell, "Aliyah," p. 108.

39. Goren, *Dissenter in Zion*, p. 218. See also Goell, "Aliyah," pp. 112–13.

40. Bentwich, *For Zion's Sake*. See also Goren, *Dissenter in Zion*, pp. 3–57. For Magnes's thoughts on Jewish-Arab cooperation, see M. Buber, J. L. Magnes, and E. Simon, eds., *Towards Union in Palestine: Essays on Zionism and Jewish-Arab Cooperation* (Jerusalem: IHUD Association, 1947). See also Susan Lee Hattis, *The Bi-National Idea in Palestine during Mandatory Times* (Haifa; Shikmona, 1970).

41. Waxman, *America's Jews in Transition*, pp. 62–103.

42. For a historical overview of the Mizrachi in the United States, see Aaron Halevi Pachenik, "Religious Zionism in America" (in Hebrew), in *Sefer Hazionut Hadatit*, ed. Yitzchak Raphael and S. Z. Shragai (Jerusalem: Mossad Harav Kook, 1977), 2:226–41. On Labor Zionism in the United States, see C. Bezalel Sherman, "The Beginnings of Labor Zionism in the United States," in *Early History of Zionism in America*, ed. Isidore S. Meyer (New York: American Jewish Historical Society and Theodor Herzl Foundation, 1958), pp. 275–88; Aaron Alperin, "Seventy Years of Labor Zionism in America," trans. Irving Heller (New York: Labor Zionist Alliance, 1976), pp. 1–28; see also L. Spizman, "Stages in the History of the Zionist Labor Movement in the United States," in *History of the Labor Zionist Movement in the United States* (in Yiddish), ed. L. Spizman et al. (New York: Yiddisher Kemfer, 1955), 1:81–292.

43. Samuel Koenig, "The Socioeconomic Structure of an American Jewish Community," in *Jews in a Gentile World*, ed. Isacque Graeber and Steuart Henderson Britt (New York: Macmillan, 1942), pp. 200–242.

44. Ibid., p. 224.

45. Waxman, *America's Jews in Transition*, pp. 104–34.

Chapter 5

1. Hyman B. Grinstein, *The Rise of the Jewish Community of New York, 1654–1860* (Philadelphia: Jewish Publication Society, 1945), p. 451.

2. Salo Wittmayer Baron, *Steeled by Adversity: Essays and Addresses on American Jewish Life* (Philadelphia: Jewish Publication Society, 1971), p. 219.

3. David Ben-Gurion, *Rebirth and Destiny of Israel* (New York: Philosophical Library, 1954), p. 535.

4. The organization is cited in Moshe Davis, *From Dependence to Mutuality: The American Jewish Community and World Jewry* (in Hebrew) (Jerusalem: Magnes Press, 1970), p. 80. There is absolutely no relationship between this organization and the much later Israeli political party of the same name.

5. S. N. Eisenstadt, *Israeli Society* (New York: Basic Books, 1967), p. 29.

6. The origins of Hehalutz are discussed in Margalit Shilah, "The First Sparks of the Idea of the Moshav: 'Haikar Hatzair,' the American Collective during the Second Aliya" (in Hebrew), *Cathedra*, no. 25 (October 1982): 79–98. Its subsequent

development is nostalgically sketched in *Pioneers from America—75 Years of Hehalutz, 1905–1980* ed. David Breslau et al. (Tel Aviv: Bogrei Hehalutz America, 1981).

7. Shilah, "The First Sparks," p. 82.

8. P. E. Lapide, *A Century of U.S. Aliya* (Jerusalem: Association of Americans and Canadians in Israel, 1961), p. 132.

9. Ibid.

10. Calvin Goldscheider, "American Aliya: Sociological and Demographic Perspectives," in *The Jew in American Society,* ed. Marshall Sklare (New York: Behrman House, 1974), p. 348.

11. Breslau, *Pioneers from America,* pp. 201–3.

12. Walter Laqueur, *A History of Zionism* (New York: Holt, Rinehart and Winston, 1972), p. 299.

13. Charles S. Liebman and Eliezer Don-Yehiya, *Civil Religion in Israel* (Berkeley: University of California Press, 1983), p. 30.

14. Aaron Antonovsky and Abraham David Katz, *From the Golden to the Promised Land* (Darby, Pa.: Norwood Editions, 1979), pp. 23–25. Antonovsky and Katz are careful to point out that all of their data pertain to those American immigrants who remained in Israel. A not insignificant percentage of Americans who immigrated to Israel returned to the United States, and we have no way of knowing whether their patterns are identical to those of American olim who remained in Israel.

15. Ibid., p. 24.

16. Ibid., p. 26.

17. Ibid., p. 30.

18. Ibid., pp. 28–29.

19. Ibid., pp. 39, 45.

20. Ibid., pp. 52–53.

21. Ibid., p. 72, n. 2.

22. See, e.g., the selections in Breslau, *Pioneers from America.*

23. Lapide, *A Century of U.S. Aliya,* pp. 91–96.

24. Gerald Engel, "North American Jewish Settlers in Israel," *American Jewish Year Book* 71 (1970):161–87. For more detailed analyses of specific aspects of the population in this study, see Gerald Engel, "Comparison between American Permanent Residents of Israel," Parts I-III, *Journal of Psychology* 71 (1969):133–42; 72 (1969): 135–39; and 73 (1969):33–39; "Comparison between Americans Living in Israel and Those Who Returned to America," Parts I-III, *Journal of Psychology* 74 (1970): 195–204; 75 (1970):243–51; and 76 (1970):117–23. This study should be utilized very cautiously because it has a number of serious methodological problems.

25. Engel, "North American Jewish Settlers in Israel," p. 165.

26. Ibid., p. 172.

27. See pp. 80–81, above.

28. Engel, "North American Jewish Settlers in Israel," p. 164.

29. Ibid., p. 166.

30. For the educational patterns of American Jews at that time, see Sidney Goldstein, "American Jewry, 1970," *American Jewish Year Book* 72 (1971):60–68.

31. Engel, "North American Jewish Settlers in Israel," pp. 166–67.
32. Ibid., p. 161.
33. Ibid., p. 162.
34. Ibid., p. 167.
35. Ibid., pp. 170–71.
36. Ibid., p. 172.
37. Ibid., pp. 172–74.
38. Ibid., pp. 176–77.

Chapter 6

1. See Chapter 5, above.
2. Calvin Goldscheider, "American Aliya: Sociological and Demographic Perspectives," in *The Jew in American Society*, ed. Marshall Sklare (New York: Behrman House, 1974), table 2, p. 353. Because of the different sources, there is a slight difference between Goldscheider's figures and those reported in Table 2 above.
3. Aaron Antonovsky and Abraham David Katz, *From the Golden to the Promised Land* (Darby, Pa.: Norwood Editions, 1979), p. 26.
4. Goldscheider, "American Aliya," pp. 358–59. Actually, Goldscheider's findings are not that different from those of Antonovsky and Katz. The reason they indicated that the olim were disproportionately from the New York area and other big cities is that they incorrectly assumed the American Jewish geographic dispersion and, especially, deurbanization to be greater than it actually was at the time.
5. Gerald S. Berman, *The Experience of Aliyah among Recently Arrived North American Olim* (Jerusalem: Hebrew University, Work and Welfare Institute, 1977), table 1, p. 19.
6. Goldscheider, "American Aliya," p. 361.
7. Harry Lieb Jubas, "The Adjustment Process of Americans and Canadians in Israel and Their Integration into Israeli Society" (Ph.D. diss., Michigan State University, 1974), p. 98.
8. Kevin Avruch, *American Immigrants in Israel: Social Identities and Change* (Chicago: University of Chicago Press, 1981), pp. 40–41.
9. Berman, *The Experience of Aliyah*, p. 19.
10. *Immigration to Israel 1986*, special series no. 808 (Jerusalem: Central Bureau of Statistics, 1987), table 5, p. 9, and table 11, p. 15.
11. Goldscheider, "American Aliya," pp. 362–63.
12. *Immigration to Israel 1984*, special series no. 773 (Jerusalem: Central Bureau of Statistics, 1985), p. xi and table 10, p. 13; Neil C. Sandberg, *Jewish Life in Los Angeles* (Lanham, Md.: University Press of America, 1986), p. 22.
13. See above, p. 79.
14. Gerald S. Berman, *The Work Adjustment of North American Immigrants in Israel* (Jerusalem: Hebrew University, Work and Welfare Research Institute, 1978), table 1, p. 19.
15. See Goldscheider, "American Aliyah"; *Immigration to Israel 1984*, table 9, p. 12; and *Immigration to Israel 1986*, table 12, p. 16. The designation "early middle age" is used because there is some question about those between the ages of thirty

and thirty-five. Goldscheider's age cohort, which shows an overrepresentation of males, 54.2 percent, runs from thirty-five to forty-four. The Central Bureau of Statistics age cohorts showing an overrepresentation of males run from thirty to forty-four.

16. Chaim I. Waxman, *America's Jews in Transition* (Philadelphia: Temple University Press, 1983), p. 145.

17. Jay Y. Brodbar-Nemzer, "Sex Differences in Attitudes of American Jews toward Israel," *Contemporary Jewry* 8 (1987):55.

18. Steven M. Cohen, *American Modernity and Jewish Identity* (New York: Tavistock Publications, 1983), pp. 116–17.

19. *Immigration to Israel 1986*, table 13, p. 17, and table 18, p. 22.

20. Goldscheider, "American Miyah," pp. 365–66.

21. Waxman, *America's Jews in Transition*, pp. 166–73.

22. *Immigration to Israel 1986*, table 18, p. 22.

23. Waxman, *America's Jews in Transition*, pp. 144–46.

24. Goldscheider, "American Aliyah," p. 367.

25. Ibid. See also Sidney Goldstein, "Jews in the United States: Perspectives from Demography," *American Jewish Year Book* 81 (1981):49.

26. Cohen, *American Modernity and Jewish Identity*, table 4(1), p. 81.

27. For the political patterns of America's Jews, see Waxman, *America's Jews in Transition*, pp. 98–103, 147–51.

28. Zvi Gitelman, *Becoming Israelis: Political Resocialization of Soviet and American Immigrants* (New York: Praeger, 1982), p. 209.

29. Ibid.

30. See above, p. 159.

31. See above, p. 84.

32. Goldscheider, "American Aliyah," p. 377.

33. Jubas, "The Adjustment Process," table 4.11, p. 102.

34. Gerald S. Berman, "Why North Americans Migrate to Israel," *Jewish Journal of Sociology* 21, no. 2 (December 1979):135–44.

35. Avruch, *American Immigrants in Israel*, pp. 50–51.

36. For American Jewry, see Waxman, *America's Jews in Transition*, pp. 187–89. For the American olim, see Goldscheider, "American Aliyah," pp. 377–79; Jubas, "The Adjustment Process," table 4.17, p. 108.

37. S. Y. Lache, Dorota Teczniczek, Beatriz Mann, and Ron Lahav, *The Absorption Problems of Older Immigrants in Israeli Society* (Jerusalem: Henrietta Szold Institute, research report no. 183, publication no. 536, February 1976), pp. 48–51.

38. Goldscheider, "American Aliyah," pp. 381–82.

39. *Survey on Absorption of Immigrants: Immigrants of the Seventies–the First Three Years in Israel* (Jerusalem: Central Bureau of Statistics, special series no. 771, 1986), pp. 14–15. Also see Sergio DellaPergola, "Demographic Trends of Latin American Jewry," in *The Jewish Presence in Latin America*, ed. Judith Laikin Elkin and Gilbert W. Merkx (Boston: Allen & Unwin, 1987), p. 126.

40. *Barkai: A Journal of Rabbinic Thought and Research* (in Hebrew), no. 4 (Spring 1987), p. 408.

41. Interview with Bobby Brown, December 30, 1986.

42. The fact that these reports suggest a big jump in the percentage of Orthodox among American olim is not altogether surprising when considered along with Steven Cohen's findings of a clear-cut intensification of attachment to Israel during the years 1983–86 among Orthodox American Jews, and a sharp decline in attachment to Israel among Reform American Jews, with the level of attachment among Conservative American Jews remaining more or less the same during those years. See Steven M. Cohen, *Ties and Tensions: The 1986 Survey of American Jewish Attitudes toward Israel and Israelis* (New York: Institute on American Jewish-Israeli Relations, American Jewish Committee, 1987), pp. 19–21.

43. S. N. Eisenstadt, *The Absorption of Immigrants* (London: Routledge & Kegan Paul, 1954), pp. 1–2.

44. Avruch, *American Immigrants in Israel*, p. 89.

45. This is what, in sociological theory, Robert Merton has called "the Thomas theorum," namely, "If men define situations as real, they are real in their consequences." See Robert K. Merton, *Social Theory and Social Structure* (New York: Free Press, 1968), p. 475. See also W. I. Thomas, *The Unadjusted Girl*, ed. by Benjamin Nelson (New York: Harper Torchbooks, 1967), p. 42, in which Thomas emphasizes the necessity of understanding "the definition of the situation" of the individual engaged in any social behavior.

46. See above, Chapter 5, Table 1.

47. Goldscheider, "American Aliyah," p. 375.

48. Jubas, "The Adjustment Process," p. 124.

49. Arnold Dashefsky and Bernard Lazerwitz, "The Role of Religious Identification in North American Migration to Israel," *Journal for the Scientific Study of Religion* 22 no. 3 (September 1983):263–75.

50. Berman, "Why North Americans Migrate to Israel," p. 142.

51. Avruch, *American Immigrants in Israel*, p. 94.

52. Ibid.

Chapter 7

1. Marshall Sklare, ed., *The Jewish Community in America* (New York: Behrman House, 1974), p. vii.

2. Melvin I. Urofsky, *American Zionism from Herzl to the Holocaust* (Garden City, N.Y.: Doubleday, Anchor, 1975), p. 1.

3. Daniel J. Elazar, *Community and Polity: The Organizational Dynamics of American Jewry* (Philadelphia: Jewish Publication Society of America, 1976), p. 288.

4. *Encyclopedia Judaica* (Jerusalem: Keter, 1971), 16:1147.

5. Steven M. Cohen, *Ties and Tensions: The 1986 Survey of American Jewish Attitudes toward Israel and Israelis* (New York: Institute on American Jewish-Israeli Relations, American Jewish Committee, 1987), pp. 36–37.

6. David Ben-Gurion and Moshe Pearlman, *Ben-Gurion Looks Back* (New York: Schocken Books, 1965), pp. 235–52.

7. Cf. Simon N. Herman, *Jewish Identity: A Social Psychological Perspective* (Beverly Hills, Calif.: Sage, 1977), pp. 115–42.

8. Marshall Sklare and Joseph Greenblum, *Jewish Identity on the Suburban Frontier*, 2d ed. (Chicago: University of Chicago Press, 1979), pp. 241–49.

9. Ibid., table 6–3, p. 225.

10. Yesha'yahu (Charles) Liebman, "The Role of Israel in the Ideology of American Jews," *Dispersion and Unity,* no. 10 (Winter 1970):23. The percentage breakdown of those agreeing with the statement that Jews should move to Israel was as follows: among the rabbis–Orthodox 69 percent, Conservative 25 percent, and Reform 10 percent; among the synagogue presidents–Orthodox 37 percent. Conservative 12 percent, Reform 5 percent. It should be pointed out that Liebman's sample of Orthodox rabbis was derived from the membership in the Rabbinical Council of America, which is composed primarily of modern Orthodox rabbis and may not be representative of sectarian or right-wing Orthodox rabbis. The differences between modern and sectarian Orthodox will be discussed in Chapter 8, below.

11. Ibid., p. 24.

12. Arnold Dashefsky and Howard Shapiro, *Ethnic Identification among American Jews* (Lexington, Mass.: Lexington Books, 1974), p. 46. Their "Index of Zionism" was composed of five statements dealing with such matters as the learning of Hebrew, consideration of living in Israel, the importance of Israel's remaining a Jewish state, the desire to visit Israel, and Israel as the spiritual homeland of the Jewish people. See ibid., table A-2, p. 139.

13. Nathan Glazer, "American Jews: Three Conflicts of Loyalties," in *The Third Century: America as a Post-Industrial Society,* ed. Seymour Martin Lipset (Stanford, Calif: Hoover Institution Press, 1979), p. 233.

14. Jonathan S. Woocher, *Sacred Survival: The Civil Religion of American Jews* (Bloomington: Indiana University Press, 1986), p. 77.

15. Eytan Gilboa, "Israel in the Mind of American Jews: Public Opinion Trends and Analysis," *Research Report,* no. 4 (London: Institute of Jewish Affairs, March 1986), p. 17.

16. Ibid., p. 18.

17. Cohen, *Ties and Tensions,* pp. 6–8.

18. Ibid., pp. 8–10.

19. Ibid., p. 17.

20. Ibid., pp. 19–21.

21. Ibid., p. 28.

22. Louis D. Brandeis, *Brandeis on Zionism* (Washington, D.C.: Zionist Organization of America, 1942), p. 29.

23. See Chapter 2, above.

24. Norman Podhoretz, "Now, Instant Zionism," *New York Times Magazine,* February 3, 1974, p. 11.

25. Ibid.

26. Ibid., pp. 42–44.

27. Ibid., p. 42.

28. Cf. the contrasting positions in the article by Israeli political scientist Shlomo Avineri, "Soured Promise: Letter to an American Friend," *Jerusalem Post,* March 10, 1987, p. 10, and the reply by the then associate national director (now director) of the Anti-Defamation League of B'nai B'rith, Abraham H. Foxman, "Reply to an Israeli Friend," *Jerusalem Post,* March 17, 1987, p. 10.

29. This implication underlies Sklare's entire chapter in the "Lakeville" study.

30. Peter L. Berger, Brigitte Berger, and Hansfried Kellner, *The Homeless Mind* (New York: Random House, 1973), p. 64.

31. Ibid., p. 67.

32. Ibid., pp. 77–79.

33. Peter L. Berger, *The Sacred Canopy* (Garden City, N.Y.: Doubleday, 1966), pp. 107–8.

34. Anton C. Zidjerveld, *The Abstract Society* (Garden City, N.Y.: Doubleday, Anchor, 1971), p. 72.

35. Berger et al., *The Homeless Mind*, p. 82.

36. Ibid.

37. Chaim I. Waxman, "Religion and State in Israel: The Perspective of American Jewry," paper presented at the conference on "Religion and State in the Perspective of Israel and World Jewry," co-sponsored by the Bar-Ilan Faculty of Law and the Argov Center for the Study of the State of Israel and the Jewish People, Bar-Ilan University, May 12, 1987.

38. Charles S. Liebman, *The Ambivalent American Jew* (Philadelphia: Jewish Publication Society of America, 1973), p. 105.

39. Christopher Lasch, *Haven in a Heartless World: The Family Besieged* (New York: Basic Books, 1977).

40. Liebman, *The Ambivalent American Jew*, p. 106.

41. It was precisely within this context that, at the outbreak of the Six-Day War, the U.S. ambassador to the United Nations, Arthur Goldberg, rejected the accusations made by Syrian ambassador Tomeh that American Jews were guilty of dual loyalty because of their support for Israel. Goldberg responded that in the United States attachment to one's "ancestral home" is not taken as "a sign of double loyalty or lack of attachment to our American institution." He then made reference to President John F. Kennedy's visit to his ancestral home and the degree to which that trip was applauded. Thus, according to Goldberg, Jewish support for Israel is part of an attachment to the ancestral home, and it is comparable to President Kennedy's attachment to Ireland. See Press Release, USUN-81, June 6, 1967, p. 8.

42. The pioneering work on the social impact of emancipation on Jewry is Jacob Katz, *Tradition and Crisis* (New York: Schocken Books, 1961). See also his *Out of the Ghetto* (Cambridge, Mass.: Harvard University Press, 1973); and Max Weiner, *The Jewish Religion at the Time of the Emancipation* (in Hebrew) (Jerusalem: Mossad Bialik and Leo Baeck Institute, 1974).

43. For a somewhat different perspective, see Aharon Lichtenstein, "Does Jewish Tradition Recognize an Ethnic Independent of Halakha?" in *Modern Jewish Ethics: Theory and Practice,* ed. Marvin Fox (Columbus: Ohio State University Press, 1975), pp. 62–88.

44. Nathan Rotenstreich, "Emancipation and Its Aftermath," in *The Future of the Jewish Community in America,* ed. David Sidorsky (New York: Basic Books, 1974), p. 47.

45. Berger, *The Sacred Canopy*, pp. 130ff.

46. Ibid., p. 138.

47. Isidor Chein, "The Problem of Jewish Identification," *Jewish Social Studies* 17, no. 3 (July 1955):219–20.

48. See above, Chapter 6, the section "Denomination."

49. Haron's findings are as yet unpublished. For a popular article about her research on American olim, see Lev Bearfield, "Making a Commitment," *Jerusalem Post Magazine,* August 14, 1987, pp. 6–7.

Chapter 8

1. Moshe Davis, *The Emergence of Conservative Judaism* (Philadelphia: Jewish Publication Society of America, 1963), p. 318. For a biographical sketch of Wilowsky, see Abraham J. Karp, "The RIDWAS: Rabbi Jacob David Wilowsky, 1845–1913," in *Sages and Saints* ed. Leo Jung (Hoboken, N.J.: Ktav, 1987), pp. 157–79.

2. William B. Helmreich, *The World of the Yeshiva* (New York: Free Press, 1982).

3. Marshall Sklare, *Conservative Judaism* (Glencoe, Ill.: Free Press, 1955), p. 43.

4. Marshall Sklare, *Conservative Judaism* aug. ed. (New York: Schocken Books, 1972), p. 264.

5. Peter L. Berger, *The Sacred Canopy* (Garden City, N.Y.: Doubleday, 1967). See also James Davidson Hunter, *American Evangelicalism: Conservative Religion and the Quandry of Modernity* (New Brunswick, N.J.: Rutgers University Press, 1983).

6. "A Bleak Outlook for Religion," *New York Times,* February 25, 1968, p. 3.

7. These are analyzed in greater detail in Chaim I. Waxman, *America's Jews in Transition* (Philadelphia: Temple University Press, 1983), pp. 124–34.

8. Mark Wischnitzer, *To Dwell in Safety* (Philadelphia: Jewish Publication Society of America, 1948), p. 289.

9. Egon Mayer and Chaim I. Waxman, "Modern Jewish Orthodoxy in America: Toward the Year 2000," *Tradition* 16, no. 3 (Spring 1977):99–100.

10. American Association for Jewish Education, "Jewish School Census 1978/79," *Information Bulletin,* no. 44 (1979).

11. Bernard Lazerwitz, "Religious Identification and Its Ethnic Correlates: A Multivariate Model," *Social Forces* 52, no. 2 (Winter 1973):204–20; Steven M. Cohen, "The Impact of Jewish Education on Religious Identification and Practice," *Jewish Social Studies* 36, nos. 3–4 (July-October 1974):316–26; Arnold Dashefsky and Howard Shapiro, *Ethnic Identification among American Jews* (Lexington, Mass.: Lexington Books, 1974); Harold S. Himmelfarb, "The Impact of Religious Schooling" (Ph.D. diss., University of Chicago, 1974).

12. Himmelfarb, "The Impact of Religious Schooling."

13. Helmreich, *The World of the Yeshiva.*

14. Jeffrey S. Gurock, *The Men and Women of Yeshiva: Orthodoxy, Higher Education and American Judaism* (New York: Columbia University Press, 1988); Gilbert Klaperman, *The Story of Yeshiva University* (New York: Macmillan, 1969).

15. Helmreich, *The World of the Yeshiva,* p. 310.

16. Solomon Poll, *The Hasidic Community of Williamsburg* (New York: Schocken Books, 1962); Israel Rubin, *Satmar: An Island in the City* (Chicago: New York Times Books, Quadrangle, 1972).

17. For a detailed analysis of the generational thesis, see Waxman, *America's Jews in Transition*, pp. 29–134.

18. Natalie Gittelson, "American Jews Discover Orthodoxy, *New York Times Magazine*, September 30, 1984, pp. 41ff.

19. Janet Aviad, *Return to Judaism* (Chicago: University of Chicago Press, 1983); M. Herbert Danziger, *The Return: A Study of the Contemporary Revival in Orthodox Judaism* (New Haven, Conn.: Yale University Press, 1989, forthcoming).

20. Reuven P. Bulka, ed., *Dimensions of Orthodox Judaism* (New York: Ktav, 1983), pp. 5–32.

21. Seymour Leventman, "From Shtetl to Suburb," in *The Ghetto and Beyond*, ed. Peter I. Rose (New York: Random House, 1969), pp. 33–56.

22. Egon Mayer, *From Suburb to Shtetl: The Jews of Boro Park* (Philadelphia: Temple University Press, 1979).

23. Chaim I. Waxman, "The Sabbath as Dialectic: The Meaning and Role," *Judaism* 31, no. 1 (Winter 1982):37–44.

24. Waxman, *America's Jews in Transition*, pp. 104–34.

25. Jackson W. Carroll, Douglass W. Johnson, and Martin E. Marty, *Religion in America: 1950 to the Present* (San Francisco: Harper & Row, 1979).

26. Peter L. Berger, " 'A Great Revival' Coming for America's Churches," *U.S. News and World Reports*, April 11, 1977, p. 70.

27. Charles Y. Glock, "Consciousness among Contemporary Youth: An Interpretation," in *The New Religious Consciousness*, ed. Charles Y. Glock and Robert N. Bellah (Berkeley: University of California Press, 1976), p. 362.

28. Robert N. Bellah, "New Religious Consciousness and the Crisis of Modernity," in Glock and Bellah, *The New Religious Consciousness*, pp. 333–52.

29. Ferdinand Tönnies, *Community and Society* (New York: Harper Torchbooks, 1957); see also Werner J. Cahnman and Rudolf Heberle, eds., *Ferdinand Toennies on Sociology* (Chicago: University of Chicago Press, 1971).

30. Robert Nisbet, *The Quest for Community* (New York: Oxford University Press, 1953), p. 15.

31. Berger, *The Sacred Canopy*, pp. 133–34; see also Peter L. Berger, Brigitte Berger, and Hansfried Kellner, *The Homeless Mind* (New York: Random House, 1973); Peter L. Berger and Richard J. Neuhaus, *To Empower People: The Role of Mediating Structures in Public Policy* (Washington, D.C.: American Enterprise Institute for Public Policy Research, 1977).

32. Dick Anthony and Thomas Robbins, "Culture Crisis and Contemporary Religion," in *In Gods We Trust: New Patterns of Religious Pluralism in America*, ed. Thomas Robbins and Dick Anthony (New Brunswick, N.J.: Transaction Books, 1981), p. 26.

33. *New York Times*, December 25, 1985, p. 1.

34. David A. Roozen, William McKinney, and Wayne Thompson, "The Big Chill Warms up to Worship," paper presented at the Annual Meeting of the

Society for the Scientific Study of Religion and the Religious Research Association, Washington, D.C., November 16, 1986.

35. Orlando Patterson, *Ethnic Chauvinism* (New York: Stein and Day, 1977).
36. Berger, *The Sacred Canopy.*
37. Hunter, *American Evangelicalism,* pp. 15–17.
38. Charles S. Liebman, "Religion and the Chaos of Modernity: The Case of Contemporary Judaism," in *Take Judaism, for Example,* ed. Jacob Neusner (Chicago: University of Chicago Press, 1983), pp. 147–64. On Orthodoxy in Israel, see Charles S. Liebman and Eliezer Don-Yehiya, *Religion and Politics in Israel* (Bloomington: Indiana University Press, 1984), pp. 119–37. See also Charles S. Liebman, "The Religious Component in Israeli Ultra-Nationalism," *Jerusalem Quarterly,* no. 41 (Winter 1987):127–44.
39. Liebman, "Religion and the Chaos of Modernity," p. 150.
40. This is an expression and an approach that Rabbi Moses Sofer frequently used in rendering decisions on religious law, halakhah. See, e.g., *Tshuvot Chatam Sofer: Orach Chaim* (Chatam Sofer, *Responsa: Orach Chaim),* responsum 181 (New York: M. P. Press, 1958), p. 68b; and *Tshuvot Chatam Sofer: Yoreh Deah* (Chatam Sofer, *Responsa: Yoreh Deah),* responsum 19 (New York: M. P. Press, 1958), p. 8a. For a biography of the Chatam Sofer, see Yehuda Nachshoni, *Rabbeinu Moshe Sofer: Hachatam Sofer* (Jerusalem: Hotzaat Mashabim, 1981); see also Jacob Katz, *Halakhah and Kabbalah: Studies in the History of Jewish Religion, Its Various Faces and Social Relevance* (in Hebrew) (Jerusalem: Magnes Press, 1986), pp. 353–86.
41. See many of the selections in Mordecai Waxman, ed., *Tradition and Change: The Development of Conservative Judaism* (New York: Burning Bush Press, 1958).
42. Berger, *The Sacred Canopy.*
43. Liebman, "Religion and the Chaos of Modernity"; Norman Lamm, *Faith and Doubt* (New York: Ktav, 1971), pp. 69–82.
44. See above, p. 114; and Berger, *The Sacred Canopy,* pp. 107–8.
45. Hunter, *American Evangelicalism.*
46. Chaim I. Waxman, "The Sabbath as Dialectic: The Meaning and Role," *Judaism* 31, no. 1 (Winter 1982):37–44.

Chapter 9

1. George D. Spindler, *Sociocultural and Psychological Processes of Menomini Acculturation* (Berkeley: University of California Press, 1955).
2. Milton M. Gordon, *Assimilation in American Life* (New York: Oxford University Press, 1964).
3. Aaron Antonovsky and Abraham David Katz, *From the Golden to the Promised Land* (Darby, Pa.: Norwood Editions, 1979), p. 72.
4. Ibid. See also Gerald S. Berman, *The Work Adjustment of North American Immigrants in Israel* (Jerusalem: Hebrew University, Work and Welfare Research Institute, 1978), p. 31.
5. Even among the majority of the pre-1956 American olim who had not previously been in Israel there were those who were, nevertheless, familiar with Israeli society and culture. Antonovsky and Katz found that about 20 percent had

spent time, usually a year, in farms located in New Jersey and Ontario that sim-
ulated life in the kibbutz. The participants received an actual taste of collective
living, learned Hebrew and about Israeli culture. See Antonovsky and Katz, *From
the Golden to the Promised Land.*

6. Jay Shapiro, *From Both Sides Now: An American-Israeli Odyssey* (Tel Aviv:
Dvir Katzman, 1983), pp. 24–25.

7. Myrna Silverman, "The Aging American Zionist in Israel: A Group
Apart" (unpublished paper based on fieldwork conducted in Israel during
the summer of 1971).

8. Sheldon Lache, Dorota Teczniczek, Beatriz Mann, and Ron Lahaz, *The
Absorption Problems of Older Immigrants in Israeli Society* (Jerusalem: Henrietta
Szold Institute, research report no. 183, publication no. 536, February 1976),
pp. 65–67.

9. See below, Chapter 11, Table 29.

10. Lache et al., *Absorption Problems,* pp. 69–74.

11. Ibid., p. 75. Compare their situation with that reflected in a joke cur-
rently popular in Israel: "What do the miracle of Chanukah and the monthly
Israeli salary have in common? Each is just enough to last eight days."

12. Ibid., pp. 77–80.

13. Kevin Avruch, *American Immigrants in Israel: Social Identities and
Change* (Chicago: University of Chicago Press, 1981), chap. 6 and 7; Silverman,
"The Aging American Zionist in Israel."

14. Steven J. Schleifer, Arthur H. Schwartz, John C. Thornton, and Sarah
L. Rosenberg, "A Study of American Immigrants to Israel Utilizing the
SRRQ," *Journal of Psychosomatic Research* 23, no. 4 (1979):250.

15. Michael Roskin and Jeffrey L. Edleson, "A Research Note on the Emotional Health of English-Speaking Immigrants in Israel," *Jewish Journal of Sociology* 26, no. 2 (December 1984):143.

16. Michael Roskin and Jeffrey L. Edleson, "The Emotional Health of
English Speaking Immigrants to Israel," *Journal of Jewish Communal Service* 60,
no. 2 (Winter 1983): 158.

17. Ibid., p. 159. Cf. Chaim I. Waxman, "The Sabbath as Dialectic: The
Meaning and Role," *Judaism* 31, no. 1 (Winter 1982):37–44, in which I suggested that Orthodox Jews do not seem to experience the loss of community
characteristic of modern society and have fewer difficulties in adjusting to a
new neighborhood because the rituals as practiced by the Orthodox provide
for a clearly defined community.

18. Roskin and Edleson, "The Emotional Health of English-Speaking
Immigrants in Israel," p. 160.

19. Ruth Tamar Horowitz, "Jewish Immigrants to Israel: Self-reported Powerlessness and Alienation among Immigrants from the Soviet Union and North
America," *Journal of Cross Cultural Psychology* 10, no. 3 (September 1979):372.

20. Ephraim Tabory, "A Sociological Study of the Reform and Conservative Movements in Israel" (Ph.D. diss., Bar-Ilan University, 1980); Ephraim
Tabory and Bernard Lazerwitz, "Americans in the Israeli Reform and Conservative Denominations: Religiosity under an Ethnic Shield?" *Review of Religious Research* 24, no. 3 (March 1983):177–87.

21. Antonovsky and Katz, *From the Golden to the Promised Land,* pp. 99–102; Avruch, *American Immigrants in Israel,* pp. 137–52.

22. See below, Chapter 11, Table 30.

23. Avruch, *American Immigrants in Israel,* pp. 140–41. For a classic "catch-22" story involving Israeli bureaucracy, see Shapiro, *From Both Sides Now,* pp. 43–59.

24. Avruch, *American Immigrants in Israel,* pp. 148–49.

25. S. N. Eisenstadt, *The Transformation of Israeli Society* (Boulder, Colo.: West-view Press, 1985), p. 352.

26. Pearl Katz, "Acculturation and Social Networks of American Immigrants in Israel" (Ph.D. diss., State University of New York at Buffalo, 1974), p. 107.

27. See above, p. 94.

28. Monica Boyd, David L. Featherman, and Judah Matras, "Status Attainment of Immigrant and Immigrant Origin Categories in the United States, Canada, and Israel," in *Comparative Social Research,* ed. Richard F. Tomasson (Greenwich, Conn.: JAI Press, 1980), 3:212–13.

29. Milton M. Gordon, *Assimilation in American Life* (New York: Oxford University Press, 1964), pp. 70–71.

30. Zvi Gitelman, *Becoming Israelis: Political Resocialization of Soviet and American Immigrants* (New York: praeger, 1982), p. 239.

31. According to Henry Valentino, director of the Federal Voting Assistance Program of the U.S. Department of Defense, some fifty to sixty thousand Americans who were not government employees voted in Israel for the 1984 U.S. presidential election. Personal interview, August 25, 1987.

32. Ibid., p. 241.

Chapter 10

1. There seems to be no neutral way to refer to the land captured by Israel in the Six-Day War. The closest to such is probably "the Territories," without any adjective such as "occupied" or "administered." The Territories encompass what is Biblically called Judea and Samaria, as well as the Gaza Strip. Those who do not accept the legitimacy of Israel's claims over Judea and Samaria continue to call them by their pre-1967 Western name, "the West Bank."

2. See, e.g., Janet O'Dea, "Gush Emunim: Roots and Ambiguities," *Forum* (Fall 1976):38–50; Amnon Rubinstein, *The Zionist Dream Revisited* (New York: Schocken Books, 1984); Zvi Raanan, *Gush Emunim* (in Hebrew) (Tel Aviv: Sifriyat Poalim, 1980); Danny Rubinstein, *On the Lord's Side: Gush Emunim* (in Hebrew) (Tel Aviv: Hakibbutz Hameuchad, 1982); Charles S. Liebman and Eliezer Don-Yehiya, *Civil Religion in Israel* (Berkeley: University of California Press, 1983), pp. 200–206; Ehud Sprinzak, *Gush Emunim: The Politics of Zionist Fundamentalism in Israel* (New York: American Jewish Committee, Institute of Human Relations, 1986), pp. 8ff.; Uriel Tal, "Totalitarian Democratic Hermeneutics and Policies in Modern Jewish Religious Nationalism," in *Totalitarian Democracy and After: International Colloquium in Memory of Jacob L. Talmon* (Jerusalem: Israel Academy of Sciences and Humanities, Magnes Press, 1984), pp. 137–57.

3. See, e.g., Marie Syrkin, "False Messianism from Brooklyn," *Midstream* 30, no. 10 (December 1984):40–42.

4. Myron J. Aronoff, "The Institutionalisation and Cooptation of a Charismatic, Messianic, Religious-Political Revitalisation Movement," in *The Impact of Gush Emunim: Politics and Settlement in the West Bank*, ed. David Newman (London: Croom Helm, 1985), pp. 46–69.

5. Gershon Shafir, "Institutional and Spontaneous Settlement Drives: Did Gush Emunim Make a Difference?" in Newman, *The Impact of Gush Emunim*, pp. 153–71.

6. Meron Benvenisti, *The West Bank Data Project: A Survey of Israel's Policies* (Washington, D.C.: American Enterprise Institute for Public Policy Research, 1984), p. 64.

7. The sample consisted of one hundred adult men and women, one per family unit, from thirty-eight different settlements throughout the Territories. At the time, it was estimated that there were some thirty to thirty-five thousand Israeli settlers, and that the Americans among them constituted approximately 12 to 15 percent of the total. The field research for the project was made possible by grants from the Foundation for Middle East Peace, Inc. (Washington, D.C.), the Jerusalem Center for Public Affairs, and the Sociology Department of Tel Aviv University.

8. Chaim I. Waxman, *America's Jews in Transition* (Philadelphia: Temple University Press, 1983), pp. 98–103, 147–51.

9. Zvi Gitelman, *Becoming Israelis: Political Resocialization of Soviet and American Immigrants* (New York: Praeger, 1982), pp. 305–40.

10. Waxman, *America's Jews in Transition*, pp. 144–46.

11. See above, Chapter 6, Tables 4 and 5.

12. See above, p. 97.

13. Waxman, *America's Jews in Transition*.

14. Gitelman, *Becoming Israelis*.

15. Ibid., pp. 65–69.

16. Shafir, "Institutional and Spontaneous Settlement Drives."

17. Benvenisti, *The West Bank Data Project*.

18. Leon Festinger, *A Theory of Cognitive Dissonance* (Stanford, Calif.: Stanford University Press, 1957).

19. Ibid., p. 13.

20. Ibid., p. 3.

21. Kach is the ultra-nationalist organization founded by Meir Kahane, an American Israeli who had previously founded the Jewish Defense League. Kach has been widely condemned, in Israel and abroad, as being anti-democractic and racist. The official position of the Kach movement is presented in Meir Kahane, *They Must Go* (New York: Grosset & Dunlap, 1981). Supporters of Kach are believed to engage in even more extreme and violent activities than those officially proposed.

22. Gitelman, *Becoming Israelis*, pp. 333–34.

23. See, e.g., Sammy Smooha, "The Tolerance of the Israeli Jewish Majority toward the Arab Minority: A Comparative Perspective," in *Is It Indeed Hard to Be an Israeli?* (in Hebrew), ed. Alouph Hareven (Jerusalem: Van Lear Institute, 1983), pp. 91–107.

24. For an account of the entire episode written by one of those involved, convicted, and imprisoned, see Haggai Segal, *"Dear Brothers"* (Jerusalem: Keter, 1987).

25. It should be emphasized that these were the immediate responses conveyed within days after the arrests. It is possible that some of the opinions expressed underwent change during the course of the detention and trials of the Underground.

26. See above, Chapter 8.

27. Ibid.

Chapter 11

1. An analysis of American olim who immigrated to Israel between the years 1969 and 1972, conducted by Dashefsky and Lazerwitz, indicated that at least 37 percent had returned. The Israel Central Bureau of Statistics finding is a 39 percent return rate for those who were in Israel less than five years. See Arnold Dashefsky and Bernard Lazerwitz, "The Role of Religious Identification in North American Migration to Israel," *Journal for the Scientific Study of Religion* 22, no. 3 (September 1983): 265; Israel Central Bureau of Statistics, *Monthly Bulletin of Statistics,* Supplement D, January 1986.

2. Gerald Engel, "North American Jewish Settlers in Israel," *American Jewish Year Book* 71 (1970): 161–87. For more detailed analyses of specific aspects of the population in this study, see Gerald Engel, "Comparison between American Permanent Residents of Israel," Parts I–III, *Journal of Psychology* 71 (1969):133–42; 72 (1969): 135–39; and 73 (1969):33–39; idem, "Comparison between Americans Living in Israel and Those Who Returned to America," Parts I–III, *Journal of Psychology* 74 (1970): 195–204; 75 (1970):243–51; and 76 (1970):117–23.

3. Engel, "North American Jewish Settlers in Israel," p. 183.

4. Harry Lieb Jubas, "The Adjustment Process of Americans and Canadians in Israel and Their Integration into Israeli Society" (Ph.D. diss., Michigan State University, 1974).

5. Ibid., chap. 7, pp. 189–245.

6. Ibid., p. 191.

7. Ibid., pp. 195–96.

8. Mario I. Blejer and Itzhak Goldberg, "Return Migration–Expectation versus Reality: A Case Study of Western Immigrants in Israel," Maurice Falk Institute for Economic Research in Israel, discussion paper no. 7812, Jerusalem, September 1978, p. 3.

9. Ibid., pp. 26–28.

10. Dashefsky and Lazerwitz, "The Role of Religious Identification."

11. Ibid., pp. 268–69.

12. Ibid., p. 270.

13. J. J. Mangalam and Harry K. Schwarzweller, "Some Theoretical Guidelines toward a Sociology of Migration," *International Migration Review* 4, no. 2 (Spring 1970):10.

14. Engel, "Comparison between Americans Living in Israel and Those Who Returned to America," Part II, Israeli Background.

15. Dashefsky and Lazerwitz, "The Role of Religious Identification," p. 272.
16. Aaron Antonovsky and Abraham David Katz, *From the Golden to the Promised Land* (Darby, Pa.: Norwood Editions, 1979), pp. 93–120.
17. Zvi Sobel, *Migrants from the Promised Land* (New Brunswick, N.J.: Transaction Books, 1986), p. 174.
18. Dashefsky and Lazerwitz, "The Role of Religious Identification," p. 272.
19. Kevin Avruch, *American Immigrants in Israel* (Chicago: University of Chicago Press, 1981).
20. A Havurah is a prayer and study fellowship which typically developed as an alternative to the formal synagogue structure.
21. Chaim I. Waxman, *America's Jews in Transition* (Philadelphia: Temple University Press, 1983), p. 188.
22. Dashefsky and Lazerwitz, "The Role of Religious Identification," p. 272.
23. Sobel, *Migrants from the Promised Land.*

Chapter 12
1. Nahum Weissman, "In the Beginning," *Bridge* (APAI newsletter) 8, nos. 1 and 2 (Summer-Fall 1984 [5745]):1–2; "Message from the President," *Bridge* (March 15, 1976):1–4. Unless part of a direct quote, all references to the organization will be as PNAI, the current name, which was adopted at the tenth annual convention to reflect the inclusion of Canadian members.
2. Personal interview, January 15, 1987.
3. Weissman, "In the Beginning," p. 1.
4. Quoted in Matthew Nesvisky, "Hard Is Where the Home Is," *Moment* (January-February 1985):54.
5. Ruth Seligman, "When Your Child Goes on Aliyah," *Pioneer Woman* (January-February 1985):6.
6. Terry Brodie, "Helping Their Children and Themselves," *Newsview* (Israel), May 17, 1983, p. 26.
7. Ephraim Tabory, "Accounting for 'Deviants': Parents of American Migrants to Israel" (unpublished paper, 1986). For a brief summary of Tabory's findings, see his article "Aliyah's Impact on Family Ties," *Bridge* 9, no. 2 (Rosh Hashanah 1985 [5746]):4.
8. Tabory, "Acounting for 'Deviants,' " pp. 8–9.
9. Irwin Shaw, "Proposal for a Program to Reduce Parental Opposition to Aliyah," *Bridge* 10, no. 2 (Succoth 1986 [Fall 5747]):10.
10. Debbie Weissman, "When Aliyah Conflicts with Parents' Wishes," *Bridge* 9, no. 1 (Spring 1985 [5745]):14.
11. Tabory, "Accounting for 'Deviants,' " pp. 10–11.
12. Ibid., pp. 12–13.
13. On the geographic mobility of America's Jews, see Waxman, *America's Jews in Transition*, pp. 137–41.
14. *The World's Telephones: A Statistical Compilation as of January 1984* (Indianapolis: AT&T, 1986), pp. 22–24, 37–41.
15. *Bridge* 8, nos. 3 and 4 (Winter 1984–85 [5745]):16.
16. *Bridge* 7, no. 2 (Summer 1983 [5743]).

17. *Bridge* 8, no. 1 (Spring 1984 [5744]):2.

18. Editorials, *Bridge* 9, no. 1 (Spring 1985 [5745]):2, and in various other issues of that newsletter.

19. Nesvisky, "Hard Is Where the Home Is," p. 57.

20. Tabory, "Accounting for 'Deviants,' " p. 22.

Chapter 13

1. Gerald S. Berman, *The Experience of Aliyah among Recently Arrived North American Olim: The Role of the Shaliach* (Jerusalem: Hebrew University, Work and Welfare Institute, 1977), rable 15, p. 35.

2. Ibid., pp. 12–13.

3. For a detailed analysis of the Jewish Agency, see Daniel J. Elazar and Alysa M. Dortort, eds., *Understanding the Jewish Agency: A Handbook* (Jerusalem: Jerusalem Center for Public Affairs, 1984).

4. *Report and Recommendations of Caesaria Commission on Aliya* (Jerusalem: October 1983), p. 3.

5. Ibid., I borrowed the term from Title II, Part A, Section 202(a) of the U.S. Economic Opportunity Act of 1964.

6. *Report of the Public Committee for the Examination of the Emissary System of the World Zionist Organization* (draft English translation), Jerusalem, December 1985, typescript.

7. Synopsis of letter from Bernice S. Tannenbaum, chairman of the World Zionist Organization–American Section, to Judge Moshe Landau, March 4, 1985.

8. See, e.g., F. Bechhofer, ed., *Population Growth and the Brain Drain* (Edinburgh: Edinburgh University Press, 1969).

9. Paul Ritterband, *Education, Employment, and Migration: Israel in Comparative Perspective* (Cambridge: Cambridge University Press, 1978).

10. Ibid., pp. 120–22.

Index

Abraham Gershon of Kitov, Rabbi, 38
Abraham of Kalisk, Rabbi, 38
Acculturation, 20; of American Israelis, 139–49
Adams, John, 53
Adaptationism, 132
Adler, Cyrus, 70
Agudath Israel, 123
Ahad Ha-am, 66, 67, 69, 70, 71, 72, 73
Alcharizi, Yehuda, 36
Ali, Muhammad, 41
Aliya: as entailing psychological difficulties, 142–43; from establishment of Israel to Six-Day War, 81–87; ideological perspective on American, 17–18; institutional structure of, 195–202; as international migration, 15–23; low priority of American Jewish communal agenda, 200–202; nineteenth century American, 59–60, 77; nonkibbutz motivation of, 87; pre-State of Israel 20th-century American, 80–81; pre-20th-century, 36–38; push and pull factors, 17, 19, 79, 83, 85, 86, 100–102, 160; rate of American since 1950, 82; religiosity and, 20, 80, 81, 84, 100–102; role of shaliach in, 196–97, 199–200; since Six-Day war, 16–17; social scientific perspective on, 18; Zionist affiliation and, 83, 97, 158. *See also* American olim
Alkalai, Rabbi Yehuda, 40, 42–45, 46, 56, 57
Al-Khazari, 30

Alliance Israelite Universelle, 41
Almohades, 31, 33, 36
American Jewish Year Book, 89, 94, 105
American Jews: beginnings of community, 50–51; contemporary conditions of, 16, 18–19; early contact with Holy Land, 52–61; size of population at American revolutionary war, 51
American olim: acculturation of, 139–49; age, 91; denominational distribution, 98–100; education, 80, 93–94, 147; fulfillment of expectations of, 147; generational status, 89–90; identificational assimilation, 147; Jewish education, 98; marriage and family, 80, 92; motivations for aliya, 80–82, 100–102; occupational distribution, 94, 147; pensioners, 141; political behavior, 94–96; regional distribution, 89; sex, 91–92; social readjustment of Soviet olim and, 143; socioeconomic status, 87; structural assimilation, 147; in "the Territories," 150–68; visits to Israel prior to aliya, 139; Zionist organizational membership, 83, 97 *See also* Aliya
American Zionist Federation (AZF), 200
Anglo-Saxons, 140
Anti-Semitism, 16, 160
Antonovsky, Aaron, 80, 81, 84, 89, 91, 93, 177
Arab, 31, 36, 107, 164–65, 166
Ararat, 55–56
Ari. *See* Luria, Rabbi Isaac
Aronoff, Myron J., 150
Ashkenazim, 38, 65

Index

Assimilation: identificational. *See* American olim, identificational assimilation

Assimilation: structural. *See* American olim, structural assimilation

Association of Americans and Canadians in Israel (AACI), 144, 186, 193

Association of Parents of American Israelis (APAI). *See* Parents of North American Israelis (PNAI)

Avruch, Kevin, 90, 97, 100, 102, 144, 145, 180

Bartenura, Rabbi Ovadiah, 37

Basle, 61, 65

Begin, Menachem, 107

Beijer, G., 16

Belkin, Samuel, 123

Ben-Gurion, David, 48, 77, 108

Benvenisti, Meron, 150, 162

Berger, Peter L., 113–15, 120, 127, 128–29

Berman, Gerald, 89, 90, 91, 97, 98, 101, 197

Besht. *See* Rabbi Israel Baal Shem Tov

Bierer, Ruben, 48

Black power, 126

Blejer, Mario, 170

Bloch, Rabbi Eliyahu Meir, 122

Bnai Jeshurun, Congregation, 54, 72

Boro Park, Jews of 124–25

Boston, Jewish community of 93–94

Bovenkerk, Frank, 21

Brandeis, Louis D., 68; definition of Zionism, 111–12

Bratslav (Breslov), 35

Bridge, 187, 188, 192

Brit Shalom, 74

Brodbar-Nemzer, Jay, 92

Bureaucracy: impact on return of American olim, 170; pervasiveness of in Israel, 144–46; as related to modernization, 113–15, 128

Caesaria Process, 197–98, 201

Canada, 83–84

Carter, Jimmy, 127

Central Bureau of Statistics (Israel), 90, 91, 92, 94, 99, 170, 171, 172

Central Conference of American Rabbis (CCAR), 61, 123

Chabad, 45. *See also* Lubavitch

Chasidism, 35, 38, 124

Chatam Sofer. *See* Sofer, Rabbi Moses

Chein, Isador, 117

Chofetz Chaim, Yeshiva, 121

Civil religion, 109, 126

Civil rights movement, 100, 126

Clinton, Gov. George, 53

Cognitive dissonance, 125, 162–63

Cohen, Abraham (Albert), 41

Cohen, Samuel, 52

Cohen, Steven M., 92, 107, 110, 111

Community: loss of in modern America, 128–29; Orthodox Judaism as presupposing, 135–36

Compartmentalization, 113–18, 131, 132, 133–34

Conference of Presidents of Major Jewish Organizations, 106

Conservative Judaism, 67, 108–9; as adaptationism, 132; attachments to Israel, 111; leaders' conceptions of Zionism, 67–76

Council of Jewish Federations, 198, 201

Cresson, Warder, 59–60

Cults, 127

Dashefsky, Arnold, 101, 109, 144, 171, 176, 178, 179, 182

Davis, Moshe, 69

Day schools, 83, 98, 121–22

De Haas, Jacob, 66, 67

Demography, 89–100

Denomination, 84, 98–100

Dulzin, Arye, 198

Eastern European Jewry: concepts of religion and culture, 66; as contrasted with German Jewry, 65–66; migration to America, 65–66; and Zionism, 66

Edleson, Jeffrey L., 142, 143

Eisenstadt, S. N., 17, 100, 146, 290

Elazar, Daniel J., 106

Elijah, Rabbi (Gaon of Vilna), 38, 40

Emissaries: in 18th century, 52–53; Isaac Leeser's attitudes toward, 58–59; of World Zionist Organization, 195–200

Encyclopedia Judaica, 106

Engel, Gerald, 83–87, 98, 169, 171, 176, 177

Entis, Barbara, 187

Ethnicity, rise of public, 127, 129–30

Evangelicals, 133
Eventov, Yakir, 106
Expansionism, 131, 132–35
Extremism, 150, 161

Federation, Jewish: and aliya efforts, 198, 201
Federation of American Zionists (FAZ), 66–69, 70
Festinger, Leon, 162
Field, Irwin, 198
Finifter, Ada, 16
Finzi, Rabbi Yaacov, 42
Frank, Suzanne, 187
Frank, Wendy, 187
Frankists, 39
Friedenwald, Harry, 67
Friedlaender, Israel, 67, 69, 75
Fundamentalism, 150

Galut, views on in traditional Judaism, 29–30, 34
Gaza Strip, 21, 134, 150–68
Gemeinschaft, 128
Gilboa, Eytan, 109, 110
Gitelman, Zvi, 94, 96, 147, 148
Glazer, Nathan, 109
Glock, Charles, 127
Goell, Yohai, 74
Goldberg, Itzhak, 170
Goldscheider, Calvin, 78, 89, 90, 91, 92, 93, 94, 97, 99, 101, 158
Goldstein, Sidney, 94
Gordon, Milton M., 139, 147
Gorki, Maxim, 73
Gottheil, Richard, 66, 67
"Green Line," 21, 134, 149, 159, 161
Gush Emunim, 150, 162, 165–67

Haam, 48
Haikar Hatzair, 78
Halakhah, 47, 132, 134, 163
Halevi Rabbi Yehuda, 29–31, 34
Haley, Alex, 130
Halpern, Ben, 67
Hamagshimim, 200
Haron, Miriam, 118
Hashomer Hatzair, 79
Hatchiya, 164
Havurah, 181
Hebrew, knowledge of 107, 140, 141
Hebrew Educational Society, 58
Hebrew Union College, 72
Hebron, 38

Hegel, 49
Hehalutz, 78
Herzl, Theodor, 66, 69, 70; as Messiah, 47, 48
Heschel, Abraham J., 28
Hess, Moses, 41, 45–47, 57
Himmelfarb, Harold, 122
Hirsch Rabbi Samson Raphael, 116, 133
Holocaust, 112, 124, 126, 161
Homelessness, 115–16
Horowitz, Ruth Tamar, 143
Hovevei Zion, 62
Hunter, James Davidson, 133

Identity, Jewish and American, of American olim, 141–42, 148–49
IHUD, 74
Immigrants, potential, 88, 172, 173, 174
Intermarriage, 83
Isaacs, Samuel Myer, 58
Isolation, feelings of among American olim, 140–41
Israel Aliya Center, 200
Israel Baal Shem Tov, Rabbi (Besht), 35, 38
Israel Bonds, 106, 183
Israel Independence Day. See Yom Haatzmaut
Israel, Michael Boaz. See Cresson, Warder
Israel, State of: American Jews' knowledge of society and culture, 107; legal system, 144; political structure, 144; religious structure, 144; role of in American Jewish life, 105–18. See also Bureaucracy

Jackson, J. A., 20
Jaffe, Eliezer L., 78
Jerusalem, 27, 28, 30, 31, 34, 37, 44, 52, 97, 140
Jerusalem Post, 140
Jerusalem Program, 105, 108
Jewish Agency, 106, 197
Jewish education, 121–23; and aliya, 83–84
Jewish Hospital, the, 58
Jewish identity, 129–30. See also Zionism: and Jewish identity
Jewish Publication Society, 58
Jewish Theological Seminary (JTS), 67, 69, 70
"Jewish Underground," 166–67

Job opportunities and satisfaction, 141, 169, 175–77
Johnson Immigration Acts, 65
Jubas, Harry L., 90, 97, 98, 101, 144, 170, 171, 176, 177, 244
Judah the Saint, 38
Judea, 21, 134, 150–68, 211–40

Kabbalah, 37
Kach, 166–67
Kalischer, Rabbi Zvi Hirsch, 40–42, 46, 57
Kalmanowitz, Rabbi Abraham, 122
Kaplan, Mordecai M., 70–71, 73, 75, 112
Karigal, Rabbi Chaim Isaac, 52
Katz, Abraham David, 80, 81, 84, 89, 91, 93, 177
Katz, Jacob, 39
Katz, Rabbi Mordechai, 122
Katz, Pearl, 147
Koenig, Samuel, 75–76
Kol Israel Chaverim, 45
Kook, Rabbi Abraham Isaac, 49, 133
Korean War, 83
Kotler, Rabbi Aaron, 121, 122
Kuzari, 29–31

Lache, Sheldon, 98, 141
Ladino, 42
Lahav, Ron, 141
Lakeville, 108
Lamm, Norman, 133
Landau Commission, 198–200
Landau, Moshe, 198–99
Lapide, P. E., 78
Laqueur, Walter, 79
Lasch, Christopher, 115
Lazerwitz, Bernard, 135, 101, 144, 171, 176, 178, 179, 182
Leeser, Isaac, 57–60; as proto-Zionist, 58–59; and restoration, 58
Leff, Leopold, 47
Liebman, Charles S., 71, 108–9, 131–33
Lilienthal, Benjamin, 60
Loew, Rabbi Judah ben Bezalel of Prague (Maharal), 29, 33–35
Lubavitch, 38, 123
Luria, Rabbi Isaac ("Holy Ari"), 37
Lurie, Chaim, 41

Maccabean, 66
McCarthyism, 83
Machal, 82–83

Magnes, Judah L., 67, 72–75
Maharal. *See* Loew, Rabbi Judah
Maimonides, 29, 36; attachments to Zion, 31–33; and messianism, 39
Maimonides College, 58
Malki, Rabbi Moses, 52
Mangalam, J. J., 175
Mann, Beatriz, 141
Marx, Karl, 45
Mayer, Egon, 121, 124–25
Menachem Mendel of Peremishlyany, Rabbi, 38
Menachem Mendel of Vitebsk, Rabbi, 38
Meshulachim. *See* Emissaries
Messianism, 27; and the forerunners of Zionism, 39–49; political, 150, 161, 166
Migration, international: aliya as, 15–23; push and pull factors in 15; typology of, 16, 18
Mikveh Israel, 42
Mikveh Israel, Congregation, 54, 58, 59
Mizrachi, 48, 68, 75
Modernity, 127–29
Monroe, James, 54
Montefiore, Moses, 41
Motivation. *See* American olim: motivations for aliya
Muddahy, Chaim, 52
Nachman of Bratslav, Rabbi, 29, 35–36
Nachman of Horodenka, Rabbi, 38
Nachmanides, 37
National Advocate, 54
National Religious Party, 198
National Society for Hebrew Day Schools, 121–22
Neotraditionalism, 131, 132
Nesvisky, Matthew, 193
New Left, 126
Newport, 52
Nisbet, Robert, 128
Noah, Mordecai Manuel, 54–58, 60; and establishment of Ararat, 55–56; as "pre-Zionist," 54; Jewish response to, 57
North American Aliya Movement, 200

Occident, 58, 59, 60
Orthodox Judaism: and adjustment to Israel, 135–36, 142; attachments to Israel, 111; impact of modernization on, 131–34;

increasing percentage of among American olim, 84, 98–100, 101–2; as monopoly in Israel, 144; as presupposing community, 135–36; renaissance of American, 119–36

Pappo, Rabbi Eliezer, 42
Parents: anxieties of, about children's aliya, 191; attitudes of, toward their children's aliya, 189–90; resources of and adjustment to children's aliya, 190; views of their children's motivations for aliya, 188–89
Parents of North American Israelis (PNAI), 186–93
Peoplehood, 101
Peres, Shimon, 107
Petersen, William, 16, 18
Philanthropy: Zionism in terms of, 66
Phillips, Jonas, 54
Pittsburgh Platform, 61
Pluralization, 113–16
Poalei Zion, 68
Podhoretz, Norman, 112
Political behavior. See American olim: political behavior
Pollard, Jonathan, 113
Protestantism, 133
Prushim, 38

Rabbi Jacob Joseph School, 121
Rabbinical Assembly, 123
Rabbinical Council of America, 123
Rambam. See Maimonides Ravenstein, Ernst G., 21
Reconstructionist Judaism, 70, 108
Reform Judaism, 54, 108–9; attachments to Israel, 111; 19th-century attitude toward Zionism, 60–62
Reines, Rabbi Isaac Jacob, 48
Religious consciousness, rise of, 127–29
Remaining in Israel: confidence in staying and, 171; ideological motives for aliya and, 169; religiosity and, 171
Rephaim, Emek, 59
Residents, temporary, 88
Restorationism. See Leeser, Isaac Returnees from Israel to America, 21–22, 142; aliya intentions upon

arrival among, 174–75; attitudes toward Israel and aliya among, 182–85; economic difficulties and, 177; expectations and, 170; occupational status of, 173; previous research on 169–71; professional opportunities and, 177; push and pull factors in decision to return, 179–80; religious and Jewish communal commitments among, 180–83; reported reasons for return of, 176–79
Rheinische Zeitung, 45
RIDVAZ. See Wilowsky, Rabbi Jacob David
Ritchey, P. Neal, 22
Roper, Elmo, 110
Roskin, Michael, 142, 143
Rotem, Cvi, 106
Rotenstreich, Nathan, 116
Rothchild, Asher Anshel (Anselm Mayer), 40, 41
Rothschild family, 44

Sabbath, 135
Sabbatian, 38
Sadducees, 131
Safed, 27, 37, 38, 40, 52
Salzman, Bernice M., 187
Samaria, 21, 134, 150–68
Schechter, Solomon, 69, 70, 72, 75
Scholem, Gershom, 37
Schwarzweller, Harry K., 175
Secularization, 113–18
Seder, 27
Seixas, Rev. Gershom Mendes, 53–54
Seligman, Ruth, 187
Sephardim, 50, 65
Shabbtai Zvi, 39
Shafir, Gershon, 150, 162
Shapiro, Howard, 109
Shapiro, Jay, 140
Shapiro, Yosef, 198
Shave Zion, 62
Shaw, Irwin, 188
Shearith Israel, Congregation, 50, 52, 53
Shilah, Margalit, 78
Shlichim. See Emissaries
Shmuel Bar Nachmani, Rabbi, 39
Shulchan Aruch, 189
Silverman, Myrna, 141
Six-Day War, 16–17, 77, 87, 88, 106, 126, 161, 196

Sklare, Marshall, 68, 120
Sobel, Zvi, 183
Society for the Colonization of
Palestine, 41, 45
Sofer, Rabbi Moses, 132
Spindler, George, 139
Stamford, Conn., Jews in, 75–76
Stern, Malcolm H., 61
Stiles, Ezra, 52

Tabory, Ephraim, 188, 189, 191, 193
Tagar, 200
Tammany Hall, 54
Tannenbaum, Bernice, 199–200
Teczniczek, Dorota, 141
Tehillah, 200
Tehiya, 78
Telem, 200
Temple Emanu-El, 72
Territories, American Israelis in
Administered: age and sex
distribution of, 151; American
political background of 159;
attitudes toward equal rights for
Israel Arabs among, 166; attitudes
toward Gush Emunim among,
165–66; attitudes toward "Jewish
Underground" among, 166–67;
attitudes toward Kach among,
165–66; belief that now is period of
Messiah among, 166; educational
status of, 152; feelings about the
U.S. among, 159–60; ideas on
dealing with Arabs in Territories
among, 164–66; influence of
American political and social
values among, 167–68; Jewish
education of, 155–56; Jewish youth
group affiliations of 157–58;
number of children of 151–52;
parents' denominational affiliation
of 154; period of aliya of, 159;
popular perception of, 150–51;
primary reasons for settling,
160–62; support for democracy as a
value among, 163–64
Tiberias, 33, 38
Tishah B'av, 31
Tönnies, Ferdinand, 128
Torah Umesorah. *See* National Society
for Hebrew Day Schools
Torah Vedaath, Yeshiva, 121
Torah Ve-Emuna, Yeshiva, 121
Tosafists, 36

Union of American Hebrew
Congregations (UAHC), 61, 123
Union of Orthodox Jewish
Congregations of America, 123
Union of Traditional Conservative
Judaism, 132
United Israel Appeal, 198
United Jewish Appeal (UJA), 106,
183, 198
United Synagogue of America, 123
Urofsky, Melvin I., 106

Vietnam War, 100, 128

Washington, George, 51
Watergate scandal, 128
Waxman, Chaim I., 98, 121
Weissman, Debbie, 189
Weissman, Nahum, 186–87
Weissman, Sylvia, 186–87
Weizman, Ezer, 164
West Bank, 150
Wilowsky, Rabbi Jacob David, 119
Wise, Isaac Mayer, 60
Woocher, Jonathan, 109
World Zionist Organization (WZO),
42, 48, 65, 99, 102, 105, 106, 195–200

XYZ Affair, 53

Yaacov Yukel of Mezhibuz, Rabbi, 38
Yachad, 164
Yale University, 52
Yalkut Shimoni, 28
Yeshiva, 119; as facilitating aliya, 135;
growth of in America, 121–24
Yeshiva University, 123
Yiddish, 107, 115
Yiddishkeit, 119
Yom Haatzmaut, 42, 107
Yom Kippur War, 112
Yonatan, Rabbi, 39
Yordim, 258, 183

Zijderveld, Anton, 115
Zion, emphasis on in Jewish culture,
27–38
Zionism, American: as distinct from
European and Israeli, 112;
sociological and ideological
development of, 66–69

Zionism, and Jewish identity, 101–2; as distinct from pro-Israelism, 108–18; as integral to Judaism, 70; political, 70
Zionism, cultural, 68, 70, 71–72
Zionism, general, 68, 69
Zionism, philanthropic, 66
Zionism, religious, 48, 68, 69, 75, 109. *See also* Mizrachi

Zionism, secular, 47, 48, 75, 79
Zionism, socialist, 68, 69, 75, 79
Zionism, spiritual, 70
Zionist Congress, 61, 65, 68, 105
Zionist Organization of America (ZOA), 68
Zohar, 40

www.ingramcontent.com/pod-product-compliance
Lightning Source LLC
Chambersburg PA
CBHW050351270326
41926CB00016B/3689